AF515653

India Unlimited

Also by the author

India's Tryst with Destiny (2012)

India Unlimited

reclaiming the lost glory

ARVIND PANAGARIYA

HarperCollins *Publishers* India

First published in India in 2020 by
HarperCollins *Publishers* India

4th Floor, Tower A, Building No 10, DLF Cyber City,
DLF Phase II, Gurugram, Haryana – 122002
www.harpercollins.co.in

6 8 10 9 7 5

Copyright © Arvind Panagariya 2020

P-ISBN: 978-93-5357-666-0
E-ISBN: 978-93-5357-667-7

The views and opinions expressed in this book are the author's own and the facts are as reported by him, and the publishers are not in any way liable for the same.

Arvind Panagariya asserts the moral right to be identified as the author of this work.

All rights reserved. No part of this publication may be reproduced, stored in a retrieval system, or transmitted, in any form or by any means, electronic, mechanical, photocopying, recording or otherwise, without the prior permission of the publishers.

Typeset in 12/16 Adobe Garamond at
Manipal Technologies Limited, Manipal

Printed and bound at
Replika Press Pvt. Ltd.

This book is produced from independently certified FSC® paper to ensure responsible forest management.

To

Ananth and Ajay

CONTENTS

PREFACE

IN THE FISCAL YEAR 2017–18, India's Gross Domestic Product (GDP) reached $2.6 trillion. This means that the country will comfortably reach the third-highest place in GDP rankings worldwide in less than a decade. Yet, only fifteen years ago, most analysts would have summarily dismissed this possibility as pure fantasy. Even a decade ago, commenting on the title of my book, *India: The Emerging Giant*, a reviewer had recalled with a touch of scepticism the remark by political scientist Stephen Cohen that one is tempted to ask whether 'India is always destined to be "emerging" but never actually arriving'.[1]

India's poor economic performance during the first four decades of Independence had justifiably left even many of its early admirers pessimistic about its future. But it needs reminding that for much of the known history of mankind, the country has been home to one of the largest and richest economies of the world. During the first one-and-a-half millennia of the Common Era, India accounted for a quarter or more of the global income. Indeed, till as late as 1820, it accounted for one-sixth of the global income and was second in size only to China. True, the Industrial Revolution, which occurred

1 See Kishore, 2008, and Cohen, 2001, p. 2.

in Europe and later spread to North America, was responsible for the relative decline of India and China during the 19th and 20th centuries. But it was the self-serving and exploitative policies of the British that greatly impoverished India even in absolute terms. By the time the British were forced out, the country had been reduced to the worst poverty any nation may have experienced.

Therefore, India's present pursuit of prosperity is not an excursion into the unknown; instead, it is a quest to reclaim its lost glory. The difference, however, is that unlike in the past, India has many competitors in the world today. Rather than lead, it is playing catch-up. Therefore, it needs to foster policies that allow its entrepreneurs to take advantage of available technologies while also innovating new products and processes to deliver double-digit growth.

In *India: The Emerging Giant*, I had been comprehensive. That book was over 500 pages long and covered nearly all aspects of the economy, including a detailed history of post-Independence economic policies. Subsequently, in response to continued scepticism towards the centrality of growth to poverty alleviation among many scholars and policy analysts, I offered a comprehensive case for growth as the single most important instrument to combat poverty in my 2012 book *Why Growth Matters* (published in India as *India's Tryst with Destiny*) jointly authored with Jagdish Bhagwati.

Today, I need not be as comprehensive as I was in *India: The Emerging Giant*. Indeed, doing so will only lead to undue repetition. With the importance of growth now gaining wide acceptance, there is no need to comprehensively make the case for it either. Therefore, in this book, I concentrate on the question of how India can achieve sustained rapid growth for two to three decades while also creating well-paid jobs for its vast workforce that has limited skills. As a by-product, I also answer the question of how India can transform its primarily agricultural, rural and traditional economy into an industrial, urban and modern one.

Part I of the book serves as introduction to Indian economy. It makes the case that India can return to being a major world economy within the next one to two decades, as it had been during the entire first millennium and four-fifths of the second. It also takes a brief look at India's development experience in the post-Independence era, principally to take stock of what worked and what didn't as far as growth and poverty alleviation are concerned.

Parts II and III constitute the core of the volume. Part II, containing three chapters, systematically documents the existence of widespread underemployment or low-productivity employment in all sectors of the economy—agriculture, industry and services. It argues that there is no way to significantly improve the lives of agricultural workers without moving half or more of them into industry and services. It further shows that even within industry and services, the bulk of the workforce is employed in tiny low-productivity enterprises in which they earn, at best, subsistence-level incomes. Part II argues that the only way to create well-paid jobs for the masses is for India to create a business environment in which many more medium and large firms can emerge, especially in employment-intensive sectors such as apparel, footwear, furniture and other light manufactures. It concludes by arguing that creation of good jobs in large numbers would require capturing a significantly larger share of the world export market and that neither the current wave of protectionism nor rising automation renders the export-led and manufacturing-fed growth model irrelevant.

Part III, consisting of eight out of a total of thirteen chapters in the volume, discusses specific policy reforms in the key areas necessary to launch India into a near-double-digit growth trajectory and to create well-paid jobs. These include trade liberalization, trade facilitation, labour and land market reforms, urban development, development of securities market, banking reform, improvements in governance and a miscellaneous set of reforms such as privatization of public-sector enterprises, consolidation of rural subsidies into a single cash transfer, scaling down the Food Corporation of India, and a set of macroeconomic reforms. Each of these subjects is discussed in considerable detail.

Reflecting my comparative advantage, the focus of the volume is on policies rather than programmes and projects. Therefore, I do not discuss the important subject of infrastructure, including the creation and expansion of digital platforms. Luckily, the present government is already moving at a fast pace in building infrastructure and spreading the role of digitization. Acceleration in growth, which would increase revenue collection, will help the government speed up this process yet further.

Additional important areas that I do not cover in the book, beyond a brief section on the reform of the Right to Education Act, are school education, health, environment and energy. These are all very important areas and progress in them has a direct bearing on growth. A good case can be made for their inclusion in a book like the present one. But I felt that the book had already become overly long and I should resist the temptation to add yet more chapters.

I am indebted to my brilliant former student Rana Hasan, who currently works in a senior position at the Asian Development Bank, for extremely helpful comments on Parts I and II of the book. I also wish to thank B. Venkatesh Kumar for his excellent comments on the chapter on higher education, Rahul Ahluwalia for providing estimates of workforce across broad sectors of the economy and Radhicka Kapoor for estimates of employment by firm size in manufacturing. As with my 2008 book, the excellent online data depositories on the website of the Reserve Bank of India, especially the digital RBI Handbook of Statistics on Indian Economy, have been extremely helpful in writing this volume. The RBI has done an excellent job of providing extensive time-series data on nearly all aspects of Indian economy in an accessible form. I am grateful to the RBI staff, especially Rajiv Ranjan, who promptly responded to all my data queries in the course of preparing the manuscript.

Finally, as usual, I must thank my wife, Amita, who served as the first reader for many draft chapters. Whenever I felt that some part of a draft chapter may be lacking clarity, I sought her advice. The book is fondly dedicated to my two children, Ananth and Ajay, who have grown up loving India just as much as the country of their birth, the United States. I am sure they too will contribute to building bridges between the two nations in their own ways.

PART I

A BRIGHT FUTURE AWAITS

1

RECLAIMING THE LOST GLORY

According to estimates by economic historian Angus Maddison (2006), India accounted for nearly 30 per cent of the world's Gross Domestic Product (GDP) from AD 1 to AD 1000 (Figure 1.1). Though this share declined subsequently, it remained approximately a quarter of the world GDP until AD 1700. As recently as AD 1820, India used to contribute a hefty 16 per cent of the global GDP.[1] China was the other major economy of the world during this period with the two nations together accounting for half of the global GDP during the two millenniums until 1820.

By the early 19th century, the Industrial Revolution had been well under way and the centre of gravity of the global economy had begun to shift from India and China to Europe. Simultaneously, with the East India Company acquiring control of much of the country, India was in decline. The situation remained unchanged after the control of India passed from the hands of the East India Company to the Crown in 1858. With the policy framework designed entirely to serve the interest of the colonial power, per capita incomes in India saw hardly any

---

1 Estimates by Maddison are in 1990 purchasing parity dollars using the Geary-Khamis method. For details on the Geary-Khamis method, see https://stats.oecd.org/glossary/detail.asp?ID=5528 (accessed on 10 February 2018).

improvement during the first half of the 20th century. Consequently, by the time the British left India, its share in the world GDP had fallen to 4.2 per cent.

Although India managed to accelerate growth in the post-Independence era by making the national interest the objective, because of the dirigiste policy regime it adopted, it failed to achieve its full potential. Indeed, India continued to grow slower than the rest of the world during early decades of its independence, with the result that its share dropped yet further to 3.1 per cent by 1973. Only after the oil crisis led to a substantial slowdown in the global economy and India began to shift to a more liberal policy regime did the declining trend reverse. According to the original Maddison estimates, by 2001, India's share in the global GDP had climbed back up to 5.4 per cent.

After 1820, China's share in the global GDP declined as well. From 33 per cent that year, it fell steadily to just 4.6 per cent in 1973. Since then, China too has recovered its share. According to Maddison, this share rose to 12.3 per cent in 2001.

Figure 1.1: GDP Shares of Major Countries and Regions

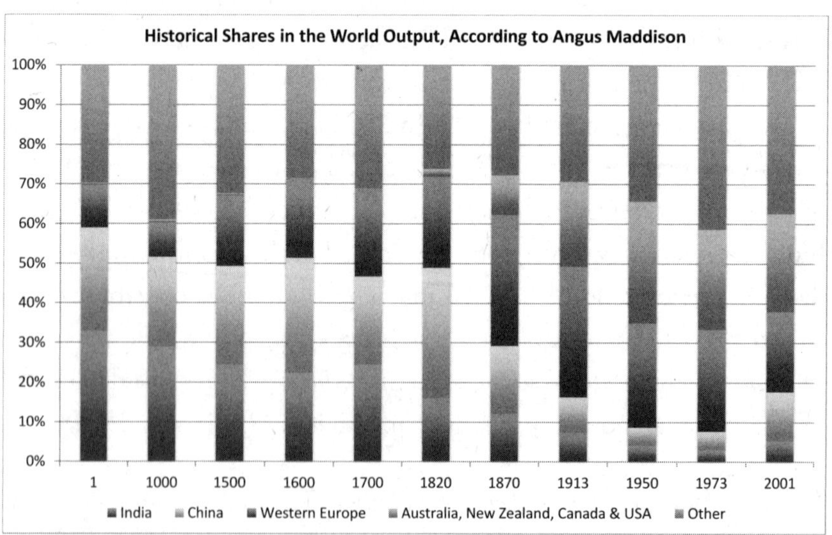

Source: Author's construction using estimates by Maddison, 2006, Table 8b, p. 639

The robust picture of India until 1820 is tempered by the fact that despite its large share in the global GDP, the country enjoyed only a marginal advantage over other countries in terms of per capita GDP and that too until AD 1000. A large population was thus the principal driver of the country's large GDP share in the world economy. By 1500, the country's per capita GDP fell significantly below most of West European countries. According to Maddison, the per capita GDP of India in AD 1000 was $450 at 1990 prices and purchasing power parity exchange rate as compared to $400 in Europe and Latin America and $425 in Japan. But by AD 1500, per capita GDP in India at $550 had been surpassed by Western Europe at $771. Indeed, by this time, even the world's per capita GDP at $556 had come to exceed that of India.

The Promise of the Future

In thinking about India's future, we must keep this historical context in mind. Barring a period of 200 years, India has been a large contributor to the global output. Now that India has opened its economy, introduced numerous pro-growth reforms and created a large GDP base, it can aspire to return to the prominent position it enjoyed in the global economy for the better part of the last two millennia. Given where India stands currently, a prima facie case for the realization of such an ambition can indeed be made.

During the fifteen years ending with fiscal year 2017/18, India's real GDP at market prices grew at the annual rate of 7.7 per cent in real rupees and 9.9 per cent in real dollars.[2] This is true despite the

2 Throughout the book, I use a slash (/) to indicate India's fiscal year, which begins on 1 April and ends on 31 March. Therefore, 2017/18 refers to the period beginning 1 April 2017 and ending on 31 March 2018. Growth in real rupees is based on the GDP series at 2004/05 for years 2003/04 to 2011/12 and at 2011/12 prices for years 2012/13 to 2017/18. Growth in real dollars is derived as follows: using the nominal GDP data from

fact that policy mistakes had led to a significant decline in the growth rate during 2011/12 to 2013/14. With its GDP at $2.6 trillion in 2017/18, globally, India ranked sixth in GDP terms in 2017.[3]

Against this background, consider the implication of an 8 per cent average annual growth in real dollars, an outcome well within India's grasp. Such growth would raise India's GDP to $7.1 trillion by 2030/31. This would be sufficient to place the country comfortably in the third position in GDP rankings worldwide. The GDP of Japan, currently the third largest economy, is placed at $4.9 trillion in 2017. Today, it is predicted that Japan will not grow faster than 1.5 per cent annually in real dollars from 2017 to 2030. At this pace, its economy would rise to only $6 trillion by 2030.

With India's population in 2030 estimated to be 1.5 billion, a GDP of $7.1 trillion would translate into an annual per capita GDP of $4,730 in 2017/18 constant dollars. This figure would still be far from the per capita GDP of developed countries, but enough to virtually eliminate abject poverty from India and bring prosperity to a large proportion of its population. Seen this way, India's prospects for becoming a prosperous nation at home and a leading economic power globally are excellent.

Yet, one thing India's own economic history teaches is that nothing can be taken for granted about the country. By 2010/11, India's economy had already seen an above 8 per cent growth for eight years

---

2002/03 to 2010/11 at 2004/05 prices and from 2011/12 to 2017/18 at 2011/12 prices and applying the corresponding average annual dollar-rupee exchange rate, the nominal dollar GDP in India grew at the average annual rate of 11.9 per cent from 2003/04 to 2017/18. With the growth in the GDP deflator in the United States averaging 2 per cent during the same period, annual GDP growth in real dollars in India works out to 9.9 per cent.

3 India's nominal GDP in 2017/18 was ₹167.73 trillion. The average exchange rate during 2017/18 being ₹64.4549 per dollar, this figure translates into $2.6 trillion.

and it had come out of the global financial crisis of 2008 unscathed. It seemed then that nothing could slow down this large economy advancing at a fast pace. Yet, cumulative policy mistakes of the then government administered a major blow to the economy and the growth rate first fell to 6.6 per cent in 2011/12 and then plummeted to 5.5 per cent in 2012/13.

Growth has two main sources: growth in resources such as labour and capital that are used to produce goods and services, and growth in productivity, which measures the volume of goods and services that can be produced from a given basket of resources. The amount of capital is constrained by savings and labour by demography. Growth in productivity, which allows more GDP to be produced from the same volume of resources, critically depends on economic policies. When policies reduce the efficiency of use of resources, reforming them promotes greater efficiency and higher levels of productivity. This is the central reason why sustaining and accelerating economic reforms is essential to sustaining and accelerating growth in the forthcoming years.

Accordingly, the central objective of *India Unlimited* is to outline reforms that the country must undertake in the forthcoming years to eliminate abject poverty and bring prosperity to large sections of its population. As India pursues these objectives, as a by-product, it must also urbanize and modernize its economy in a major way in the next two decades. With new technologies associated with the Fourth Industrial Revolution emerging at an accelerated pace, the task of modernization assumes special significance.

Before I turn to a detailed discussion of the necessary reforms, however, it is useful to briefly outline the post-Second World War experience of a handful of countries that have successfully transformed their economies. Even though the economic and technological environment today is significantly different from that of the decades immediately following the Second World War, the experience of these economies will provide useful lessons for India.

Lessons from the Miracle Economies of East Asia

Six East Asian entities—Japan, Hong Kong, Singapore, South Korea, Taiwan and China—grew at rates ranging from 8 to 10 per cent on a sustained basis following the Second World War. These countries successfully achieved the kind of transformation within three decades that took Western economies a century or longer to achieve. Table 1.1 provides the growth rates and the associated periods of transformation in these countries.

Table 1.1: Growth Rates in Miracle Transformers

Country	Period	Average Annual Growth Rate
Japan	1946-75	8.80%
Hong Kong	1961-80	9.95%
Singapore	1961-80	9.80%
Taiwan	1962-89	9.30%
South Korea	1963-96	8.30%
China	1981-2013	10%

Source: Ito and Weinstein 1996, Table 1, p. 209 for Japan and author's calculations using online World Development Indicators, World Bank for other countries

The growth experiences of these countries have several features in common. They all witnessed an exceptionally rapid growth of exports. They also witnessed a rapid rise in the share of manufacturing in the GDP, especially of labour-intensive products. Accelerated manufacturing growth, which gave rapidly rising purchasing power to the citizens, expanded the demand for services and, thus, accelerated the growth of services as well. The rapid expansion of manufacturing and services pulled workers out of agriculture (except in Hong Kong and Singapore, where agriculture had, at best, limited presence) in vast numbers and led to rapid urbanization. Productivity grew sufficiently fast in this process to raise the wages in manufacturing and services by 8 to 10 per cent annually at the same time that workers migrated in large numbers into these sectors. Poverty levels saw a rapid decline in relatively short periods of time.[4]

The Experience of South Korea

The experience of South Korea, summarized in Figures 1.2 to 1.5, best illustrates the process of transformation in these economies. In 1963, when the country began growing rapidly, the share of exports in the GDP was less than 5 per cent (Figure 1.2). During the following decades, the share grew exceptionally rapidly, reaching 38.3 per cent in 1987. With the GDP itself growing at an 8 per cent plus rate, exports had to grow at an average rate exceeding 20 per cent to produce such a large increase in the exports-to-GDP ratio.

Figure 1.2: Exports-to-GDP Ratio in South Korea, 1960–1987

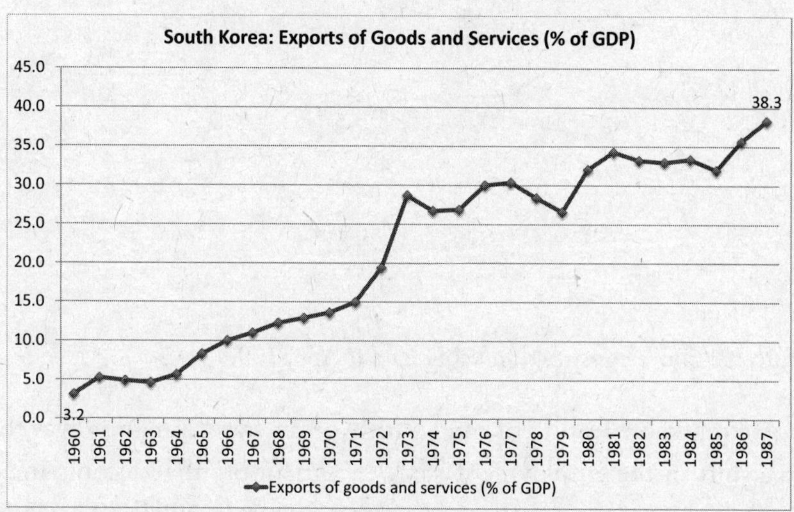

Source: Based on the author's calculations using online World Development Indicators, World Bank

4 The detailed experiences of these countries, except Japan, are documented in Panagariya, 2019.

This export growth was accompanied by a rapid expansion of manufacturing initially. But as incomes rose and the demand for services expanded, growth of services accelerated as well (Figure 1.3). The share of agriculture in the GDP, which stood at 39 per cent in 1965, fell to just 9 per cent by 1990. Industry and services came to account for more than 91 per cent of the GDP in 1990. Within twenty-five years, South Korea went from being an agrarian economy to one dominated by industry and services.

Figure 1.3: Output Shares of Different Sectors in South Korea: 1965–1990

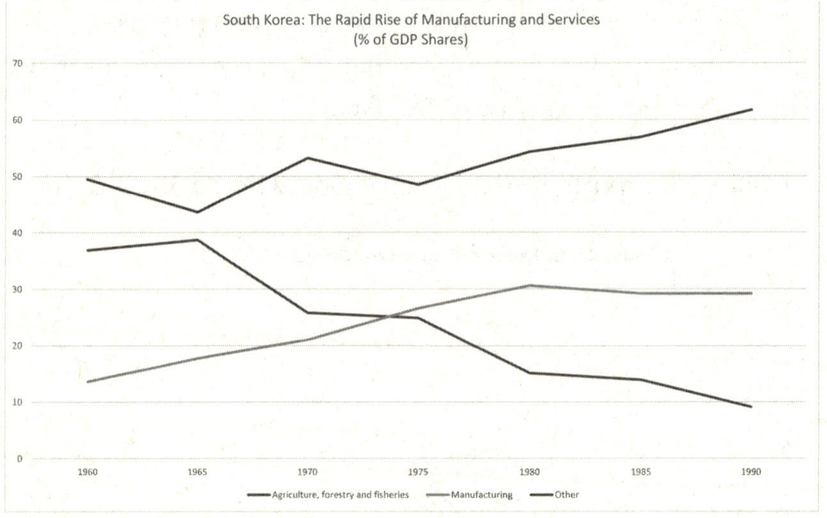

Source: Author's construction using data in Yoo, 1997

A remarkable feature of the South Korean transformation was the large shift in the employment share of agriculture that accompanied the huge shift in the output share of that sector. In 1965, 59 per cent of the Korean workforce was employed in agriculture (Figure 1.4). By 1990, this share had dropped to 18 per cent. Even as manufacturing and services absorbed such large volumes of workers, with the rapid rise in productivity, the real wages paid by them rose by approximately 10 per cent annually.

Figure 1.4: Employment Shares of Broad Sectors in South Korea: 1965–1990

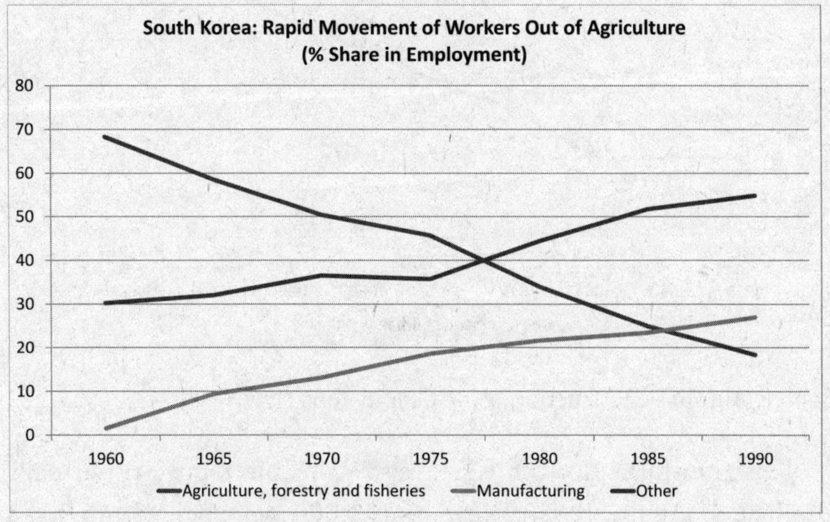

Source: Author's construction using data in Yoo, 1997

The movement out of agriculture and into manufacturing and services was accompanied by urbanization. In the mid-1960s, the urban population in South Korea was 29 per cent of the total (Figure 1.5). But once growth accelerated and workers began shifting from agriculture to manufacturing and services, urbanization spread rapidly. By 1990, urbanization in South Korea had crossed the 74 per cent mark and by 1999, it had reached 88.3 per cent. This urbanization took place not just because workers moved from rural to urban areas but also because many of the previously rural regions became urban, alongside the shift in the pattern of employment in favour of non-agricultural activities.

Figure 1.5: Urbanization in South Korea, 1955–1999

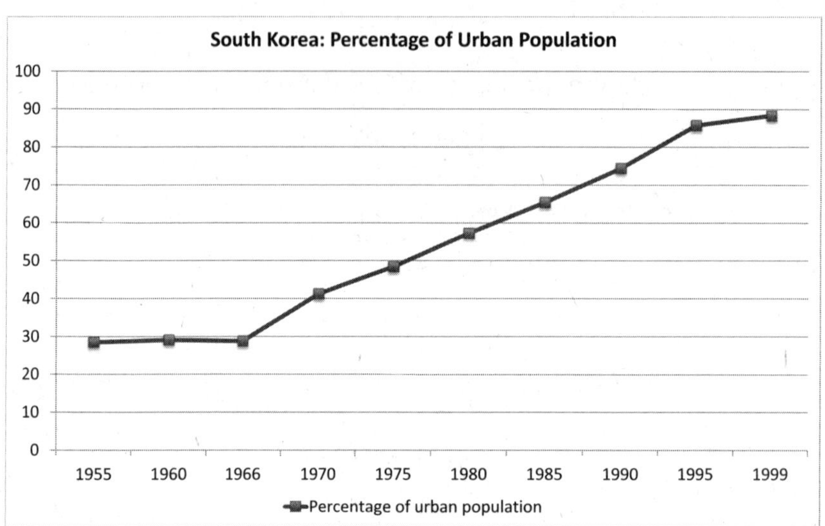

Source: Author's construction using data in Yoo, 1997

This transformation of Korea also saw abject poverty virtually eliminated. At the poverty line of 121,000 won per month for a household of five members, the proportion of households below poverty line fell from 40.9 per cent in 1965 to 14.8 per cent in 1976 and 7.6 per cent in 1991. In rural areas, poverty fell from 54.9 per cent in 1965 to 18.1 per cent in 1976 and 8.7 per cent in 1991. In urban areas, the reduction was from 35.8 per cent in 1965 to 11.7 per cent in 1976 and 2.8 per cent in 1991.[5]

Remarkably, this decline in poverty took place almost entirely through growth, since very few Koreans benefited from anti-poverty programmes. In 1961, Korea had introduced a public assistance programme, which was based on strict means tests. In 1965, the programme covered 13.66 per cent of the population. But this

5 Kwon and Yi, 2008, Table 2

proportion fell to 3.77 per cent in 1975 and then modestly rose to 5.26 per cent in 1990.[6]

Concluding Remarks

Historically, India and China have been the two largest economies in the world. Until as recently as 1820, they jointly contributed half of the world's GDP. But as the Industrial Revolution lifted per capita incomes, first in Europe and then in the United States, the economic centre of gravity of the global economy shifted to those regions.

In India, with the British following policies that were entirely designed to serve the interest of their own country's economy, there was prolonged stagnation or decline during the second half of the 19th and first half of the 20th century. The country's share in the global GDP fell from 16 per cent in 1820 to just 4.2 per cent by the time the British left in 1947. Once a national government committed to promoting the country's interest came to the helm, per capita incomes did begin to rise. But the choice of a command and control model, driven by the socialistic thinking of the leadership of the day, failed to deliver the high rates of growth that the country needed during the first four decades of Independence to rid itself of abject poverty.

A review of the fast-growing economies of East Asia shows that an important key to near double-digit growth remains openness. A detailed look at the development of South Korea from the early 1960s to 1990 shows that once this country opened its economy to the world markets, the growth in exports of labour-intensive manufacturing initially and in services subsequently allowed it to move the workforce out of agriculture into non-agricultural activities. Wages that rose at approximately 10 per cent per year accompanied this movement and helped eliminate poverty in the country.

6 Kwon and Yi, 2008, Table 1

Stories of the transformation of other miracle economies, which include China, Hong Kong, Singapore and Taiwan, although they are different in details, are similar in substance. They also opened up to international trade and built their successes on the rapid expansion of exports and imports. Large global markets allowed them to scale up their export industries and reap the economies of scale. Competition against the best manufacturers in the global economy and exposure to new products and technologies allowed them to achieve quick productivity growth. The result was near double-digit growth and a sharp decline in abject poverty.

Until the 1980s, many analysts had argued that exports could serve as the engine of growth only for small economies such as Singapore, Hong Kong, Taiwan and South Korea. In particular, populous countries such as China and India could not achieve high growth rates on the back of the world market. But after China opened its economy and more or less repeated the performance of the four smaller economies of East Asia, this argument lost its force. Eventually, beginning in 1991, when India too decided to open to the world markets, albeit cautiously and gradually, its experience turned out to be no different from that of China. This is the story I turn to in the next chapter.

2

FROM COMMAND AND CONTROL TO A MORE LIBERAL ORDER: 1950–2018

INDIA EXHIBITED A VERY different growth trajectory than the four East Asian miracle economies during the early decades of development. In spite of a rapidly expanding global economy, which helped pull up per capita incomes at significantly high rates in many developing countries, India saw only a modest turnaround in its performance. The progress it achieved during these decades was superior only to its abysmal performance during the first half of the twentieth century, when the entire policy and administrative apparatus had been geared towards serving the interest of the mother country.

As was true of other developing countries around the time, India had started out extremely poor. But unlike some countries such as Singapore, South Korea and Taiwan, which successfully overcame much of their abject poverty during the first few decades following the Second World War, India remained mired in it. As late as 1980, economist Garry Fields described India as a 'miserably poor country' whose poverty problem was so acute that it was 'debatable whether any internal policy change short of a major administrative overhaul and major redirection of efforts might be expected to improve things substantially'.[7]

An Overview of Post-Independence Growth Experience

In broad terms, the economic history of India from 1950/51 to 2017/18 can be divided into four distinct phases (Table 2.1).[8] In Phase I, spanning three decades from 1950/51 to 1980/81, India grew 3.7 per cent annually, with per capita income growing at just 1.6 per cent per annum. In Phase II, the transition phase and therefore the shortest of the four, spanning 1981/82 to 1987/88, the GDP growth rate accelerated to 4.9 per cent. During Phase III, covering years 1988/89 to 2002/03, there was further acceleration in GDP growth to 5.7 per cent. Finally, in Phase IV, encompassing the years 2003/04 to 2017/18, India grew at a yet higher rate of 7.7 per cent.[9]

7 Fields, 1980, p. 204

8 In Table 2.1 and the remainder of the book, periods such as 1951–81, when used in the context of India, refers to the period spanning fiscal years 1951/52 to 1980/81 with the end point years included. In the context of other countries, unless otherwise specified, data usually relates to the calendar year and a period such as 1951–81 refers to the period 1951 to 1981.

9 Until 2011/12, growth rates in Table 2.1 are calculated as simple averages of annual growth rates of the GDP at constant 2004/05 market prices. Beginning in 2012/13, India began measuring growth using a new series based on 2011/12 as the base year and incorporating several methodological improvements. Growth rates from 2012/13 onward are calculated using this new GDP series.

Table 2.1: Four Phases of Growth in India

Period	**Growth in Real GDP at Market Prices**	**Growth in Real Per-capita GDP at Market Prices**
Phase I (1951–81)	3.7	1.6
Phase II (1981–88)	4.9	2.8
Phase III (1988–2003)	5.7	3.7
Phase IV (2003–18)	7.7	6.4

Source: Author's calculations based on CSO GDP data

This summary of growth rates illustrates the varied performance of the economy during nearly seven decades beginning in 1950/51. Indeed, a finer division of the period shows even more variation. In my earlier book, *India: The Emerging Giant,* I further subdivided Phase I into two parts: 1951/52 to 1964/65, when the economy grew 4.3 per cent annually, and 1965/66 to 1980/81, when it grew only 3.2 per cent per year.[10] Indeed, since the population during the latter period grew faster, the difference in per capita income growth between the two sub-periods was event larger: 2.3 versus just 0.9 per cent per year. From an economic standpoint, the period from 1965/66 to 1980/81 was by far the worst with a hardly perceptible change in standard of living.

To help the reader better appreciate the implications of the varied performance over four phases, Figure 2.1 shows the evolution of per capita income at constant 2004/05 prices from 1950/51 to 2013/14 with per capita income in 1950/51 set at 100. I have terminated Figure 2.1 at 2013/14 because a continuous GDP series for the same base year, 2004/05, is available only until 2013/14.

The slow growth during Phase I translated into per capita income rising just 56 per cent points over three decades. In 1980/81, the index

10 Panagariya, 2008, Chapter 1

of per capita income stood at just 156 compared with 100 in 1950/51. In contrast, the modest acceleration and slightly higher base ended up yielding a rise of 61 per cent points in per capita GDP during the 1980s over the level prevailing in 1950/51. Acceleration during the 1990s yielded another rise of 90 per cent points. Finally, an over 8 per cent growth for nine years beginning in 2003/04 and the higher base of per capita income allowed the economy to add as many as 307 per cent points during the first thirteen years of the 21st century. Put another way, while India added just 207 per cent points to per capita income over its 1950/51 level during the entire second half of the 20th century, it managed to add 307 per cent points in just thirteen years during the 21st century.

Figure 2.1: Evolution of Per Capita Income in India: 1950/51 to 2011/12

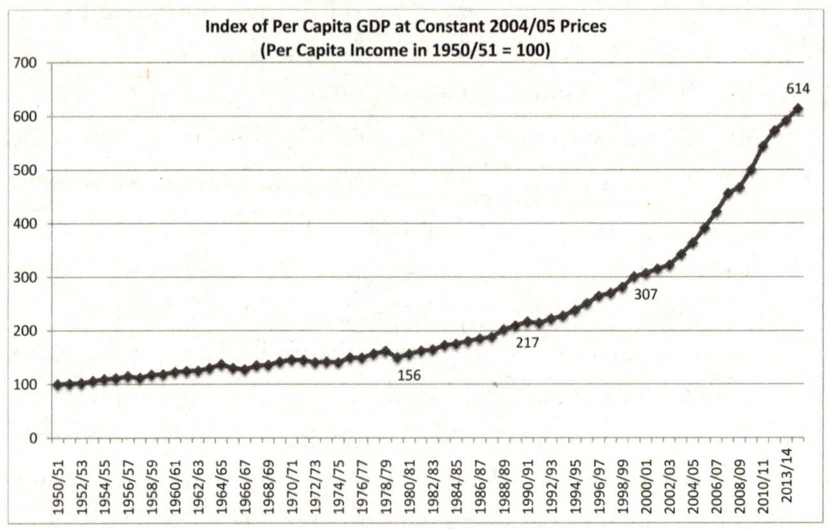

Source: Author's construction using the CSO data

According to estimates by Maddison, between 1913 and 1950, the GDP in India grew by a mere 0.23 per cent per year. Judged against this performance, the growth rate of 3.7 per cent during the first three decades of development may seem satisfactory. Some may even characterize it as a big leap. But such comparison is what one astute commentator has called 'both fatuous and facetious' because the near lack of growth during 1913 to 1950 was the result of a policy designed to serve solely the interest of Great Britain.[11] Any policy that placed the interest of India at its centre was likely to produce some acceleration in growth. The real question is whether the policies India adopted in the immediate post-Independence era fully exploited its growth potential. As the experience of the East Asian economies testifies and India's own superior performance following the post-1991 economic reforms demonstrates, India's potential went badly unrealized during those early decades of development.

Policy Mistakes and Corrections

In the early 1950s, South Korea, Taiwan, Singapore, China and India had comparable per capita incomes. The first three switched to outward-oriented policies in the early to mid-1960s, resulting in wholesale economic transformation during the following three decades. China and India remained inward-oriented and found themselves at significantly lower per capita income levels in the late 1970s. With its per capita income slightly below that of India, China too made a switch to outward-oriented policies in the late 1970s. Within three decades, it managed to achieve a transformation similar to what South Korea, Taiwan and Singapore had achieved. India persisted in maintaining its inward-looking policy regime much longer and therefore saw its transformation much delayed. In the following pages, I briefly review the policies India pursued during various periods, their rationale and the eventual shift away from them.[12]

---

11 Khatkhate, 2006, p. 2204

12 The review below is kept deliberately brief. Readers interested in details should consult my earlier books, *India: The Emerging Giant* and *Why Growth Matters*.

The Lost Decades: 1950/51 to 1980/81

The two key objectives underlying the development model that India's political leadership favoured in the 1950s were self-sufficiency and industrialization. In the immediate post-Independence era, it was natural for the leadership to seek to reinforce the hard-won political independence with economic independence. Industrialization, on the other hand, was seen as synonymous with development and modernization and essential for accelerated growth. Growth, in turn, was viewed as the key instrument for ridding India of its abject poverty.

A movement towards self-sufficiency also found broad support among Indian and foreign economists of the day, though for a very different reason. The policy instincts of these economists were rooted in what has been called 'export pessimism'. They held that the comparative advantage of developing countries lay in primary products. Therefore, reliance on trade as the engine of growth would mean that these countries would specialize in and export primary products.

But this was a losing proposition for two reasons. First, world demand for primary products was not very responsive to a given price change. Therefore, in order to get industrial countries to buy more of these products, prices would have to drop by a large magnitude. It followed that the benefits of any expansion of exports of these products following trade liberalization or productivity enhancement would pass on to importing industrial countries through substantially lower prices. Second, as incomes rise, demand shifts away from primary towards manufacturing products. This meant that by shifting demand away from primary products, rising incomes in industrial economies would drive down their prices. As such, specialization in primary products would not pay. The case for import substitution industrialization (ISI), which relied on protection to industry and a movement of the economy away from specialization in primary products, followed.

Nearly all developing countries including South Korea, Taiwan, Singapore, China and India began with ISI in some form in the 1950s. What distinguished the first four of these countries was that one by one, they decisively opted out of this model. They could escape the curse of 'export pessimism' by specializing in and exporting light manufactures, which did not suffer from price reduction that threatened primary product exports.

Unfortunately, India persisted much longer with the ISI model. In the early post-Independence decades, there were two key elements of the industrial policy that it pursued. First, it gave the public sector a dominant role in the development of heavy industry. This was premised, arguably erroneously, on the assumption that efficient operation in heavy industry would require investment on a scale that was beyond the capacity of the private sector. Second, the policy regulated private sector investment flows through strict licensing. This decision was premised on the assumption that without licensing, private investment would follow profits and would therefore flow into sectors that did not necessarily serve the national interest and priorities.

Combined with the self-sufficiency objective, this industrial policy gave rise to a highly inefficient economy. Self-sufficiency required that India quickly diversify its production basket to align it with its consumption basket. If bicycles were needed, their assembly at home was not sufficient; the parts used in them, the steel used in the parts and machines necessary to produce the parts had to be produced at home as well. Given limited resources, such wide diversification came in the way of exploiting scale economies. Many products were also beyond the technological capability of the country, which resulted in abysmal product quality.

Employment being an important objective, the leadership of the day also decided to leave the production of light manufactures to small household enterprises collectively called the 'cottage industry' in those days. It was expected that much of the available capital would be absorbed by formal, heavy industry, which was unviable without some minimum scale of operation. Therefore, light manufactures would have to be produced with minimal capital, principally using labour, in a cottage-industry setting.

The decision was therefore made that the government would give investment licences only for products such as chemicals, fertilizers, machinery and consumer durables that could not be produced by small household enterprises. Later, beginning in 1967, Prime Minister Indira Gandhi formalized this policy via the introduction of the small-scale industries (SSI) reservation. Under SSI reservation, a list of labour-intensive products was drawn up, with these products reserved for exclusive manufacture by small enterprises. In turn, small enterprises were defined as those with an investment ceiling of just ₹750,000 or, at the prevailing exchange rate of ₹7.5 per dollar, $100,000.

On the surface, this was a coherent strategy to stimulate growth and employment while promoting self-sufficiency. In practice, it undermined both growth and employment creation by undermining efficiency. The strategy greatly underestimated the productivity gains associated with specialization according to comparative advantage and competition in the world markets. Specialization in a handful of products, which can be partially exchanged in the world markets for products not produced at home, allows the firms to achieve high productivity through several channels:

- Insofar as the country specializes in the export of labour-intensive manufactures in the early stages of development and is consequently able to import machinery and other capital-intensive products, it is better able to utilize its scarce capital.
- Firms that operate in export markets are inevitably exposed to competition with the most efficient producers in the world. This fact forces them to continuously update their

technologies, management practices and product quality to remain competitive.

- Large world markets also allow the exporting firms to achieve a scale that makes it attractive for them to employ machinery, which in turn creates skills and raises labour productivity and wages. The usage of extra machinery does not undermine the employment objective since, employment per unit of capital is large in labour-intensive products that the country exports and the vast world market allows exporting firms to operate on a large scale.
- World markets also give the firms access to high-quality inputs and machinery, which in turn allows them to produce high-quality products demanded by sophisticated global customers.
- Continuous upgrading of technology and management by export-oriented firms also gives rise to continuous upgrading of skills and thus better prepares the workforce for the next generation of technologies and innovations in management techniques.

Confined predominantly to the domestic market in the early decades, Indian firms remained stuck in old technologies, low-quality products and low levels of productivity. The greatest loss of efficiency was in light manufactures, precisely the products in which the country had potential comparative advantage because of its vast labour force. Hamstrung by the investment cap of just $100,000, these products could neither achieve an efficient scale nor take advantage of the technological progress or advances in product quality that were taking place elsewhere in the world.

A look at the evolution of exports as a proportion of GDP over time illustrates the detrimental effect that India's policies had on export performance (Figure 2.2). As in South Korea, this ratio was low in India in the 1950s. But in contrast to South Korea, it declined over time in India, even though the GDP exhibited a mildly rising trend. For the first time in 1958/59, the ratio fell below 5 per cent and remained there every year until as late as 1974/75. In contrast, in South Korea, the ratio rose steadily after the mid-1960s and reached above 25 per cent in 1973. A declining exports-to-GDP ratio in a growing economy is rare and symptomatic of near-autarkic trade policies and a highly overvalued domestic currency.

Figure 2.2: Exports as a Proportion of the GDP in India: 1950/51 to 2011/12

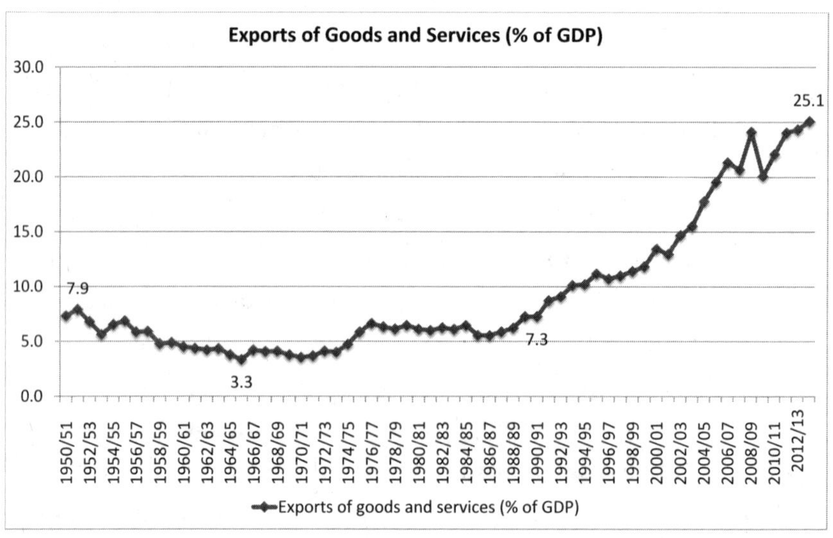

Source: Author's construction using data from RBI Handbook of Statistics, 2014

With limited access to external sources of financing, imports into India were constrained by revenues generated by exports. Therefore, imports exhibited a pattern mirroring exports (Figure 2.3). They were subject to a declining trend from the late 1950s to the mid-1970s. As payment from Great Britain for India's contribution to the Second World War, India had some sterling balances available to it during the decade immediately following Independence. These balances allowed its imports to exceed exports by a small margin. Imports as a proportion of the GDP especially declined after 1957/58, when the sterling balances dried up. During the 1960s and the first half of the 1970s, imports remained in the neighbourhood of 5 per cent of the GDP. The fortuitous appearance of remittances by workers migrating to the Middle East following the oil price hike gave imports some boost in the second half of the 1970s, but they did not return to the 1950s' peak of 10 per cent until after the liberalizing reforms of 1991.

Figure 2.3: Imports as a Proportion of the GDP in India, 1950–2012

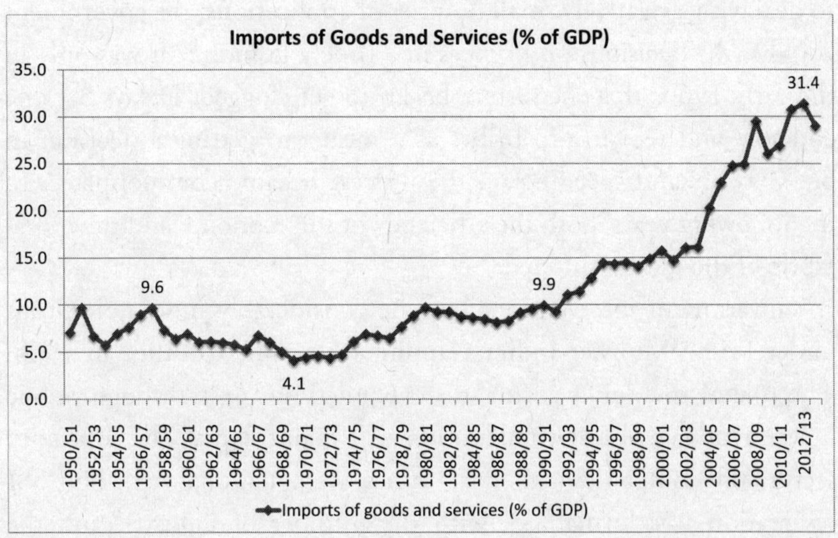

Source: Author's construction using data from RBI Handbook of Statistics, 2014

During 1951–65, the GDP grew by 4.3 per cent annually. This was a significant acceleration in growth over the first half of the 20th century. There were three broad reasons why this acceleration could be achieved:

First, unlike during the British era, national interest rather than the interest of the colonial power now guided economic policy. All efforts were directed towards serving India's interests rather than Britain's. A concerted effort was made to increase investment, build infrastructure and promote industrial development. This was bound to yield some positive results.

Second, overall, policies during the first one-and-a-half decades were less constraining and their impact less damaging than what was to come. The availability of the sterling balances from Britain allowed India to maintain a relatively liberal import regime till at least 1957/58, when these balances dried up. Nehru had inherited a liberal foreign investment regime from the British and liberalized it further.

Finally, in the early years when the economy was small and it had to deal with a relatively small number of applications, the government could make decisions on licences in a timely fashion.[13] It was only in the early 1960s that the system began to get clogged. Delays became endemic and recourse to bribes as a means to getting a decision in one's favour and speeding up the process became commonplace. In the following years, both the efficiency of the economy and the moral fabric of the nation suffered.

Government interventions became considerably more ubiquitous under Prime Minister Indira Gandhi, who came to office in 1966. The role of the public sector was expanded not only through public investment but also nationalization. All major banks, the insurance sector, oil companies and coal mines were nationalized. The SSI reservation was formalized, with the number of industries on the list growing over time. Licensing reigned supreme in virtually all industries. Entry and expansion of firms came to be governed by a series of lists of products subject to a complex web of rules.

The years 1966–76 also saw a significant tightening of rules governing foreign investment. With some exceptions, foreign companies were asked to dilute foreign equity to 40 per cent and register in India as Indian companies. Two major foreign companies, IBM and

---

13 For a more detailed account of policies during 1951/52 to 1964/65, see Panagariya, 2008, Chapter 2

Coca-Cola, exited India as a result. Investments by big business houses and large enterprises were confined to a narrow range of industries. The government also introduced ceilings on urban landholdings and effectively prohibited worker layoffs in factories with one hundred or more workers.

A final set of notable interventions in manufacturing concerned price and distribution controls. With imports tightly controlled and licences issued only to a handful of producers in view of the existence of scale economies, the government was apprehensive that those lucky enough to get investment licences would earn monopoly profits. That in turn led the government to impose price controls in many cases. At the controlled prices, demand usually far exceeded the licenced production capacity, forcing the government to introduce distribution controls. Under the latter, using a set of opaque criteria, the government assumed effective control of who would get to buy the product and who would be excluded from it. Products such as sugar, telephones, cement, scooters and cars thus became subject to administrative allocation by the government via permits. Products such as telephones, cars and scooters saw the creation of years-long wait-lists. Bribes and black markets proliferated in response. The result of these dirigiste policies was that growth fell to 3.2 per cent per year during the period 1965–81.[14]

Prime Minister Nehru was focused squarely on developing industry to the neglect of agriculture. After he died in 1964 and before his daughter Indira Gandhi came to office, Prime Minister Lal Bahadur Shastri briefly ruled the country. During his short stint from June 1964 to January 1966, Shastri successfully shifted the focus of government policy from heavy industry to agriculture. He sowed the seeds of the Green Revolution and launched the following important institutions—the Agricultural Price Commission, Food Corporation of India (FCI) and the National Dairy Development Board (NDDB).

---

14 For details, see Panagariya, 2008, Chapter 3

These institutions subsequently played a key role in the development of agriculture and remain robust till today. Indira Gandhi supported the initiative for the Green Revolution by Shastri, which proved extremely important in making India self-sufficient in food.

Hesitant Liberalization: The Transition Decade of the 1980s

The fact that the licensing system was becoming a stumbling block to the growth of industry had begun to be recognized by some in the government by the mid-1970s. The sector had experienced an annual average growth of just 2 per cent from 1970 to 1975, compared with 6.7 per cent from 1951 to 1965. This plummeting of industrial growth and pressures by industrialists who had been hamstrung by shortage of inputs helped create a small constituency for liberalization. The appearance of remittances from the Middle East became a facilitating factor, since it led to a modest easing of the foreign exchange constraint.

Consequently, India began taking some baby steps towards the liberalization of industrial and import controls in the second half of the 1970s. The process saw a slight acceleration in the 1980s, especially beginning in the mid-1980s. But since there was not enough political will to recognize that the command-and-control model was fundamentally flawed, there was no effort to change the policy framework. Instead, the changes were made through small alterations in rules and regulations within the existing policy framework. Unsurprisingly, liberalization was quite limited and has been rightly labelled as 'reform by stealth'.[15]

Of course, limited action produced only limited returns. The growth rate from 1981 to 1988 edged up to 4.9 per cent. Fiscal expansion and a long-overdue depreciation of the rupee during the second half of the 1980s, which helped boost exports, reinforced the effect of the modest

---

15 For details, see Panagariya, 2008, Chapter 4

domestic liberalization and temporarily pushed the growth rate up to 7 per cent during the last three years of the decade, 1988–91. But the large fiscal deficits, partially financed by borrowing abroad, also carried the seeds of a balance-of-payments crisis. The crisis became a reality in the wake of the First Gulf War in early 1991. An accelerating economy came to a sudden stop. The real GDP at market prices grew just 1.4 per cent in 1991/92.

Deeper Reforms During 1991–2004

The 1991 balance-of-payments crisis provided the occasion for more systematic and deeper reforms. In June 1991, Prime Minister P.V. Narasimha Rao came to the helm. Within a short period, his government substantially devalued the rupee to make Indian goods competitive in the world markets, abolished investment and import licensing (except on consumer goods imports), and threw open the door to direct foreign investment. It also stabilized the economy macro-economically, bringing down the fiscal deficit significantly.

Later, the government steadily lowered tariffs, opened civil aviation and telecommunication to the private sector, eased the entry of private domestic and foreign banks and reduced financial repression via reduction in the Statutory Liquidity Ratio (SLR) and Cash Reserve Ratio (CRR). By 1995/96, the highest industrial tariff rate had been brought down to 50 per cent (with the exception of some peak tariffs) from 355 per cent in 1990/91; personal income tax rates had been unified into three rates, 20, 30 and 40 per cent; and corporate profit tax had been reduced to 40 per cent from 50 per cent for widely held companies and from 55 per cent for closely held companies.

Occasional observers have described the Rao reforms as the continuation of a process that had been begun in the late 1970s and accelerated in the 1980s. This characterization not only undermines Rao's contribution; it is wholly misleading. The earlier measures had all been taken within the existing policy framework. In contrast, the

1991/92 reforms entirely abandoned that framework. In a single stroke, the statement of industrial policy dated 24 July 1991 did away with investment licensing and myriad entry restrictions on firms. It also ended public sector monopoly in most sectors and initiated a policy of automatic approval of foreign direct investment up to 51 per cent. So robust was this policy framework that the government has not had to replace it by a new one till today.

In a similar vein, entry into private sector in telecommunications and civil aviation broke new ground. For the first time since Independence, it threw open the doors of two sectors reserved for the public sector to private players. On the one hand, the reform established the principle of entry of the private sector into areas that were the exclusive preserve of the public sector in the past, and on the other it laid the foundation of yet more reforms and future revolutions in telecommunications and civil aviation.

The National Democratic Alliance (NDA) government under Prime Minister Atal Bihari Vajpayee, which served in office from March 1998 to May 2004, took the reform process initiated by Rao considerably forward. On the external front, it ended import licensing on consumer goods, brought the top industrial tariff rate down to 20 per cent by 2004/05 (later reduced to 10 per cent by 2007/08 by its successor, the United Progressive Alliance [UPA] government) and opened the door to direct foreign investment much wider, allowing 100 per cent foreign investment in a large number of sectors. On the internal front, it made significant progress in dismantling the small-scale industries reservation, abolishing it entirely for firms exporting 50 per cent or more of their output in 2000. It brought corporate profit tax down to 30 per cent; included services in the tax net for the first time; rationalized the indirect tax system by compressing the then-existing eleven excise tax rates into three rates of 8, 16 and 24 per cent; introduced the principle of Value-Added Tax in the states; and considerably improved tax administration.

Of particular significance under the NDA government were reforms in the area of macroeconomic policy. The government ended administered interest rates with one or two exceptions. It continued reducing financial repression by lowering the SLR and CRR further. It improved prudential regulation of banks, recapitalized them and encouraged them to raise their own equity by disinvestment up to 49 per cent. It enacted the important Securitization and Reconstruction of Financial Assets and Enforcement of Security Interest Act, 2002. Finally, it also enacted the Fiscal Responsibility and Budget Management Act, 2001, committing the government to a roadmap of fiscal consolidation.

The Vajpayee government also gave greater play to the private sector. It undertook genuine privatization of several public sector enterprises (PSEs) leading to a jump in their efficiency and profitability.[16] It opened life and general insurance to the private sector with 26 per cent stake by foreign companies allowed. It introduced the open skies policy, giving further impetus to private players in airline industry.

The New Telecom Policy (NTP), 1999, unleashed the mobile revolution in India. It greatly strengthened the Telecom Regulatory Authority of India (TRAI) and created the Telecom Dispute Settlement and Appellate Tribunal (TDSAT), giving the latter the entire responsibility for settling disputes involving consumers and providers. The NTP introduced a revenue-sharing regime, transferred the service provision function of the Department of Telecommunications to the newly created Bharat Sanchar Nigam Limited (BSNL), freed up entry into domestic and international long-distance service and introduced a unified licence for the provision of fixed-line and mobile telecom services. These changes kicked off an unstoppable revolution in the

---

16 Economist Nandini Gupta compared the PSEs privatized under Vajpayee with similar PSEs that had been identified for privatization but not privatized. She found that the former outperformed the latter by a wide margin along key dimensions. See Gupta, 2012.

telecommunications sector, with tele-density rising from just 2.8 in 1999/2000 to 78.7 per hundred persons in 2011/12.

In the area of infrastructure, the government broke new ground. It launched the National Highway Development Project (NHDP), under which it undertook the Golden Quadrilateral project that converted two-lane highways connecting Delhi, Mumbai, Chennai and Kolkata to four lanes. Alongside, the Prime Minister's Gram Sadak Yojana (PMGSY), which has become a major source of connectivity for rural India today, was also initiated. In civil aviation, domestic private airlines were given entry into international aviation, breaking the monopoly of Air India. The 2003 amendment of the Airport Authority of India (AIA) Act, 1994, allowed the entry of private airports, which led to transformational changes under the UPA government.

In agriculture, the State APMC (Development and Regulation) Model Law was introduced. Although the implementation of this law was unfortunately half-hearted, it made some positive contribution in some states by bringing more remunerative prices to farmers. Kisan credit cards were introduced in 1998. By the end of 2003/04, the government had cumulatively issued more than forty million Kisan credit cards. For the first time, India also introduced genetically modified organism (GMO) seeds in cotton. Subsequently, the pest-resistant Bt cotton revolutionized cotton farming in Gujarat, Andhra Pradesh and Maharashtra.

In the social sector, the government launched the Sarva Shiksha Abhiyan (SSA) or, literally translated, universal education mission. It led to massive expansion of elementary school enrolment. For the first time, the expenditure on education exceeded 4 per cent of the GDP and did not fall below 3.5 per cent in a single year under the Vajpayee government. The constitutional amendment making education a Fundamental Right was also passed. In the area of health, the Complete Sanitation Campaign was launched. The Integrated Child Development System (ICDS) was extended to all 5,652 blocks.

The Food-for-Work programme and Antyodaya Anna Yojana for ten million poorest households were introduced. There was also massive expansion of urban housing during this period.

Miracle Growth and A Major Blow to Abject Poverty

The reforms during the Rao and Vajpayee eras had a major impact on the economy. Opening up the economy to the world reflected itself in the rapid growth of exports and imports. From the peak of 7.9 per cent in 1951/52, exports of goods and services as a proportion of GDP had fallen below 5 per cent in 1958/59 and did not cross the 7 per cent mark again until as late as 1989/90. But after the 1991 reforms, they rose steadily and reached the impressive 25.1 per cent level in 2013/14 (Figure 2.2). Likewise, imports as a proportion of GDP, which crossed the 10 per cent mark for the first time in 1992/93, rose to a peak of 31.4 per cent in 2012/13 (Figure 2.3). From a near-autarkic economy, India came close to being a free-trade economy. This openness was accompanied by faster growth. Between 1992/93 and 2002/03, the economy grew at the average annual rate of 5.8 per cent. This was significantly higher than what had been experienced during the earlier periods.

Indeed, a much bigger impact on growth was seen beginning 2003/04. This was the last year of the Vajpayee government and growth shifted to a new 8 per cent-plus trajectory. Although the successor government under Prime Minister Manmohan Singh did not carry forward the process of reforms and the global economy faced a major financial crisis in 2008, the lagged effect of what the Rao and Vajpayee governments had done sustained growth in India at the average level of 8.2 per cent for nine years from 2003/04 to 2011/12.

The accelerated growth in turn helped combat poverty. It did so through two channels. First, it created employment opportunities and raised wages, which helped reduce poverty directly. Increased income allowed the poor better access to not only items of daily needs such as food, clothing and shelter but also quality services in areas such as education and health.

Second, higher growth placed larger volume of revenues in the hands of the government than would have been possible if growth had been slower. These revenues allowed the government to increase social spending. It was on the strength of this 8 per cent-plus growth during the period 2003–12 that the UPA government was able to introduce the Mahatma Gandhi National Rural Employment Guarantee Act (MGNREGA) scheme, under which the government guaranteed one adult member of every rural household one hundred days of employment each year. Increased revenues also paved the way for the Right to Education Act, 2009, and the National Food Security Act, 2013. Under the former, all children aged six to fourteen years were guaranteed school education and under the latter, the availability of highly subsidized food grains was extended to 75 per cent of the population in rural areas and 50 per cent of the population in urban areas.

Empirical evidence on the evolution of poverty during the post-reform era reinforces these analytic arguments. No matter how we dissect the data, there is unequivocal evidence of significantly faster poverty reduction alongside faster growth. For starters, research has shown that during the early decades of development, the trend in poverty exhibited no decline. Poverty fell during the years of good monsoon but rose during the years of drought with the trend staying flat.[17] Given that India started with an extremely low per capita income in 1950/51 and the increase in the latter in the early decades was very slow, this trend is consistent with the hypothesis of no poverty reduction at low per capita income without substantial growth.

By 1990/91, per capita income had reached slightly more than double of what its level was in 1950/51. Therefore, prospects for poverty reduction with further increases in per capita income had improved. Evidence shows that poverty declined with growth in the post-1991

17 Panagariya, 2008, pp. 131–36.

era and it declined faster with faster growth. Most remarkably, when we look at well-defined groups within the population, this pattern holds up for all of them.

Figures 2.4 to 2.6 show poverty ratios at the official poverty line at the aggregate level in urban and rural India, across different social groups and in the twenty-one largest states, respectively, in 1993/94, 2004/05 and 2001–12. Three observations follow from these figures. First, the reduction in poverty at the national level is larger for all groups shown during the seven years from 2004/05 to 2011/12 than during the eleven years from 1993/94 to 2004/05. Recall that the period 2004/05 to 2011/12 also happens to be that of fastest growth. Second, during the period shown, poverty has declined for all groups, Scheduled Castes, Scheduled Tribes, and all areas, rural and urban. Finally, poverty has declined between 1993/94 and 2011/12 for all states, as shown in Figure 2.6. At the group level, growth has not left anyone behind.

Figure 2.4: Poverty in Rural and Urban India

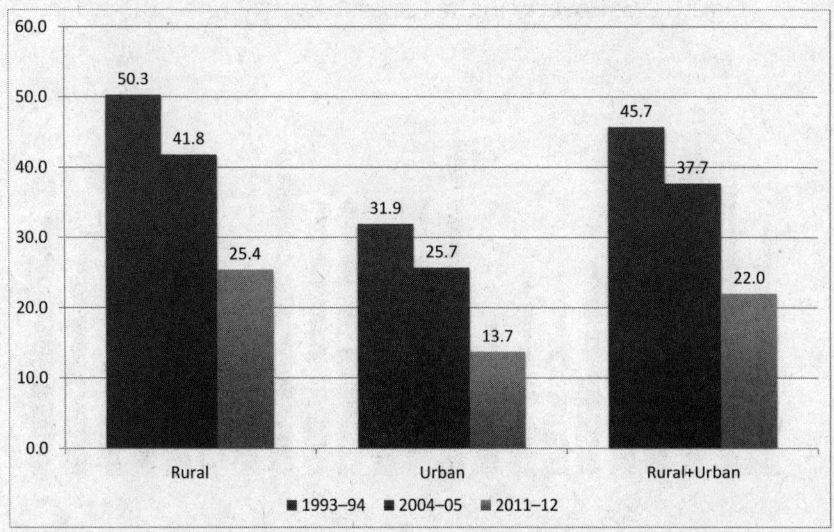

Source: Author's construction based on estimates in Panagariya and More, 2014

Figure 2.5: Poverty among Scheduled Castes and Scheduled Tribes

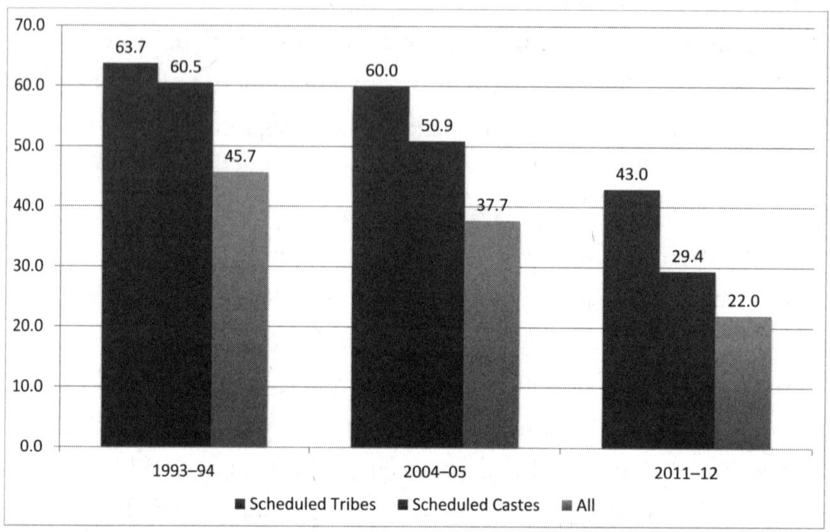

Source: Author's construction based on estimates in Panagariya and More, 2014

Figure 2.6: Poverty in the Largest Twenty-one States

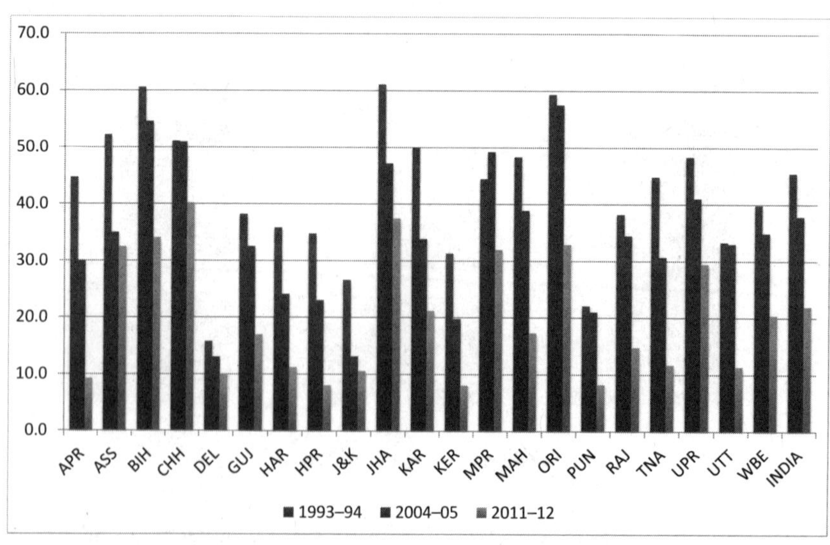

Source: Author's construction based on estimates in Panagariya and More, 2014

Renewed Policy Mistakes Culminating in a Setback to Growth: 2004–14

The Congress-led UPA government under Prime Minister Manmohan Singh, which came to power in 2004, focused principally on social programmes. Taking advantage of accelerating revenues that came with high growth, it initiated new social programmes while also expanding those it had inherited from the previous government. Programmes in the former category included the MGNREGA scheme and compulsory education for children from the ages of six to fourteen years under the Right to Education Act, 2009. Programmes under the latter category were numerous, with the notable ones being rural electrification, Prime Minister's Rural Roads Programme and the public distribution system (PDS) providing highly subsidized foodgrains to the poor.

Unfortunately, however, the Singh government did not maintain the pace of reforms necessary to sustain high growth. The main reforms by the UPA over ten years of its rule included reduction in the highest non-agricultural tariff rate from the 20 per cent it had inherited to 10 per cent (with some sectors retaining higher rates) by April 2007; further liberalization of foreign direct investment; further financial sector liberalization; trimming of the SSI reservation list; pension reform; entry of private players in the construction and running of airports; deregulation of petroleum prices; and, most importantly, the launch of the biometric identity project Aadhaar.

Apart from the slowdown in reform, the UPA also took some decisions that were detrimental to growth, especially during its second term from 2009 to 2014. It introduced retrospective taxation, which hit a number of multinationals particularly hard and sent a chill down the spines of foreign investors. It also enacted the Land Acquisition Act, 2013, which made land acquisition both time-consuming and financially costly. It passed the Right to Education Act, 2009, which laid down norms for recognition of schools that were based solely on inputs. Many of these norms had no relationship to the quality of education and threatened the survival of low-budget private schools that provided better education than their public counterparts in the same geographical area. Finally, through the passage of the Food Security Act, 2013, the UPA extended a corrupt and leaky public distribution system to 75 per cent of the rural and 50 per cent of the urban population. This spread the available resources for transfer to the poor thinly over a large population, which included many who did not suffer from any deprivations identified in the Socio-Economic Caste Census.

During the last year of the first term and early years of the second term, the UPA government also abandoned fiscal discipline, incurring large fiscal deficits. The deficits eventually fuelled inflation and widened the current account deficit to alarming levels. In response, the Reserve Bank of India (RBI) raised the interest rate on thirteen consecutive occasions between 19 March 2010 and 25 October 2011. Alongside, environmental clearances for large projects came to a standstill and decision-making in the central government suffered a general paralysis.

These factors led to a decline in the growth rate from 10.3 per cent in 2010/11 to 6.6 per cent in 2011/12 and then to 5.5 per cent in 2012/13. The relative weakness of the macroeconomic situation and prospects of the United States returning to a tighter monetary policy during the summer of 2013 led to large capital outflows and depreciation of the rupee by a wide margin. Although there was some recovery in 2013/14 with the growth rate rising to 6.4 per cent, the economy remained fragile. These were the circumstances under which Prime Minister Narendra Modi took charge of the government.

Setting the House in Order and Back to Reforms: 2014–18

In May 2014, having won a landslide victory in the parliamentary elections on a development platform, Prime Minister Narendra Modi came to office. His government immediately took several measures to restore confidence. It credibly committed to initiating no new cases of retrospective taxation, though it stopped short of repealing the measure altogether. It speeded up environmental clearances and ended the paralysis that had characterized the decision-making process in the central government. The government also made a concerted effort to improve the ease of doing business in the central government as well as at the level of the states. A large number of projects that had been stuck for a variety of reasons were unblocked. Above all, the government revived and invigorated the process of reforms.

Key reforms by the Modi government included the introduction of a much-needed modern bankruptcy law through the Insolvency and Bankruptcy Code; replacement of myriad indirect taxes by a single nationwide uniform Goods and Services Tax (GST); replacement of fragmented and leaky chains of distribution of government social benefits by direct benefit transfers (DBT) using the instrumentalities of the biometric Aadhaar identity and near-universalization of bank accounts; a systematic assault on corruption in the central government; provision of fixed-term labour contracts resulting in greater flexibility in employment; end to subsidy on diesel; autonomy to well-ranked universities and colleges; adoption of inflation targeting; stricter rules governing defaults by bank borrowers; creation of cost-effective digital platforms through the Unified Payments Interface (UPI) system; and near-universalization of toilets in rural households. For the first time, the Modi government also took systematic steps to combat corruption. Most prominent among these steps was the demonetization of high-denomination currency notes.

Improved decision-making and reforms helped return India to higher growth path. During the first four years of the Modi government, India clocked an annual average rate of growth of 7.7 per cent. It is a fair assessment that the full impact of many of the reforms by the government is yet to be realized. But as the recent slowdown illustrates, the government cannot take sustained growth for granted. To bring prosperity to all, it will need to stay the course on reforms.

Concluding Remarks

Historically, India has been among the largest economies of the world. But over time, especially under the British rule, it lost the prime place in the global economy that it had enjoyed for almost two millennia. With the Industrial Revolution concentrated in the West, India lost even greater ground in relative terms. Happily, in recent years, India has begun to regain its position among the large economies. Between 1990 and 2005, it was entirely absent from the top ten countries of the world by GDP. But in 2010, it became the ninth-largest economy in the world and quickly climbed to the seventh position in 2015 and sixth in 2017.

In 2017/18, India's GDP was $2.6 trillion in 2017 dollars. If India grows by 8 per cent in real dollars–a perfectly plausible assumption–it can more than double its GDP in less than ten years. If the Japanese economy remains as tepid as it has been in recent decades, this would comfortably make India the third largest economy in the world by 2027.

But achieving 8 per cent or faster growth would require avoiding the past mistakes and staying the course on reforms. An analysis of how other economies have grown rapidly and India's own past experience points to the critical importance of openness to trade. Ultra-tight control of investment and imports in the past, especially from 1951–81, held back India's growth. Releasing controls on the economy, both internally and externally, has allowed India to gain its potential more fully. India must build on this success to transform itself into a prosperous and modern economy. The remainder of this volume is about the reforms India must undertake to achieve this objective.

PART II

UNDERSTANDING THE CHALLENGE OF TRANSFORMATION

3

UNDEREMPLOYMENT IN AGRICULTURE

THE LARGEST PROPORTION OF India's workforce is employed in agriculture. Therefore, any analysis of policy reform in India must begin with this sector. The analysis cannot end with prescriptions aimed at improving farm incomes, however; a significant part of improving the lives of today's farmers lies in helping a large proportion of them to exit to more productive jobs in industry and services.

Much of the public policy discussion on agriculture in India implicitly assumes that this sector is synonymous with the rural economy. This may have been approximately true during the early decades following Independence, but it is not so anymore. One would think that politicians who seek rural votes would appreciate the difference and equally address the needs of farmer and non-farmer populations in rural India. But at least in their public pronouncements, they continue to focus disproportionately on farmers and neglect the non-farmer rural population.

In 1977/78, the earliest year for which sectoral employment shares are readily available, agriculture had a share of 80.6 per cent in the male workforce and 88.1 per cent in the female workforce in rural India. At these shares, the assumption that the rural workforce was largely agricultural could be defended. But in the subsequent years, these figures steadily fell. In 1993/94, they were estimated at 74.1 and 86.2 per cent for male and female workforces, respectively. By 2017/18, the latest year for which we have the estimates, the shares had fallen to 55.0 and 73.2 per cent respectively.[18] In this year, the employment share of agriculture in the total rural workforce was 59.4 per cent.[19] The assumption that rural workforce is all about agriculture can no longer be defended.

A further complication is that though agriculture is predominantly a rural activity, some agricultural activity also takes place in urban India. The proportion of urban workforce in agriculture was 10.6 per cent for males and 31.9 per cent for females in 1977/78. These proportions fell to 5.38 and 9.07 per cent respectively in 2017/18.[20] The share of agriculture in the total urban workforce stood at 6.14 per cent in 2017/18.[21]

These employment estimates imply that though there is a large overlap between agriculture and the rural economy, the two are far from synonymous. As a matter of approximation, we may say that agriculture is a wholly rural activity. But it would be a stretch to say that rural economic activity is all about agriculture. As of 2017/18, two-fifths of the rural workforce was employed in non-agricultural activities.

Unfortunately, the National Accounts Statistics of India does not separate sectoral GDP data by rural and urban areas. Therefore, it is not possible to analyse agriculture separately as a rural or urban activity. Likewise, we lack the GDP data associated with non-agricultural employment in rural India. Therefore, strictly speaking, our analysis

18 National Sample Survey Office, 2019, Statement 16, p. 65

19 National Sample Survey Office 2019, Table 26, p. A-150

20 National Sample Survey Office 2019, Statement 16, p. 65

21 National Sample Survey Office 2019, Table 26, p. A-150

below is purely sectoral in nature, applying to rural and urban areas taken jointly. At most we can say that what happens in agriculture largely impacts the rural population. But agriculture does not tell us the full story of the economic fortunes of rural India. These nuances must be kept in mind throughout this chapter.

A Brief Overview of Agricultural and Rural Policies

The Bengal famine of 1943, the subsequent continuing food shortages and repeated bouts of food inflation were foremost on the minds of policymakers following Independence. Therefore, the key objective guiding agricultural policy at the time was the achievement of self-sufficiency in foodgrain production. During the years that Prime Minister Jawaharlal Nehru ruled, the government sought to achieve this objective through an institutional approach that consisted of land reforms and farm and service cooperatives.[22]

In the event, both land reform and cooperative movements were largely unsuccessful and, with rising population, food shortage became more acute in the 1960s. India came to depend heavily on food aid from the United States. Nehru died in 1964 and Prime Minister Lal Bahadur Shastri succeeded him. Around this time, food shortage became sufficiently serious for Shastri to call upon the nation to forego at least one meal every week. Subsequently, after Shastri passed away in 1966 and Indira Gandhi came to the helm, India faced virtual humiliation at the hands of United States President Lyndon B. Johnson for becoming dependent on food aid from his country. Partially irked by India's lack of support for his Vietnam policy, Johnson vowed to keep India on a ship-to-mouth policy whereby he would release ships carrying foodgrain only after food shortage reached a point of desperation. An episode reported by Ravi V. Prasad, son of Sharada

22 Varshney, 1995, Chapter 2

Prasad, press secretary to Gandhi, captures the anguish Gandhi felt when dealing with Johnson in these terms:

> My father was present when she [Indira Gandhi] was on the telephone with Lyndon Johnson regarding the food shipments when India was living from ship to mouth. She was clenching her fists in anger while she was all sweetness over the phone with Johnson in a gentle voice at her persuasive best. She then vowed in fierce determination that she would see to it that India became self-sufficient in food, and that no Indian leader would ever have to beg for aid again.[23]

By this time, India had switched from its earlier institutional approach towards agricultural policy to one that was based on technology and remunerative prices for farmers. At the centre of this policy were imported high-yielding varieties of seeds. Thanks to the resounding success of the new policy, India was able to usher in the Green Revolution, which led to the fulfilment of the objective of self-sufficiency in food. By the mid-1980s, India's foodgrain imports had dropped to nil.

With self-sufficiency achieved, the implicit goal of India's agricultural policy changed to the improvement of the lot of farmers. Regardless of which party or coalition ruled, this objective has guided its policy since the mid-1980s. Accordingly, over the years, the government has launched an impressive array of schemes and programmes aimed at benefiting the rural population, of which farmers are the largest group. Consider some of the more important of these schemes and programmes in force today:

---

23 Prasad, 2015. Author Denis Kux reports the same incident in these words, 'The Prime Minister [was] clenching her fingers tightly on the telephone. Talking to Johnson, she was friendly and charming, but when she hung up, she said angrily, "I don't want us to ever have to beg for food again."' See Kux, 1992, p. 257.

- Under the National Food Security Act (NFSA), a nationwide network of public distribution system (PDS) provides 5 kilogrammes of wheat at ₹2 per kilogramme or rice at ₹3 per kilogramme per person per month to 75 per cent of rural households. The poorest of the poor among these 75 per cent receive 35 kilogrammes of wheat or rice per household at these subsidized prices. With 75 per cent of rural households covered, the programme has the potential to benefits all poor farm households.
- The government has a massive procurement programme under which it buys a substantial proportion of wheat and rice at the minimum support prices (MSP), which are set well above corresponding market prices. Foodgrain so procured is then distributed through PDS shops to beneficiaries at subsidized prices. Therefore, as sellers, farmers can receive high prices and as buyers, they need pay only nominal prices for foodgrains.
- The Mahatma Gandhi National Rural Employment Guarantee Act (MGNREGA) scheme offers guaranteed employment up to 100 days per year to one adult per rural household at a specified wage. The programme serves as a source of employment during lean seasons. Workers hired under it help build public assets at the local level.
- The government has a major fertilizer subsidy scheme. Under it, farmers can purchase urea at a pre-specified below-market price. In 2017/18, this subsidy amounted to ₹700 billion. Farmers in most states also receive free electricity. Alongside, a separate scheme provides crop insurance to farmers at highly subsidized premiums.
- Finally, the government runs a variety of schemes and programmes that benefit farmers, directly or indirectly. Below is a partial list:

- Under the Prime Minister's Housing Scheme, the government provides ₹120,000 and ninety days of free MGNREGA labour to build pucca houses for households living in kuccha houses;
- Under the Ujjwala scheme, ₹1,600 is given to poor households to obtain a connection for cooking gas;
- Under the Prime Minister's Rural Roads Scheme, the government has been building rural roads since 2000/01 to provide connectivity to unconnected habitations with 570,000 kilometres of roads already constructed;
- A rural electrification programme has brought electricity to all villages and nearly all households;
- Under the Prime Minister's Irrigation Scheme, massive amounts have been spent on expanding cultivated areas under irrigation;
- There are separate schemes to promote white (milk) and blue (fisheries) revolutions;
- Free primary education is provided under the National Education Mission;
- Since the 1960s, the government has built a network of sub-centres, primary health centres and community health centres to provide free primary health-care services in rural India; and
- During elections, governments waived massive volumes of farm loans at the expense of the exchequer.

Perpetual Farmer Distress

Notwithstanding these numerous programmes aimed at addressing different aspects of lives of farmers and others in rural India, it is commonplace to come across stories of distress, especially those relating to farmers. There thus remains a sharp contrast between the resources and efforts successive governments have put into bringing relief to farmers and the dominant narrative in the media and among intellectuals. How is this contradiction to be explained?

There are two hypotheses. First, since stories of distress grab public attention more easily, the media has a vested interest in exaggerating them. Being overly critical of the government of the day, it also disproportionately focuses on negative stories. Since television is a visual medium, it has a great advantage in translating an isolated story of suffering into generalized distress across the length and breadth of the nation. In contrast, hard data is costly to collect, requires specialized skills and often does not get traction with viewers.

Second, it is possible that the stories of recurring, even perpetual, distress afflicting the rural population, especially farmers, on a large scale, are real. Despite significant reduction in abject poverty, the overall level of income in India remains low. Indeed, going by the 2011/12 NSSO expenditure survey, which is the latest such survey available to date, the per capita expenditure of 80 per cent of the rural population at prices prevailing that year was ₹59 per day or less. The corresponding expenditure in urban India was significantly higher at ₹111.5.[24] In all likelihood, the expenditure in urban areas is greatly underestimated on account of the wealthiest households going unrepresented in the sample from which the estimates are derived.

I would argue that the reality is somewhere between these two extremes, though closer to the latter. It cannot be denied that the media exhibits a tendency to pick episodes of distress and depict them as representing generalized distress across the entire nation. For example, just as suicides cannot be eliminated entirely from the non-farmer

---

24 National Sample Survey Office (2014a). *Level and Pattern of Consumer Expenditure 2011–12*, NSS Report No. 555, Ministry of Statistics and Programme Implementation, Government of India, Table T3, p.18. Expenditure figures quoted in the text are based on the Modified Mixed Reference Period method of measurement, which is judged to provide the most accurate estimates of consumer expenditure.

population, they cannot be eliminated from farmer population. But many journalists and non-governmental organizations (NGOs) use the existence of farmer suicides by itself as compelling evidence of widespread distress among farmers in their press writings and television appearances. For instance, a little-appreciated fact is that farmer suicide rates in the poorest states of Bihar, Odisha and Uttar Pradesh have been minuscule in comparison to the richer states such as Kerala, Karnataka and Maharashtra. Likewise, overall farmer suicide rates are far lower than the rates exhibited by the non-farmer population.

This being said, to make progress, the first thing we need to do is recognize that rural incomes, including those of farmers, remain low. Rapid growth in the past two decades has surely helped reduce abject poverty on a significant scale but this is not the same as saying that the rural population has achieved comfortable levels of income. Per capita expenditure data cited above testifies to this fact. Therefore, the question we must investigate next is why this is so.

Why Have Agricultural Incomes Remained Low?

Rural incomes, which are predominantly derived from agriculture, have not done well. The explanation for this phenomenon is as follows. A robust, stylized fact of growth and development is that a declining share of agriculture in the GDP accompanies rising per capita incomes. India has been no exception. In most countries experiencing rising per capita incomes, as agriculture's share in GDP declines, its share in employment also does so commensurately. The latter decline in India has been, at best, modest. As a result, too many households in India now depend on too small a share of agriculture in the GDP. This problem is compounded by the fact that as family farms have been divided with rising population over the generations, landholdings have become progressively smaller. Half of the landholdings today are half a hectare or smaller. To appreciate the magnitude of the problem, let us consider these phenomena in some detail.

Growth in Agriculture Lagging Behind Industry and Services

As a long-term trend, without exception, the share of agriculture in GDP declines as per capita incomes rise. For instance, it fell from 27 per cent in 1990 to 8 per cent in 2017 in China; from 26 per cent in 1970 to 8 per cent in 1990 and then 2 per cent in 2017 in South Korea; and from 39 per cent in 1990 to 15 per cent in 2017 in Vietnam. In developed countries, the share stands at extremely low levels today: 1.5 per cent in France in 2017; 1 per cent in Japan and the United States in 2016; and 0.5 per cent in the United Kingdom in 2017.[25]

This pattern is the result of slower growth in agriculture than in industry and services. The impetus for acceleration in growth invariably originates in industry and services. As a result, the faster the rise in per capita income, the faster is the decline in the share of agriculture in GDP.

The process of declining share of agriculture in GDP has been under way in India as well, at least since Independence. In the initial decades, industry and services grew slowly so that the decline in the share of agriculture was also slow. But once growth in industry and services accelerated, the process of decline speeded up. Table 3.1, which provides the growth rates in agriculture, industry, services and the GDP from 1951–52 to 2016–17, captures this feature of India's post-Independence experience. The table divides these years into three periods showing slow, moderate and fast growth of GDP.

For the present purpose, two key features of the table may be noted. First, the growth rate in agriculture has been consistently lower than in industry and services. This fact has meant that the share of

---

25 These figures have been taken from the World Development Indicators of the World Bank, available at https://data.worldbank.org/indicator/NV.AGR.TOTL.ZS (last accessed on 17 December 2018).

agriculture in the GDP has consistently shrunken over time. Second, while growth rates in industry and services rose successively and significantly in the second and third periods, agriculture experienced a modest acceleration in the second period but lost a large part of that gain in the third period. Acceleration in agriculture in the second period resulted from the Green Revolution but the momentum could not be sustained.

Table 3.1: Growth Rates in Agriculture, Industry and Services, 1951/52 to 2016/17

Period	Agriculture	Industry	Services	GDP
1951/52 to 1979/80	2.1	5.4	4.5	3.5
1980/81 to 1999/2000	3.8	6.1	6.8	5.8
2000/01 to 2016/17	3.0	7.2	8.4	7.1
1951/52 to 2016/17	2.9	6.1	6.2	5.1

Source: Author's calculation using CSO data on GDP at factor cost at constant 2004/05 prices until 2011/12 and at constant 2011/12 prices thereafter

Note: Throughout this volume, unless explicitly stated otherwise, agriculture includes allied activities and services include construction

The result of this pattern of growth has been that the level of GDP in industry and services taken together greatly diverged from that in agriculture in the second and third periods. The divergence was particularly pronounced during the third period because industry and services continued to accelerate while agriculture decelerated. This 'growth' effect on divergence has been reinforced by a 'level' effect. Once the absolute level of combined GDP in industry and services came to exceed that in agriculture, each percentage point increase in the former resulted in a larger absolute increase than that in the latter.

Figure 3.1, which depicts the evolution of GDP in the three sectors from 1950/51 to 2013/14, graphically brings out the uneven performance of agricultural and non-agricultural sectors. The graph ends in 2013/14 because the CSO series on sectoral GDP at constant prices in a common base year is available only up to this year. To emphasize the divergence between industry and services on the one hand and agriculture on the other, Figure 3.1 shows sectoral outputs in a stacked form: the middle curve represents GDP in agriculture plus industry and the top one represents GDP in all three sectors combined. As can be seen, the gap between agriculture and other sectors has become progressively larger.

Figure 3.1: Sectoral GDP at Factor Cost in Constant 2004/05 Prices from 1950/51 to 2011/12

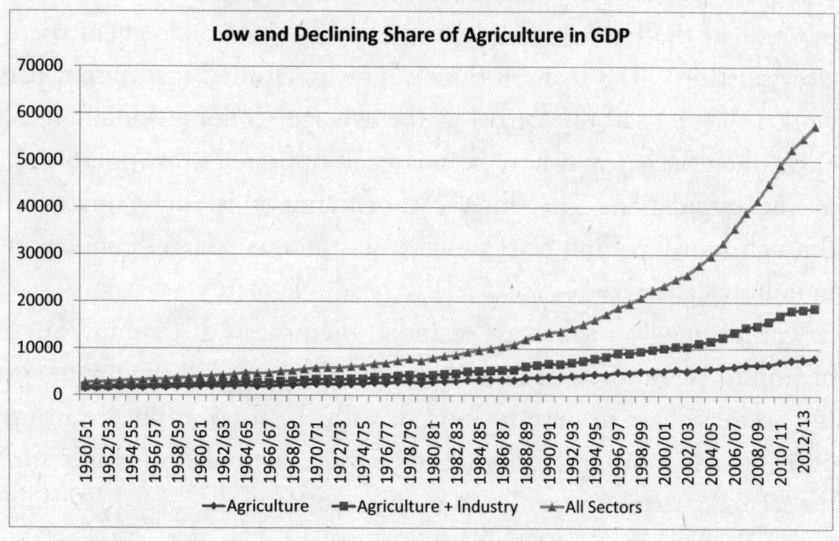

Source: Author's construction using CSO data

Until the early 1980s, the three sectors saw minimal divergence because industry and services had a slight lead over agriculture in terms of growth rate and agriculture had begun with larger than half the share in the GDP in 1950/51. But by the beginning of the second period, not only had the share of agriculture in the GDP fallen well below half, industry and services growth rates acquired substantially greater advantage over it. This process accelerated further in the third period. The result was that the share of agriculture in the GDP fell from 53.1 per cent in 1950/51 to 36.1 per cent in 1980/81 and then plummeted to 14.4 per cent in 2011/12.

A More Stubborn Share of Agriculture in Employment

Most of the countries that enjoy high incomes and therefore exhibit a low share of agriculture in GDP have also seen a large decline in the proportion of the workforce employed in agriculture. For example, this proportion stood at 5 per cent in South Korea, 3.5 per cent in Japan, 2.9 per cent in France, 2 per cent in the United States and 1 per cent in the United Kingdom in 2017.[26] Low employment share alongside low GDP share in these countries ensured that output per worker did not fall too far below the average economy-wide figures. Even when the gap may have been large, it impacted a tiny proportion of the population. Therefore, compensating this tiny population through transfers from taxes raised from the much larger population in industry and services was a relatively simple matter.

Unfortunately, in the case of India, the process of the movement of workforce out of agriculture has not kept pace with the decline in this sector's share in output. Indeed, with the total workforce rising over time, at least until 2004/05, the absolute number of workers in the sector saw an increase. It is only after 2004/05 that a sharp decline in female labour participation rates has yielded a modest decline in this figure.

---

26 These figures represent modelled International Labour Organization estimates as reported in the World Development Indicators at https://data.worldbank.org/indicator/SL.AGR.EMPL.ZS (last accessed on 17 December 2018).

Estimation of the absolute level of employment in different sectors at the national level in a consistent manner requires unit-level observations from the large Employment–Unemployment surveys. The latter are available from the National Statistical Office (NSO) from 1987/88 to 2017/18 at approximately five-year intervals. Accordingly, Figure 3.2, which shows the absolute number of workers employed in agriculture, begins in 1987/88 and ends in 2017/18. Between 1987/88 and 2004/05, the workforce in agriculture increased by a hefty 25 per cent. This number finally saw a decline beginning in 2011–12 with its level in 2017/18 falling barely a hair's breadth below that in 1987/88.

Figure 3.2: Total Number of Workers in Agriculture, Industry and Services in 1987/88, 1993/94, 1999/2000, 2004/05 and 2011/12

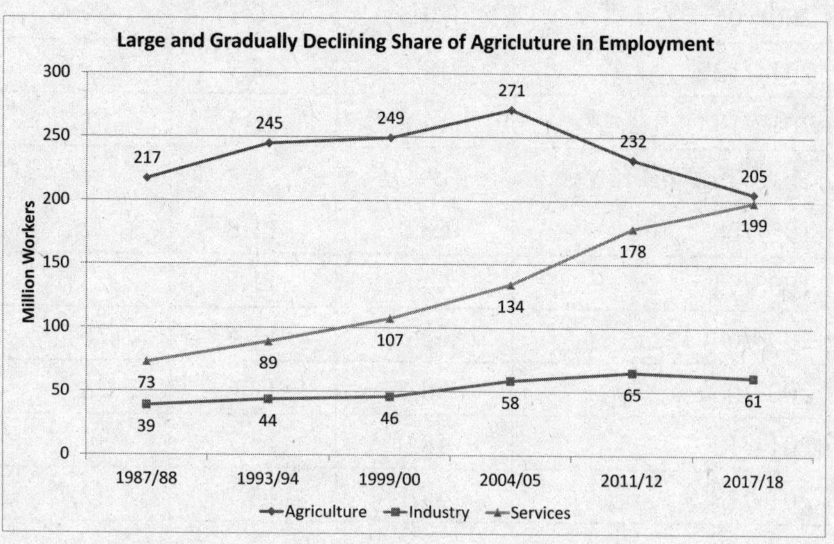

Source: Author's construction based on estimates by economist Rahul Ahluwalia from Employment–Unemployment and Period Labour Force Surveys by the National Statistical Office

Table 3.2 shows the evolution of the shares of the three sectors in GDP and workforce to further emphasize the slow pace of change in the composition of workforce relative to GDP. Between 1987/88 and 2017/18, the share of agriculture in GDP fell by more than half, from 30 per cent to 14.8 per cent. But the decline in the workforce share was far less sharp, from 66 per cent to 44.1 per cent.

Table 3.2: Shares of Agriculture, Industry and Services in GDP and Workforce

Year	Agriculture	Industry	Services
Share in GDP			
1987/88	30.0	20.1	49.8
1993/94	28.3	20.1	51.5
1999/00	23.3	20.4	56.4
2004/05	20.3	20.1	59.6
2011/12	18.5	22.9	58.6
2017/18	14.8	23.5	61.7
Share in Workforce			
1987/88	66.0	11.8	22.2
1993/94	64.6	11.5	23.5
1999/00	62.0	11.4	26.7
2004/05	58.5	12.6	28.9
2011/12	48.9	13.7	37.5
2017/18	44.1	13.1	42.7

Source: Author's calculations using CSO data on GDP and workforce estimates by Rahul Ahluwalia from Employment–Unemployment and Periodic Labour Force Surveys

Note: GDP data is at constant 2004/05 prices until that year and at 2011/12 prices thereafter

A very large part of the decline in the workforce share took place between 2004/05 and 2011/12, when the total workforce grew just 2.6 per cent due to a precipitous fall in female worker participation rate in rural areas. This growth in workforce between 2004/05 and 2011/12 compares with 15.5 per cent growth between 1999/2000 and 2004/05. If not for the large decline in female worker participation rate in rural areas, workforce share of agriculture in 2011/12 would have remained significantly higher than 48.9 per cent. Equally disturbing is the fact that the modest decline in workforce share of agriculture between 2011/12 and 2017/18 has also been substantially due to a further decline in female worker participation rate.

Large and Widening Gap in Per Worker Output between Agriculture and Other Sectors

To make further transparent the implications of continued high share of agriculture in the workforce in relation to agricultural GDP, Table 3.3 reports per worker GDP in industry, services and all sectors relative to per worker GDP in agriculture. The slow transition of the workforce out of agriculture even during the decades preceding 1987/88 meant that by that year, industry and services had already come to enjoy a GDP per worker that was respectively 3.8 and 4.9 times that in agriculture. In the subsequent years, these proportions rose, reaching 4.6 in industry and 5.9 in services in 2004/05. A revised GDP estimation methodology led to some shift in output proportions in favour of industry over services, but the gap between agriculture and non-agricultural GDP rose steadily. This is reflected in the output per worker in all sectors taken together, relative to that in agriculture rising from 2.2 in 1987/88 to 3.0 in 2017/18. Output per worker in industry and services stood at more than four times that in agriculture in 2017/18.

Table 3.3: Per Worker Productivity in Industry, Services and All Sectors Relative to Agriculture

Year	Industry	Services	All Sectors
1987/88	3.8	4.9	2.2
1993/94	4.0	5.0	2.3
1999/00	4.8	5.6	2.7
2004/05	4.6	5.9	2.9
2011/12	4.4	4.1	2.6
2017/18	5.3	4.3	3.0

Sources: Author's calculation using CSO GDP data and estimates of employment by economist Rahul Ahluwalia

Note: GDP data is at constant 2004/05 prices until that year and at 2011/12 prices thereafter

Low Absolute Level of Per Worker Output in Agriculture

These per worker output gaps would not matter much had the proportion of workforce in agriculture been small or the overall per worker income high. But neither of these conditions holds in India. With more than two-fifths of the workforce in agriculture, a very large part of the population is dependent on this sector. Moreover, with overall output per worker remaining low, output per worker in agriculture is extremely low too.

Figure 3.3 illustrates this last point graphically. Per worker output in agriculture in 2017/18 was just ₹129,980 at current prices. For a family of five, this works out to just ₹71.22 per person per day. That is to say, if the entire agricultural output in 2017/18 could be equally distributed among farm workers, it would have given just ₹71.22 per family member in expenditure in households with only one agricultural worker and no other source of income. Of course, given that the supply chain delivering farm produce from farm gate to final consumer must be maintained, it is an impossibility to give the entire farm output to agricultural workers. Likewise, with no history of redistribution of income from rich farmers to poor farmers and agricultural workers, distributing agricultural income equally among all agricultural workers is also unlikely. These facts imply that most farmers who work on tiny farms—68.5 per cent of Indian farms are smaller than one hectare as per the 2015–16 Agricultural Census—cannot be helped in any significant way through market reforms leading to more remunerative prices.

Figure 3.3: Gross Value Added Per Worker in Broad Sectors in 2017/18 in Current Rupees

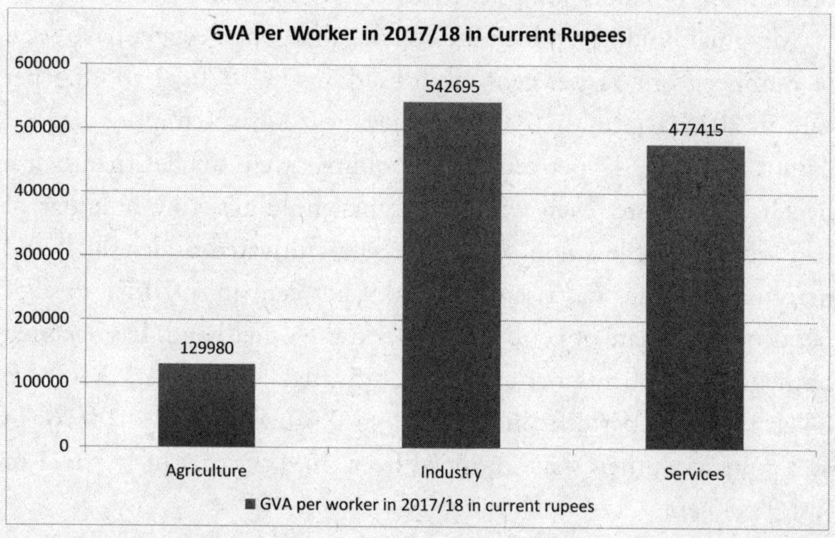

Source: Author's construction based on GVA data by CSO and workforce estimates obtained from the PLFS survey by NSO

In comparison, in South Korea, the share of agriculture stood at 2 per cent in the GDP and 5 per cent in employment in 2017. These proportions imply that output per worker in agriculture that year was two-fifths of that in all sectors taken together. But this gap impacted only 5 per cent of the workforce. In addition, with the overall level of per capita income in South Korea being high, the absolute level of income in agriculture is high enough to give farmers a decent living standard. With high per worker output overall, the scope for redistribution per farmer is also much greater.

Preponderance of Tiny Landholdings within Agriculture

The burden of low absolute sector-wide per worker GDP in agriculture is made worse by overly uneven distribution of cultivable land among farmers. The vast majority of farmers in India cultivate tiny farms that are getting tinier over time. The point is graphically brought out by Table 3.4, which reports the size distribution and operated area distribution of landholdings over time.

Marginal holdings, which are smaller than one hectare, have risen in number from 51 per cent of all holdings in 1970/71 to 68.5 per cent in 2015/16. In 2010/11, the latest year for which more detailed data is available, 47 per cent of all holdings were smaller than half a hectare. Therefore, even within marginal holdings, tiny holdings of half a hectare or less dominate. The area cultivated under small and marginal holdings has risen from 20.9 per cent in 1970/71 to 47.4 per cent. The share of large holdings, on the other hand, has declined both in terms of number and area cultivated. In number, they have fallen from 3.9 per cent in 1970/71 to 0.6 per cent in 2015/16. In area cultivated, their share dropped from 30.8 per cent in 1970/71 to just 9 per cent.

This size and operated area distribution of landholdings has serious implications for both the efficiency and plight of the bulk of the farmers. As regards efficiency, small farms have numerous disadvantages. They are unable to use high-capacity machinery and have restricted access to manifold cheaper credit from formal as opposed to informal sources. They also place the farmer at a great disadvantage when selling her produce. For example, it is the large farmers who are able to sell their produce at the minimum support prices, which are invariably higher than the market prices.

Table 3.4: Size and Operated Area Distributions of Landholdings

Size Groups	1970/71	1990/91	2010/11	2015/16
Percentage of All Holdings				
Marginal (less than 1 hectare)	51.0	59.4	67.1	68.5
Small (1 to 2 hectares)	18.9	18.8	17.9	17.7
Semi/Medium (2 to 4 hectares)	15.0	13.1	10.0	9.5
Medium (4 to 10 hectares)	11.2	7.1	4.2	3.8
Large (10 hectares or more)	3.9	1.6	0.7	0.6
All Sizes	71011	106637	138348	145727
Percentage of operated area				
Marginal (less than 1 hectare)	9.0	15.0	22.5	24.2
Small (1 to 2 hectares)	11.9	17.4	22.1	23.2
Semi/Medium (2 to 4 hectares)	18.5	23.2	23.6	23.7
Medium (4 to 10 hectares)	29.7	27.0	21.2	20.0
Large (10 hectares or more)	30.8	17.3	10.6	9.0
All Sizes	162318	165507	159592	157142

Source: Author's calculations using data from Agricultural Census 2015/16

In what is perhaps the most careful study using panel data from India, economists Andrew Foster and Mark Rosenzweig find that profits per hectare rise as farm size increases. Even within the same farm, larger plots are more profitable than smaller ones. Larger farms enjoy credit advantage and are more mechanized.[27]

The most deleterious effect of progressive fragmentation and decline in farm size relates to the welfare of farmers. With profitability itself declining with farm size, farms less than half a hectare scarcely allow a family of four or five to earn a living. Indeed, even farms that are two hectares in size offer barely a subsistence existence to a family of four or five. Sadly, a whopping 86.2 per cent of landholdings in India are smaller than two hectares. Unsurprisingly, nearly 80 per cent of India's poor households remain in rural areas and are overwhelmingly dependent on small farms for their living.

The Challenge of Bringing Prosperity to Farmers in the Short Term

The bitter reality of the current situation is that short of radical reforms, there exists no solution that can bring a decent standard of living to farmers. Multiple subsidies that tie farmers and other rural households to their inherited locations and other policies that discourage the creation of attractive jobs for them in industry and services have left too large a population stuck in low-productivity agriculture. None of the avenues to bringing prosperity to this population in the short term *within* agriculture promise to succeed. Consider in turn the main remedies commonly suggested.

Accelerating Growth in Agriculture

If the transition of the workforce out of agriculture into better-paid jobs in industry and services will remain slow, can India not bring

27 Foster, Andrew and Mark Rosenzweig, 2009

rapid prosperity to farmers through acceleration of growth within agriculture? Unfortunately, the odds in favour of the success of this approach are minuscule. As Table 3.1 shows, nationally, agriculture in India has never grown faster than 4.5 per cent over long periods. Even during the 1980s' decade, when the Green Revolution was fast spreading, it grew only 4.4 per cent annually. Since then, the growth rate has greatly moderated.

For the sake of argument, let us suppose that India could raise the growth rate of agricultural output to 5 per cent. We must then confront the question of where the resulting output will be sold. As of 2011/12, more than 70 per cent of the rural agricultural workforce was engaged in growing cereals, pulses and oilseeds. With the exception of oilseeds, India is already self-sufficient in most of these crops, so any additional output will have to be exported. But this poses two problems. First, since India provides larger subsidies on these crops through MSP than is allowed under the World Trade Organization (WTO) rules, it will face stiff countervailing duties in importing countries. Such duties will lead to a substantial decline in the net price received on exports. Second, even if we discount countervailing duties, any major expansion of exports of these crops would lead to a large decline in price. Once again, output expansion will fail to translate into commensurate income expansion for farmers.

Even if buyers of the extra output can be found, a further problem is that of ensuring that small farmers receive the lion's share of the price paid by the buyer. Marketing of produce in India remains heavily monopolized by middlemen, who continue to pocket the substantial gap between the price paid by the final consumer and what is received by the farmer. The process of marketing reforms had begun in the early 2000s but few state governments have succeeded in implementing them due to the enormous political clout the local middlemen have. The state of Karnataka is credited with having carried out most successful marketing reform through e-auctions and yet it found its farmers in enough distress to announce a large loan waiver worth ₹340 billion in July 2018.[28]

Diversification of Agriculture

Yet another solution to bring rapid prosperity to those currently engaged in farming is increased diversification within agriculture. This would involve moving land and labour out of traditional crops into high-value crops such as fruits and vegetables, as well as other commercial crops such as cotton, and into fisheries and animal husbandry. While such diversification can offer an avenue to bring some prosperity to a few farmers, it is implausible that it can bring genuine prosperity to a large farmer population.

Table 3.5 provides the distribution of cultivated area across various crops from 1980–81 to 2014–15 at intervals of ten or more years. It is remarkable that there has been no exit of land whatsoever from rice and wheat over the thirty-five years covered by the table. All we see is a small shift out of rice into wheat. The main exit has been from other cereals and millets, which constitute the healthiest grains but have lost out in popularity to rice and wheat. In addition, there has been a modest exit from pulses, which too is an unhappy outcome, since it has created a serious shortage in recent years. Fruits and vegetables have gained two percentage points and non-food crops have gained eight percentage points in cultivated area. Clearly, the shifts in cultivated area across different crops do not offer promising prospects for a rapid movement towards greater diversification. Farmers are generally

---

28 'Karnataka government announces partial farm loan waiver of ₹34,000 crore', *Times of India*, 5 July 2018. Available at https://timesofindia.indiatimes.com/india/karnataka-government-announces-partial-farm-loan-waiver-totalling-rs-34000-crores/articleshow/64866321.cms (Last accessed on 27 December 2018).

reluctant to experiment with new crops, preferring instead to go for the safety of what they have grown before.

Table 3.5: Percentage Area Cultivated Under Major Crops

Crops	1980–81	1990–91	2000–01	2014–15*
Rice	23.3	23	24.2	22.3
Wheat	12.9	12.9	13.9	16.2
Other cereals and millets	24.6	19.6	16.6	12.8
Total pulses	13.2	13.4	11.5	**10.9**
Total foodgrains	**73.9**	**68.9**	**66.2**	**62.3**
Sugarcane	1.7	2.1	2.5	2.8
Total fruits and vegetables	2.9	3.6	4.4	5
Other food crops	1.3	1.4	1.6	1.8
Total food crops	**79.7**	**75.9**	**74.7**	**72**
Total oilseeds	9.1	13.5	13.3	14.3
Total fibres (mostly cotton)	5.3	4.7	5.2	6.8
Other non-food crops	5.8	5.9	6.8	6.8
Total non-food crops	**20.2**	**24.1**	**25.3**	**28**
Total area under crops	100	100	100	100

*Figures for this year are provisional

Source: Pocketbook of Agricultural Statistics 2017, Table 4.2

Employment data does not offer any greater comfort to diversification serving as the driving force of farmer prosperity.

In 2011/12, of the 64.1 per cent rural workforce that worked in agriculture, a hefty 87.25 per cent was employed in non-perennial crops including cereals, pulses, oilseeds, vegetables, sugarcane and fibre crops such as cotton and jute. In 2017/18, the share of rural workforce in agriculture fell to 59.4 per cent but within it, the share of non-perennial crops remained 85 per cent. Non-perennial crops account for the lion's share of agricultural employment and movement out of them is extremely slow.

Perennial crops including fruits, spices and beverage crops such as tea, coffee and cocoa accounted for 3.81 per cent of the rural agricultural workforce in 2011/12 and 3.97 per cent in 2017/18. The only other substantial employer within agriculture is animal husbandry, which accounted for 5.3 per cent of the rural agricultural workforce in 2011/12 and 4.4 per cent in 2017/18. Remarkably, forestry and logging, and fishing and aquaculture, employed just 0.78 per cent of the rural agricultural workforce in 2011/12 and 0.81 per cent in 2017/18.

The main candidates for increased diversification of the workforce are fruits and vegetables, animal husbandry, and fishing and aquaculture. Can such workforce diversification serve as the instrument of farmer prosperity? The answer to this question in turn lies in answering two other questions: how much workforce diversification is feasible within a relatively short period of time, and how much can farmers themselves benefit from such diversification.

Regarding the first question, only 10.1 per cent of the rural agricultural workforce was employed in fruits and vegetables, animal husbandry and fisheries in 2011/12. In 2017/18, this proportion rose to 14.34 per cent. From these proportions, it is evident that even doubling the proportion from its 2017/18 level within a short period is unrealistic. Moreover, even if such doubling could happen, it would not go far towards bringing high returns to a large farm population, especially when we consider the effects on the prices of fruits and vegetables and animal products that would accompany such doubling.

Regarding the second question, high returns in fruits and vegetables, animal husbandry, and fishing and aquaculture arise at the processing stage. To be sure, food processing, the meat and poultry industries and export-oriented fisheries can generate high returns. But these activities can benefit farmers only if they either undertake these activities themselves or if they are employed at decent wages in them. But this is about diversification of the workforce out of agriculture, not within it.

Agricultural Marketing Reforms

I have already touched upon agricultural marketing reform but the issue is sufficiently important to require a fuller discussion. Farmers currently receive a rather small share of the price paid by the final consumer. This low share is the result of undue market power that intermediaries exercise at government-run marketplaces (mandis) where the farmer is required to sell his produce. Therefore, there is most surely scope for raising the farmer's income through marketing reforms. But this avenue to prosperity for farmers has two limitations.

First, the experience till date does not give any hope that a dramatic reform in this area can or will happen. The need for such reform has been noted for at least two decades and a model act for the reform of the Agricultural Produce Marketing Committees (APMC) Act in the states had been floated by the central government in 2003. A large number of states have passed laws to reform their original APMC Acts but have not implemented them in earnest. Consequently, at best, limited progress has been made towards shifting the share of the price paid by the final consumer in favour of the farmer.

An alternative effort to achieve the objective has been launched in the form of e-auctions at APMC-run marketplaces. Accordingly, each farmer can bring her produce to the marketplace and auction it, with market agents bidding for it without being able to discuss their bids with each other. Such an auction would give the farmer the highest price any buyer agent is willing to pay. The state of Karnataka has pioneered this model and the Government of India has adapted it for implementation in APMC-run marketplaces across all India. But from the available information, it is difficult to escape the conclusion that so far this reform too has been unsuccessful in bringing significant improvement in the conditions of the farmers. As noted earlier, the successful implementation of the model in Karnataka has not succeeded in freeing the farmers there from recurrent episodes of distress.

The second and even more compelling limitation of marketing reforms as the vehicle for bringing genuine prosperity to farmers is that output per worker in agriculture remains low. As Table 3.3 shows, per worker output in agriculture is just one-third of the per worker economy-wide GDP, which itself is quite low. Therefore, even if marketing reforms could deliver the entire value of agricultural output to farmers, their genuine prosperity would remain a distant goal. There is just not enough output in the sector to bring prosperity to the households of such a vast workforce.

Larger Redistribution from Urban to Rural Areas

The final possible remedy to bring prosperity faster to farmers is to affect yet larger transfers from taxpayers to the latter. But there are two problems with this approach. First, the feasibility of yet more transfers is seriously in question. Only one-third of the population of India lives in urban areas. Of this one-third, a small fraction has enough income to pay taxes. Redistribution from such a small population will simply not bring prosperity to the large population residing in rural areas. This is in contrast to countries such as the United States, the United

Kingdom, Japan and South Korea, where farmers account for less than 5 per cent of the workforce, income levels are high and taxpayers are numerous. Though farmer distress in the face of drought, floods and frost is a feature of these countries as well, since farmers constitute a small proportion of the workforce, the countries are well placed to alleviate such distress.

Second, it is also not clear that it is desirable to massively expand the transfers. Because such transfers are tied to farming as a profession, they discourage migration to non-farm jobs. If India is to complete the transition to a prosperous economy and all are to share in this prosperity, it is important that the agricultural workforce shrinks and non-agricultural workforce expands sooner rather than later.

What Are the Options?

There is no escaping the conclusion that the only available road to rapid prosperity for the current large workforce in agriculture goes through migration of a substantial fraction of the latter to more productive jobs in industry and services. Such migration will directly bring prosperity to those who migrate. It will also raise per worker output in agriculture by bringing down the worker-to-land ratio in agriculture. The more we delay this migration, the longer will be the period of farmer distress.

To appreciate why such migration is crucial, consider the approximate picture waiting to emerge on the output front. In the next fifteen years, the most optimistic assumption regarding annual agricultural growth we can realistically make is 3.5 per cent. The most conservative assumption regarding growth in industry and services combined would be 8 per cent. In fifteen years, these assumptions imply a fall in the share of agriculture in GDP from 14.8 per cent in 2017/18 to 8.4 per cent in 2032/33. Of course, this scenario is the most optimistic one. Realistically, agriculture is not likely to grow more than 3 per cent annually over the fifteen-year period and industry and services together would probably grow closer to 9 per cent. Under this, the share of agriculture in the GDP would decline to just 6.9 per cent by 2032/33. Under either scenario, even with a 12 to 15 per cent-point decline in agricultural workforce over this period, we face the prospect of having to continue to support nearly 30 per cent of the nationwide workforce on less than 10 per cent of the GDP. This would still leave a very large number of workers exposed to distress. Policies that accelerate the exit of farmers into other professions are urgently required.

A large part of the policy change to affect this migration lies outside agriculture, a subject I will consider in subsequent chapters. But some bold actions would be worthwhile in agriculture as well. Many of these actions have been widely discussed in the rich public-policy discourse that takes place in the Indian media, despite its excessively noisy nature. But even at the risk of repetition, I spell out the more important of these actions below.

First and foremost, India must replace procurement at MSP and the provision of subsidized food grains through PDS by an equivalent cash transfer to the relevant beneficiaries. MSP procurement is principally limited to wheat and rice and suffers from several shortcomings. First, it encourages wheat and rice crops over others and thus undermines progress towards diversification into other crops and activities. Second, it has perpetuated the growing of rice, which requires vast volumes of water, in Punjab, where water tables have fallen to abysmal levels. Third, MSP counts as trade-distorting subsidy under WTO rules and therefore undermines the ability of India to export wheat and rice. And finally, while only larger farmers growing wheat and rice benefit from procurement at MSP, income transfers associated with MSP and PDS will reach smaller farmers and landless workers and will not discriminate between those who grow wheat and rice and those who grow other crops.

In-kind transfers through PDS continue to suffer from substantial inefficiencies despite some improvements after the introduction of the Aadhaar biometric identity cards. Many beneficiaries complain that the quality of PDS grain is so poor that they prefer to forego the subsidy and buy the necessary grain from private shops. Others say that they have to make repeated trips to government shops to avail of the benefit either because of the intransigence of the shop owner or failure of the identity verification system. Income support provided through electronic transfers to beneficiary bank accounts does not suffer from these problems.

If this reform is implemented, as a by-product, the government will also be able to carry out a major overhaul of the behemoth that is the Food Corporation of India (FCI). With a huge workforce, this is a massive organization riddled with inefficiencies. Once cash transfers replace the PDS, FCI would have to fully compete with the private sector in the distribution of foodgrains. It will have to procure foodgrains at market prices and recover its costs by selling them competitively to consumers. It would be allowed to maintain only a small part of its operations at the cost of taxpayers to serve pockets where private retailers do not find it attractive to reach.

The second important reform concerns marketing of agricultural produce. This reform can only be effective if state governments successfully dilute the market power of local middlemen, who currently have a near-monopoly on local purchases of the farmers' produce. A genuine reform of the APMC Acts is critical. Organized retail, which brings new and influential buyers of agricultural produce in the marketplace, and e-commerce, which can potentially connect sellers directly to consumers, can majorly complement the APMC reform.

The third important reform is the removal of restrictions on the use of seeds based on genetically modified organisms (GMO) and the introduction of emerging gene-editing technologies. Here, the key lesson from the Green Revolution and the success of Bt. cotton needs highlighting. The beauty of seed varieties that produce high yields is that they can spread rapidly without the government having to do very much. Other productivity-enhancing measures such as improved irrigation, mechanization, crop diversification and spread of contract farming require large investments and are time-consuming. Today, with the ready availability of fertilizer and irrigation and easy access to information through digital platforms, farmers can take advantage of high-yielding seed varieties at a rapid pace.

The fourth important reform is the introduction of a transparent land-leasing law in each state. The NITI Aayog has prepared and promoted a model law that seeks to balance the rights of the tenant and the landowner, while also providing for greater transparency. Most states could greatly improve tenancy conditions by adopting this model law after modifications that take into account any specific local features of landownership pattern and political compulsions.

The case for a modern land-leasing law cannot be overstated. Today, as mentioned earlier, 68.5 per cent of landholdings are smaller than one hectare. Many farmers, struggling to make a living for families of five or more on such small landholdings, would like to lease out their land and look for superior alternatives. But they are unable to do so because the laws in most states do not permit leasing of land. As such, anyone leasing her plot runs the risk of losing it to the lessee. This situation has had two deleterious effects. One, it has perpetuated the fragmentation of landholdings and prevented their consolidation. And two, it has discouraged migration of farmers working tiny plots of land to alternative employments.

A transparent land-leasing law is also necessary to make the direct benefit transfer (DBT) intended for the actual cultivators feasible. Currently, with no formal record of tenancy, any benefit intended for the cultivator goes to the landowner, since formal records show him as the cultivator. A land-leasing law, which provides for the recording of tenancy, can overcome this problem, allowing benefits to reach the intended beneficiary.

The fifth and final reform is to end MGNREGA. From the beginning, this was a poorly conceived programme and has resulted in high wastage of taxpayers' money. Once substantial cash transfers to the poor are put in place, the original rationale for MGNREGA—providing relief work during lean season when employment opportunities on farms become scarce—will no longer remain valid. Some may argue that MGNREGA employment also serves as a means to building public assets. These proponents of MGNREGA need to be reminded that this argument reverses what was originally seen as an end and what was the means to that end. When MGNREGA was first adopted, provision of employment was the end and building public assets the means. It is bad use of public money when public projects must be imagined so that an available resource can be used. The process has to be the reverse: identify public projects which would serve important public needs and then find the right mix of resources to implement those projects.

It bears emphasizing that the reforms recommended here constitute a package. Productivity-enhancing reforms such as the introduction of GMO seeds and transparent land-leasing laws cannot succeed without the MSP reform. This is because India is already self-sufficient in foodgrains and any further increase in their output would have to be exported. Exports, in turn, would face countervailing duties in the importing country as long as the subsidy via MSP exceeds the margin permitted by the WTO, which is just 10 per cent. In a similar vein, replacing in-kind transfers in the form of subsidized foodgrain will require massively cutting back on procurement. Once beneficiaries have cash in their hands, they will no longer be restricted to purchasing foodgrain from PDS shops and will be free to switch to private shops to obtain the grain of their choice.

Concluding Remarks

It is not possible to bring genuine prosperity to farmers without moving half or more of them out of agriculture. Without such movement, there are only two ways to raise farmers' incomes: more remunerative prices to them and increased productivity in agriculture. It is easy to see that neither avenue can deliver genuine prosperity.

Today, the GDP per worker in agriculture is one-third of the economy-wide GDP per worker. But given that the economy-wide GDP per worker itself is small, GDP per-worker in agriculture is truly minuscule. Therefore, even if the farmer receives the entire price paid by the final consumer—a rather infeasible proposition since intermediation is essential to deliver the produce from the farm gate to the final consumer—it would be insufficient to help the farmer live a prosperous existence.

A moment's reflection shows that increased productivity in agriculture cannot go very far either. For example, suppose that a technological advance allows India to double its agricultural output overnight. The immediate question then would be, where would this output be sold? If it were sold at home, given that India has already achieved self-sufficiency in most grains including rice and wheat, this would result in a precipitous fall in prices. What is gained in output will be lost in price received. The final revenue receipts of farmers will not change very much. Alternatively, the extra produce could be exported. But this will attract duties from importing countries, especially since India subsidizes the production of wheat and rice through MSP.

It is thus clear that as long as the proportion of workforce in agriculture remains large, India will be unable to bring genuine prosperity to them. The movement of workers into industry and services would not only make those workers prosperous but also raise GDP per worker in agriculture, making those left behind better off.

The only feasible path to prosperity for farmers, therefore, is the creation of attractive job opportunities in industry and services. The critical question this raises is whether industry and services can provide gainful employment to a large number of workers migrating out of agriculture. This is the key question we must confront in the next chapter. As we will see, the answer is not straightforward.

4

UNDEREMPLOYMENT IN INDUSTRY AND SERVICES

FARMERS CHOOSE NOT TO exit their current occupation despite incomes that are below subsistence level partly because many of the government transfers are available only if they stay where they are. But the failure of industry and services to create sufficiently attractive jobs has also contributed to the phenomenon in a major way. If these sectors created jobs that could pay decent wages to those working half-a-hectare or smaller farms, migration out of agriculture would surely take place at a faster pace.

When it comes to low-productivity employment, vast sections of the Indian industry and services mirror agriculture. They consist of millions of tiny enterprises, each employing a small number of workers. Often, the owner and her family are the only employees of these enterprises. Even when enterprises employ hired workers, numbers are small. In 2017/18, a solid 56.5 per cent of all workers in industry and services were employed in enterprises with just five or fewer workers.[29] The income per worker in these enterprises is uniformly very low. Enterprises with twenty or more workers, which are able to pay better wages, employed only 15.9 per cent of the workers.

---

29 National Statistical Office, 2019, Table 41, p. 261

Politicians in India glorify microenterprises without realizing that they have been paddling in the same place for decades, going nowhere. Own-account enterprises, which employ no hired workers on a regular basis, account for a large part of employment in industry and services but only a small part of their output. If these enterprises were growing larger over time, their celebration would have had justification. But such is not the case.

Two characteristics of industry and services have played a critical role in causing a shortage of good jobs at the low end of skill distribution. First, sectors able to pay decent wages such as auto, auto parts, two-wheelers, machinery, pharmaceuticals, finance and software are either capital intensive or skilled-labour intensive. And second, the proportion of the workforce employed in medium and large firms in manufacturing, especially of the labour-intensive variety, is small relative to comparable countries. This has meant that India has had limited success at best in capturing the world markets and therefore creating well-paid jobs in large volumes. Any strategy to create a large volume of well-paid jobs that would help speed up the transition of workforce out of agriculture and into industry and services must address these deficiencies of the current structure of industry and services.

Low Unemployment Rates

It is a commonplace to come across journalists and analysts who point to the large number of individuals, many among them PhD holders, applying for a small number of lowest-level positions in the government, titled multi-tasking staff (MTS), as evidence of a high rate of unemployment in India. For instance, according to a September 2015 news report, more than 2.3 million candidates, including 222,000 engineers and 255 PhD holders, applied for 368 Class IV vacancies in the state secretariat of the Government of Uttar Pradesh.[30] Similar stories have appeared in the press about positions advertised by the Haryana government and Indian railways.

30 Ali, 2015

The reason for such a heavy demand for MTS positions in the government is not unemployment, however. Instead, the high salary, highest level of job security and generous housing, the pension and health-care benefits associated with this position account for the large number of applicants for it. In the Government of India, salary for the lowest-level employee begins at ₹18,000 per month. This salary comes with excellent health, housing and pension benefits; prospects for regular salary hikes regardless of performance; and complete job security for life. In case of untimely death of the employee, there even exist provisions for preference for employment in the government towards one of her children. At the same time, the duties of MTS staff are the least demanding and offer plenty of free time.

Many engineers and PhD holders are unable to find such emoluments and benefits in private sector jobs, which additionally require harder work. This makes an MTS position in the government an attractive prospect. Therefore, even if they are employed, many among engineers and PhD holders apply for MTS positions whenever the government advertises for them. Unsatisfactory employment, rather than unemployment, is what attracts them to these jobs.

In a country like India, where self-employment and informal employment dominate, overall unemployment can only be measured through large household surveys. Even the most carefully conducted censuses of enterprises fail to cover the workforce exhaustively. For example, the Census of Industries, which India has conducted periodically, fails to account for a substantial part of the workforce even within industry and services. Under such circumstances, we do not know whether what happens to the workforce covered by the censuses or surveys is offset or reinforced by changes in the workforce not covered by them.

India has conducted large household surveys approximately every five years since 1972/73. Until recently, these surveys went by the title Employment–Unemployment Survey (EUS). But beginning 2017/18, it has been rechristened Period Labour Force Survey (PLFS) and made annual. The NSO, which carries out the PLFS, now provides unemployment and related estimates annually for entire India and also on a quarterly basis for urban India.

There has been some confusion in media stories about the comparability of EUS and PLFS. A close review of sample designs of the two surveys leads to the conclusion that at the aggregate level, they are comparable, but with one important qualification. Data collection for EUS used to be done using paper schedules while that for PLFS is done using the Computer-assisted Personal Interviewing (CAPI) method with inbuilt validation rules in the software on computer tablets. For EUS, conducted using paper schedule, different levels of validation were carried out after data entry. For PLFS, validation is done automatically by CAPI's inbuilt validation rules. Unfortunately, NSO did not carry out a validation exercise to check if the two methods lead to differences in measurement. Therefore, some doubt remains regarding full comparability of EUS and PLFS.

This difference in data collection and validation methodologies assumes significance principally because PLFS has given rise to results that are at substantial variance with those yielded by multiple rounds of EUS. Two examples illustrate this point. First, EUS has rarely produced an India-wide unemployment rate exceeding 3 per cent. In comparison, PLFS has produced an unemployment rate of 6.1 per cent. Second, much of the debate on jobs and employment in India in recent years has taken place in the context of additions of eight to ten million workers to the labour force each year. But labour-force calculations based on EUS 2011/12 and PLFS 2017/18 yield additions of less than 300,000 workers per year.

There is no way to answer the question whether these anomalies have resulted from the difference in data collection and validation methods or represent real changes in the economy. Luckily, we need not answer it to proceed further. Regardless of whether the unemployment rate is 6.1 per cent in 2017/18 or lower, an inescapable conclusion is that the unemployment rate in India is low. Even the 6.1 per cent rate from PLFS for 2017/18 is close to what is viewed as the natural rate of unemployment in many countries. In effect, given the limited assistance from the state and limited economic opportunities, everyone must do something to make ends meet.

Table 4.1: Unemployment in Rural and Urban Areas, 2017/18

Area	Male	Female	Person
Rural	5.8	3.8	5.3
Urban	7.1	10.8	7.8
Rural + Urban	6.2	5.7	6.1

Source: National Statistical Office 2019, Statement 30, p. 82

With this in view, Table 4.1 reports estimates of unemployment rate in 2017/18 for male, female and all persons in rural, urban and all India. Predictably, the unemployment rate in rural areas is lower than in urban areas. Agriculture often serves as the employment of last resort. The highest unemployment rate is among urban women. But because the proportion of urban women in workforce is small, the overall urban unemployment rate is much closer to the rate among urban males.

Concentration of Employment in Informal Unincorporated Enterprises

Underemployment is the key problem India needs to target. Doing so will help cut outright unemployment as well. Underemployment manifests itself in low-productivity employment. Some of this low productivity can be observed in daily life. For instance, it is commonplace in India to find two or more workers performing tasks that one worker can do. If a home appliance such as air conditioning or television requires servicing or the plumbing needs fixing, often two or more workers show up. But only one of them will actually perform the task, with the others either carrying the tools or simply providing company. In government offices and even private companies, it is common to find workers sitting outside office doors nearly all day with little to do. Even workers in small and informal private enterprises can be seen taking long breaks or simply shirking their duties.

Concrete evidence of dominance of low-productivity jobs in India is to be found in a surprisingly large concentration of workforce in small, often tiny, and informal enterprises in both industry and services. The Indian industry and service sectors are perhaps unique in the world for being populated by such a large number of micro and small enterprises and such a small number of medium and large enterprises. The combination of low per worker productivity in micro and small enterprises and heavy concentration of employment in them translates into overall low per worker productivity in industry and services.

Before presenting the evidence, it bears noting that enterprise surveys, which are the only sources of detailed estimates on the distribution of workforce, output and wages by enterprise size, remain highly partial in coverage in India. Indeed, even the periodic Economic Censuses, which aim to collect information on a handful of variables from all enterprises in all non-agricultural enterprises, fall well short of covering the entire non-agricultural workforce. For instance, the number of non-agricultural workers reported in the latest Economic Census, conducted in 2013/14, was only 131 million, compared with 243 million based on the Employment–Unemployment Survey of 2011/12.

There are two sets of enterprise surveys in India: the Annual Survey of Industries (ASI) conducted annually by the Central Statistical Office (CSO) and the survey of unincorporated or unorganized sector non-agricultural enterprises periodically conducted by the NSO. The former is confined to manufacturing enterprises registered under certain sections of the Factories Act, 1948.[31] The latter covers unincorporated enterprises in both industry and services with some sectors such as the financial services or construction occasionally excluded. It explicitly excludes enterprises covered by the ASI. The two surveys are, thus, mutually exclusive in their coverage.

The latest NSO survey on unincorporated enterprises relates to the year 2015/16 and covers all non-agricultural sectors except construction. The enterprises account for a total of 111.3 million workers. Keeping in mind that the total number of workers identified by the 2013/14 Economic Census, which also covered incorporated enterprises, was 131 million, it can be concluded with a reasonable degree of confidence that the survey covers 80 per cent or more of non-agricultural workforce identifiable in all non-agricultural enterprises. Therefore, an extremely large part of the workforce in India remains employed in the informal sector.

To gain further insight into the characteristics of the workforce, consider the nature of the enterprises covered by the survey. These enterprises can be classified according to two criteria: employment of hired workers on a regular basis—or lack thereof—and ownership pattern. Under the nomenclature used by the NSO, enterprises that run without employing any hired worker on a regular basis are called own account enterprises (OAEs), and those employing one or more hired workers are classified as establishments. Using the ownership criterion, the enterprises are classified into proprietorship, partnership, self-help groups (SHGs) and trusts.

At an all-India level, 84.2 per cent of the enterprises in 2015/16 were OAEs. In rural areas, the share of these enterprises was even higher at 91.4 per cent. Therefore, the vast majority of the enterprises hired no workers on a regular basis. In terms of ownership, 96 per cent of enterprises were proprietorships on India-wide basis. Of the remaining, 1.4 per cent enterprises were partnerships and 1.8 per

---

31 The sections are 2m(i) and 2(m)(ii).

cent SHGs. This, once again, indicates the generally informal nature of employment.

Table 4.2: Shares of OAEs and Establishment Enterprises in the Total Workforce in Unincorporated Enterprises, 2015/16

Enterprise Type	Manufacturing	Trade	Other Services	All
		Rural		
OAE	75.9	87.9	65.1	76.5
Establishment	24.1	12.1	34.9	23.5
All (Million Workers)	18.7	16.1	15.1	49.9
		Urban		
OAE	49.0	56.4	45.2	50.4
Establishment	51.0	43.6	54.8	49.6
All (Million Workers)	17.4	22.7	21.3	61.4
		Rural + Urban		
OAE	62.9	69.5	53.4	62.1
Establishment	37.1	30.5	46.6	37.9
All (Million Workers)	36.0	38.7	36.5	111.3

Source: Author's calculations using estimates in NSO 2017, Statement 4, p. 16

Turning to employment structure in unincorporated enterprises, Table 4.2 provides the composition of workforce according to OAE and establishment enterprises across three broad sectors: manufacturing, trade and other services. Several observations follow. First, at the aggregate level, 62.1 per cent of the 111.3 million workers in these enterprises were employed in OAEs and only 37.9 per cent in establishment enterprises. Second, the share of OAEs in the total workforce was consistently higher in rural areas. At the aggregate level, this share was 76.5 per cent, compared with 50.4 per cent in urban areas. Finally, services accounted for a little more than two-thirds of the total workforce in unincorporated enterprises, while manufacturing employed slightly less than one-third of it.

Table 4.3: Gross Value Added Per Worker in Unincorporated Enterprises in 2015/16 Rupees in Broad Sectors

In 2015/16 Rupees Per Worker				
Enterprise Type	**Manufacturing**	**Trade**	**Other Services**	**All**
	Rural			
OAE	36,021	64,103	71,008	55,459
Establishment	86,296	131,947	131,227	114,024
All	48,152	72,338	91,901	69,198
	Urban			
OAE	62,822	113,541	104,324	96,718
Establishment	140,639	189,749	169,436	167,627
All	102,523	146,739	139,856	131,811
	Rural + Urban			
OAE	46,088	87,611	87,498	73,951
Establishment	122,344	180,219	157,554	152,723
All	74,379	115,885	119,947	103,744

Source: Author's calculations using estimates in National Statistical Office 2017, Statement 20, p. 30

The full impact of the concentration of non-agricultural employment in unincorporated enterprises, especially OAEs, can only be appreciated when we see it in conjunction with the gross value added (GVA) per worker. Table 4.3 provides the relevant estimates. Three features of the table may be noted at the outset. First, the GVA per worker is consistently significantly lower in manufacturing than in services. In rural areas, the gap is particularly large. Second, predictably, OAEs consistently exhibit lower GVA than establishment enterprises. And, finally, there is a large gap in per worker GVA between rural and urban enterprises. At the aggregate level, urban enterprises exhibit 1.9 times per worker GVA than rural enterprises. In manufacturing, urban GVA per worker is more than twice that in rural areas.

To appreciate how low per worker GVAs in Table 4.3 are across the board, we must compare them to the nationwide GVA per worker. In 2015/16, the latter was approximately ₹244,000 at current prices.[32] This figure is more than twice the GVA per worker at the aggregate level in Table 4.3 and uniformly higher than that in every sector and every form of enterprise. Of particular importance in this table are GVAs in rural areas. The average value of this parameter across all rural enterprises is less than ₹70,000, which is less than one-third of the nationwide GVA per worker. In the manufacturing sector, rural OAEs exhibit less than one-sixth of the GVA per worker at nationwide level. This low level of productivity relative to the national average in unincorporated enterprises is almost as bad as in agriculture. Even in urban areas, the GVA per worker in manufacturing is less than half

32 At current prices, India's GVA at factor cost in 2015/16 was ₹125,666.5 billion. The total number of workers in India was 475 million in 2011/12. Going by EUS 2011/12 and PLFS 2017/18, workforce actually fell between 2011/12 and 2017/18. Nevertheless, generously assuming that it rose by ten million workers per year, the total number of workers would be 515 million in 2015/16. Dividing GVA by this workforce figure yields ₹244,012.5 as the nationwide GVA per worker in 2015/16.

of the nationwide GVA per worker. The inevitable conclusion is that too many workers, even in industry and service, are employed in low-productivity enterprises.

Estimates of emoluments received by hired workers reinforce this picture. Because OAEs do not employ hired workers on a regular basis, we have these estimates for establishment enterprises only. Table 4.4 shows the estimates for the three broad non-agricultural sectors in rural and urban areas and for all sectors taken together. Alongside, it also shows the number of workers employed in each category. Out of a total of 111.3 million workers in unincorporated enterprises, only 29.4 million happen to be hired workers. The remaining 81.9 million workers are self-employed in their own enterprises.

Table 4.4: Emoluments and Number of Hired Workers in Unincorporated Enterprises, 2015–16

Area	Manufacturing	Trade	Other Services	All
	Annual Emoluments in 2015/16 Rupees			
Rural	56,001	63,048	94,227	74,871
Urban	85,515	83,371	104,161	92,441
Rural + Urban	75,595	80,267	101,094	87,544
	Number of Hired Workers in Million			
Rural	3.2	1.1	3.8	8.2
Urban	6.4	6.2	8.6	21.2
Rural + Urban	9.6	7.4	12.4	29.4

Source: Author's calculations using estimates in National Statistical Office 2017, Statement 23, p. 32

More strikingly, emoluments received by these workers are low by almost any measure. In aggregate, average monthly emoluments in the enterprises turn out to be only ₹7,295 in 2015/16. Emoluments in rural manufacturing turn out to be particularly low: just ₹4,667 per month. Even in urban areas, monthly emoluments at ₹7,703 reflect rather low worker productivity.

A More Detailed Picture of Manufacturing

Ongoing research by economist Radhicka Kapoor provides further insight into the phenomenon of concentration of manufacturing workforce in small, low-productivity enterprises. Combining the manufacturing component of NSO surveys of unorganized/unincorporated enterprises with those of CSO surveys of organized sector enterprises, Kapoor has constructed the full distribution of workforce across different firm sizes in manufacturing. Table 4.5 reports the results.

The estimates show that more than half of the manufacturing workforce in India has remained trapped in tiny enterprises employing five or fewer workers. Though the proportion has seen a steady decline from the hefty 67.4 per cent in 2000/01, it remained as high as 58.8 per cent in 2015/16. Traditionally, firms with fifty or fewer workers are defined as small. The proportion of workforce in these firms has ranged from a gigantic 85.4 per cent in 2000/01 to 75.4 per cent in 2015/16. India is unique in exhibiting such a high proportion of workforce in small enterprises. The only silver lining to this otherwise unhappy story is that the share of large firms, defined as those employing 200 workers or more, has been rising over the years. At 17.4 per cent in 2015/16, it still remains small when compared with other countries, but the increase from 9.7 per cent in 2000/01 is significant.

Table 4.5: Per Cent Shares of Firms of Different Sizes in Manufacturing Workforce

Firm Class Size (Number of Workers)	2000/01	2005/06	2010/11	2015/16*
1 to 5	67.4	63.6	56.6	58.8
6 to 10	9.4	9.7	8.9	7.6
11 to 20	4.9	5.7	6.2	4.8
21 to 50	3.7	4.0	4.7	4.2
51 to 100	2.4	2.9	3.8	3.3
101 to 200	2.5	2.8	4.1	3.8
>200	9.7	11.2	15.7	17.4
Total Number of Workers (Million)	44.9	45.1	46.5	48.9

*For 2015/16, ASI 2014/15 survey, the latest available, has been used for organized sector manufacturing enterprises.

Source: Estimated by economist Radhicka Kapoor

Why Large Firms Are Critical

Lower average worker productivity in smaller firms, relative to larger ones, is a common phenomenon and can be observed in all countries. Smaller firms typically employ less capital per worker than larger ones, which is sufficient to result in lower per worker productivity. What makes India's situation unique and disconcerting is the disproportionately large concentration of employment in small firms. Medium and large firms have, at best, limited presence in many sectors in India, especially in labour-intensive sectors such as apparel, footwear and other light manufactures.

A Comparison with China

A comparison of India and China best illustrates the importance of the presence of large firms in significant numbers. Figure 4.1 shows the distribution of workers in manufacturing by firm size in India and China in 2005. Whereas employment in China is predominantly concentrated in medium and large firms, that in India is concentrated in small firms. This difference also translates into a larger wage differential between small and medium firms on the one hand and large firms on the other.

Figure 4.1: Concentration of Manufacturing Employment in India in Small Firms

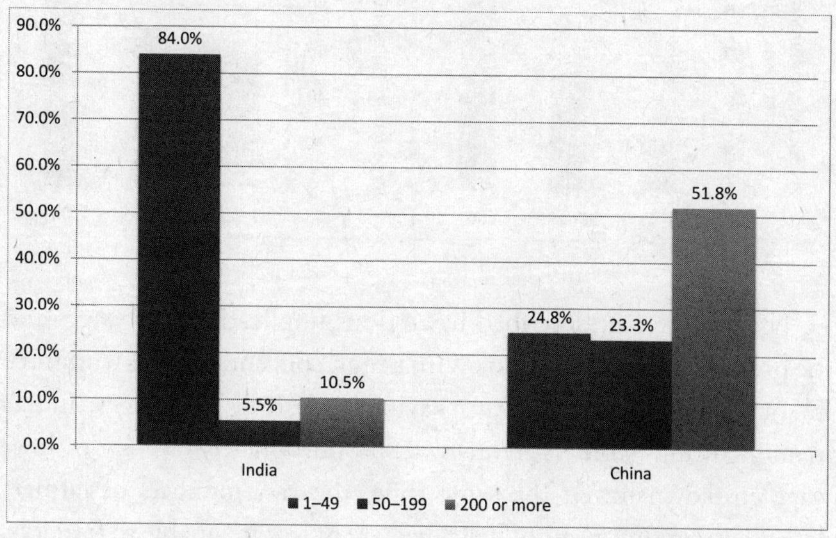

Figure 4.2 illustrates this point: wages in small firms in India are close to 20 per cent of the wages in large firms. In contrast, wages in small firms in China are 60 per cent of those in large firms. The significance of this wage difference rises yet further when we recognize that wages in large firms in China are themselves significantly higher than the corresponding wages in large firms in India. The work of economists Rana Hasan and Karl Jandoc, on which Figures 4.1 and 4.2, are based shows that this pattern holds for a wider set of countries.[33]

Figure 4.2: Low Wages in Small and Medium Firms Relative to Large Firms in India in Comparison to China

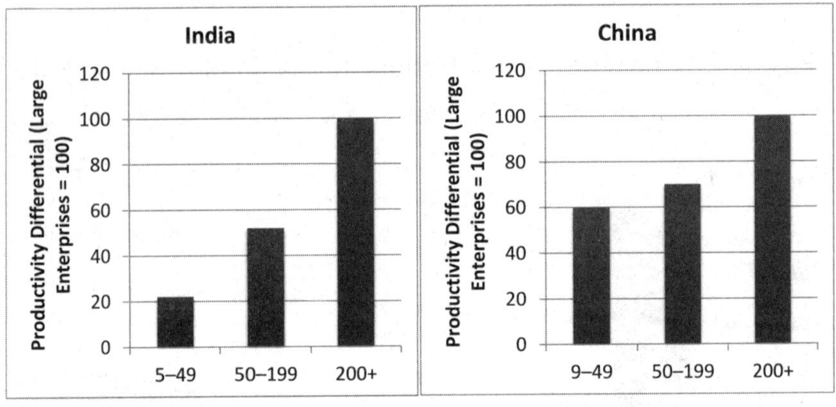

The pattern just described has serious implications for wages and the process of transformation. With a high concentration of workforce in small firms and small firms paying excessively low wages, India's manufacturing workers remain disproportionately stuck in low-wage employment. At the same time, the vast numbers of farmers dependent on tiny farms of half a hectare or less are unable to find jobs that will give them a better existence. As a result, they remain stuck in subsistence or below-subsistence farming. The transformation from a

33 Hasan and Jandoc, 2012

traditional agrarian economy to a modern industrial and urban one is advancing at snail's pace.

Large Firms, Productivity and Exports

Sectoral experience lends further support to the hypothesis that large firms are an important key to high overall productivity. Nearly all the sectors in India that have shown significant growth are those in which large firms find a substantial presence. These sectors include auto, auto parts, two-wheelers, engineering goods industries, pharmaceuticals, petroleum refining, software and telecommunications.[34] In parallel, sectors lacking a significant presence of genuinely large firms such as apparel, textiles, footwear, electrical and electronic products and other light manufactures have not done well in India, despite the abundance of labour in the country. Numerous small manufacturers of mobile phones have emerged in recent years, but none has been able to capture a significant market share.

There are many reasons why large firms are crucial to the success of an industry. For one thing, in many industries, the per unit cost of production declines with the rising scale of the firm. A larger scale makes the use of specialized cost-saving machinery viable. Small firms are either unable to deploy these cost-saving machines or are unable to utilize them at full capacity. In either case, per unit cost turns out to be higher than in large firms. Even in a labour-intensive industry such as apparel, larger firms use a lot more machinery per worker than small firms. Additionally, a larger scale allows greater specialization, which helps bring costs down through creation of skills in specific tasks.

---

34 The auto sector still remains uncompetitive in the global market because a high level of protection has shielded its inefficiency and permitted the emergence of many small plants. In India, even the larger auto firms are smaller than their counterparts in countries such as China and the United States.

Given their large output, large firms must also operate in the global marketplace. This forces them to compete against the best suppliers in the world. The process of competition compels them to be on their toes all the time so as not to lose their buyers to competitors. They must continuously adopt cost-saving technologies and management practices. Even when large firms sell their product exclusively in the domestic market, they are in direct competition with other global firms.

Furthermore, efficient large firms which operate in the global marketplace define the ecosystem around them and give rise to efficient small and medium firms. Large firms help create a skill pool from which small and medium firms benefit. They also become agents of technological change for small and medium firms. The latter become either their ancillaries or competitors. In either case, they are forced to adopt efficient practices and technologies to become cost- and quality-competitive.

A comparison of Indian and Chinese apparel industries best illustrates how the link between the presence of large firms and export performance influences the overall efficiency of an industry. Figure 4.3, also based on the work of Hasan and Jandoc, shows the distribution of employment across small, medium and large firms in the apparel industry in India and China in 2005. While 92.4 per cent of the apparel workforce in India was employed in firms with fewer than 50 workers, only 12.3 per cent of apparel workforce in China was employed in these small firms. The flip side is that India had a very small proportion of the workforce in medium and large firms while such employment dominated the Chinese apparel industry. Indeed, more disaggregated data shows that the bulk of apparel employment in India (84 per cent) was concentrated in tailor shops with seven or fewer workers. Symmetrically, employment in firms with more than

500 workers was minuscule in India (3.3 per cent) in comparison to China (29.4 per cent).[35]

Figure 4.3: Distribution of Employment in Apparel across Small, Medium and Large Firms in India and China

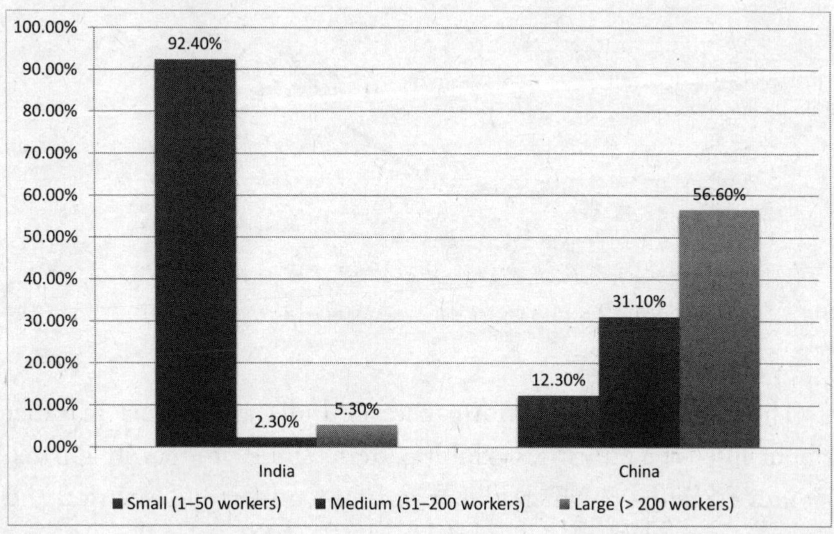

These dramatic differences in the distribution of employment across different firm sizes between India and China are matched by differences between their export performances. This is shown in Figure 4.4, which plots the evolution of exports of apparel in India and China from 1999 to 2014. In 1999, exports by China exceeded those by India by just $25 billion. Fifteen years later, this difference had grown to $109 billion. Today, exports of apparel by India have fallen below those by much smaller countries such as Bangladesh and Vietnam. Evidence shows that exporting firms even in Vietnam are significantly larger than those in India.

35 Hasan and Jandoc, 2012

Figure 4.4: Exports of Clothing and Accessories by India and China: 1999–2014

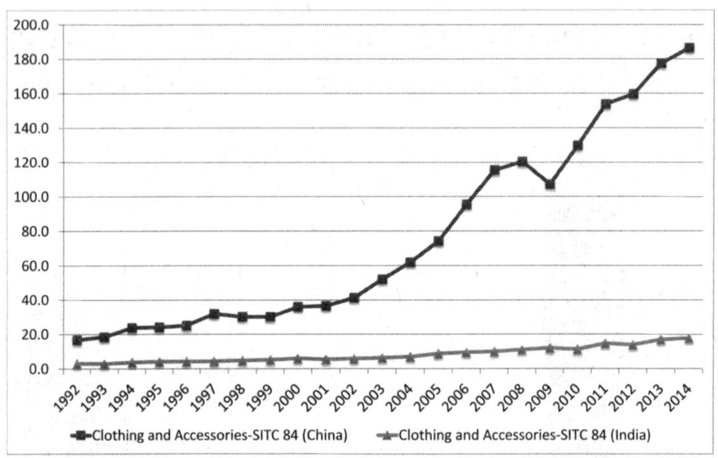

The relative export performances of India and China in other labour-intensive industries exhibit patterns similar to that in apparel. Figures 4.5 and 4.6, which plot exports of footwear and electrical and electronic products, respectively, by the two countries demonstrate this fact. Larger Chinese firms in these sectors have shown much greater dynamism than their smaller counterparts in India.

Figure 4.5: Exports of Footwear by India and China: 1999–2014

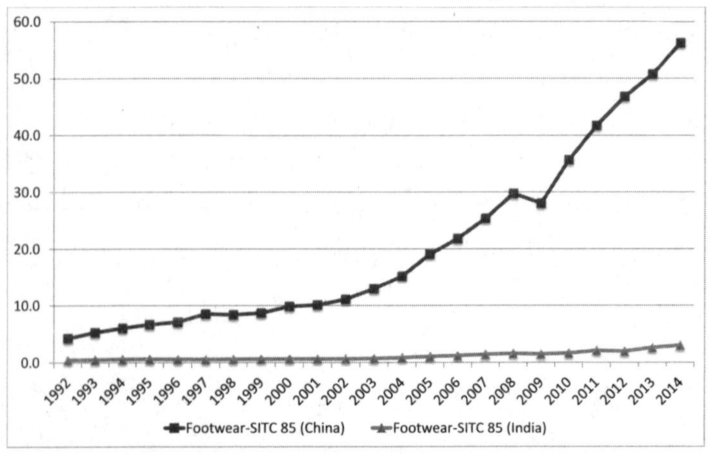

Figure 4.6: Exports of Electrical and Electronic Products by India and China: 1999–2014

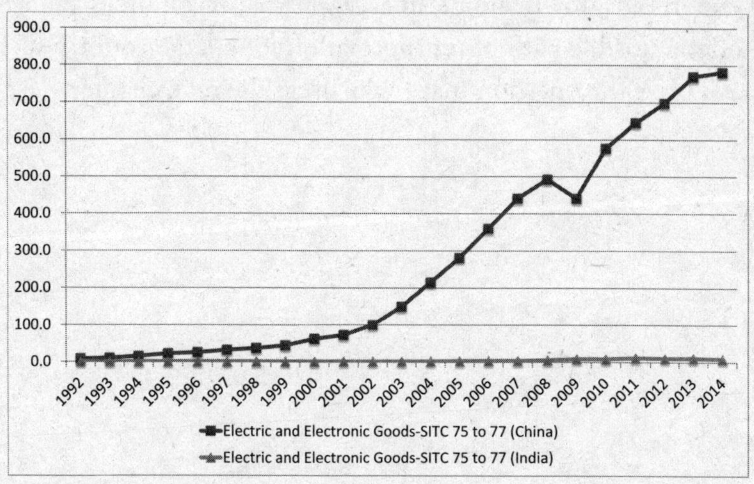

Concluding Remarks

Just as there is a preponderance of tiny farms in agriculture, there is a dominance of tiny firms in industry and services in India. This feature has resulted in low output per worker and hence low incomes for the bulk of the Indian workforce. India needs to create more productive jobs in industry and services so that workers may exit agriculture.

A key conclusion following from the analysis in this chapter is that the creation of high-productivity jobs requires the entry of significantly larger firms in industry and services than is the case. It is not merely that large-scale firms themselves are more productive; their presence also helps small and medium firms achieve high productivity. Large firms effectively become agents of change in technology, skills and management. They also demand high-quality components that small and medium firms may supply.

Therefore, the key policy question we must address is how best to facilitate the emergence and entry of large firms in India. Before I address this question, we need to confront a prior question that is being asked in the context of the current developments in the global trading system and technological developments: does the manufacturing-fed and export-led growth model that East Asian economies pioneered still offer a feasible path of transformation for a large country such as India? This is the question that I take up in the next chapter.

5

WALKING ON TWO LEGS

CAN INDIA FOLLOW THE successful East Asian model of manufacturing- and export-led growth or do the changed global market conditions and impending fourth industrial revolution point to an altogether different approach as being optimal? In discussing this important question, let me reiterate that the approach India adopts must deliver on two key objectives. One, it should accelerate the process of job creation in industry and services to help absorb new workers who have been joining the workforce and those who may migrate out of agriculture to seek better opportunities. And two, the approach India adopts must produce proportionately significantly larger number of well-paid jobs for those with no or limited skills.

Seizing on faster growth of services than manufacturing in India in recent decades, some commentators have argued that manufacturing- and export-led transformation is not an option for India and that it should simply go for primarily, even exclusively, a services-led development model. I disagree with this view and, accordingly, consider this subject in greater detail below.

The Case for Manufacturing as the Engine of Growth

Going by the experience of virtually all countries that have transitioned from low to high per-capita incomes, manufacturing, especially of the labour-intensive variety, must serve as the initial source of job creation. As manufacturing pulls workers out of agriculture, rising incomes in this sector create a demand for services. Because most services must be supplied domestically, acceleration in demand for them via manufacturing growth accelerates their growth as well. Table 5.1 provides some prima facie evidence in support of this proposition. Whenever countries have experienced an upward shift in the growth rate in manufacturing, growth rate in services has also seen a jump. In the 1960s, when a shift to outward-oriented policies led to accelerated manufacturing growth in South Korea and Taiwan, both countries also saw their services growth accelerate. On a lesser scale, India too had the same experience during its fast-growth phase from 2003–04 to 2010–11. A paper by economist Rajeev Dehejia and me has established this link econometrically using firm-level data.[36]

As the growth process progresses and per-capita incomes and wages rise, production begins to shift into more capital- and skilled-labour-intensive industries. In India, till date, manufacturing in general and labour-intensive manufacturing in particular have not fulfilled this function well. If India is to follow the well-trodden and only known path to job creation at decent wages in the early stages of development, it must take steps that would enable manufacturing, especially of the labour-intensive variety, to grow significantly faster.

A minority of commentators in India argues, however, that India is different and that it should eschew manufacturing expansion and build on its successes in services alone. However, these manufacturing sceptics do not offer a roadmap for the creation of well-paid jobs for hundreds of millions of workers with limited or no skills. The

---

36 Dehejia and Panagariya, 2016

workers are either employed in agriculture and informal-sector enterprises or are self-employed. Dynamic services sectors, such as software and finance, generate relatively fewer jobs for them. Tourism, transportation and construction hold greater promise but their potential itself greatly depends on the performance of manufacturing. For example, transportation flourishes when the manufacturing sector generates demands for its services. Likewise, tourism and construction are spurred by higher incomes generated by manufacturing. Therefore, if the creation of well-paid jobs for some of those currently employed in the agriculture and informal sectors is an important objective, reliance on services as the exclusive engine of growth will not do.

Table 5.1: Faster Manufacturing Growth Leading to Faster Services Growth

Country and Period	GDP	Agriculture	Industry	Services
South Korea				
1954–62	4.2	2.6	11.6	4.4
1963–72	9.5	4.7	17.3	10.0
Taiwan				
1951–53 to 1961–63	7.0	4.9	11.5	7.6
1961–63 to 1971–73	10.0	4.4	15.3	10.3
India				
1991–92 to 2002–03	5.6	2.3	5.6	7.1
2003–04 to 2010–11	8.4	4.1	8.0	9.7

Source: Dehejia and Panagariya, 2016, Table 1

If we agree that services alone cannot carry the day, the natural next question is whether manufacturing continues to offer the potential to create the kind of jobs India needs. Two arguments have been offered recently in support of a negative answer to this question: rising protectionism around the world and automation. Let us examine the validity of each of these arguments in turn.

Does Rising Protectionism Pose a Threat to Export-led Growth?

The first argument says that when South Korea, Taiwan and China transformed, markets were relatively open. Therefore, these countries could take advantage of scale economies in manufacturing by exporting their products in large volumes. The same option is not available today due to rising protectionism around the world.

This argument greatly overstates the problem. Notwithstanding the current trade tensions, largely of a bilateral nature between the United States and China, the global economy is far more open today than in the days when South Korea and Taiwan transformed. Indeed, it remains more open than even during the 1990s and early 2000s when China transformed. Much of the liberalization under the Uruguay Round Agreement was implemented between 1995 and 2005 and remains intact, except for tariffs imposed by the United States and China on each other, tariffs on steel and aluminum by the former, and retaliatory tariffs by a handful of the affected countries.

Total merchandise exports stood at $17.7 trillion in 2017 and have been exhibiting a growing trend. India's share in these exports was only 1.7 per cent compared with 12.8 per cent of China in 2017. Even if the export market shrinks to $15 trillion in the coming years—an unlikely prospect—India could more than double its exports by raising its share in the world market to just 4 per cent. To put the matter in perspective differently, global merchandise exports in 2002 were only $6.5 trillion. Yet China managed to export $325.6 billion worth of merchandise goods that year by capturing a 5 per cent share in the total world exports. India's problem is not a small or shrinking global merchandise export market; it is raising its own share in that market to a respectable level.

Does Impending Automation Render Export-centred Strategy Infeasible?

The second argument says that with advances in technology, manufacturing is becoming highly automated and this would lead to its move back to the developed countries. This argument too has been grossly overstated. It is true that automation is on the increase and perhaps moving at a faster pace than in the past. Yet, for many labour-intensive tasks, automation remains technically infeasible. And for many other such tasks, although automation has become technically feasible, commercially viability remains a distant dream.

Nothing illustrates the limits of automation better than the efforts by Adidas to automate its production of sneakers, traditionally one of the most labour-intensive activities. At the end of 2015, the company had opened its first high-tech speed factory in Germany, which produces sneakers using intelligent robotics technology. More recently, it has opened a shoe factory that uses 3-D printing technology.

Yet, Kasper Rorsted, the CEO of Adidas, says that full automation of sneaker manufacturing is unlikely in the next five to ten years. Currently, Adidas produces only one million out of its total production of 360 million pairs in automated factories. When asked whether manufacturing is poised to return to the United States and Europe, Rorsted says, 'I do not believe, and it is a complete illusion to believe, that manufacturing can go back to Europe in terms of volume.'[37] He adds that despite the political interest in the United States to bring back manufacturing, it is financially 'very illogical' and unlikely to happen.

What is true of shoe manufacturing is even truer of apparel, where we are still to see the appearance of the first factory that automates

---

37 Quoted in Bain, 2017

manufacturing as much as the German Adidas factory has done for shoes. And the global apparel market is huge. In 2017, total world exports of clothing and accessories amounted to $810 billion. Of this, India exported only $18.3 billion compared with China's $157.5 billion. With high and rising wages, China will not only see the current trend of declining apparel exports accelerate, it will eventually become a large importer of the product. And with its population of 1.3 billion, its potential apparel imports are large. Put another way, the world population is predicted to reach 7.3 billion in 2030. A low per-capita income nation, which becomes the dominant supplier of apparel to this population, would be able to create a vast number of good jobs in this one sector alone. Just think about each individual buying just two new shirts each year. That translates into 14.6 billion shirts every year. India can scarcely afford to pass on such an opportunity.

Even as we move beyond shoes and apparel toward more capital-intensive manufacturing, use of human labour is not about to cease entirely. Tesla recently tried to automate the assembly of its Model 3 and it backfired. Elon Musk, CEO of Tesla, had to concede, 'Excessive automation at Tesla was a mistake. To be precise, my mistake.'[38] Experts say that automation in final assembly has been tried by many in the past and failed.

Mechanization and a shift towards greater capital and skill intensity has been an ongoing process. Even when South Korea, Taiwan and Singapore industrialized, the capital intensity of production processes was higher than when Europe and the United States industrialized. When China industrialized, the capital intensity of production processes had risen relative to what had been the case when the three East Asian countries industrialized in the 1960s and 1970s. Moreover, China is a significantly larger country. Yet, by capturing the vast world market, it successfully created hundreds of millions of well-paid jobs for its workers. Over time, what has been lost for job creation by way

38 Quoted in Hull, 2018

of increased capital- or skilled-labour-intensity has been offset by rising demand due to accompanying higher incomes.

Start-ups and Micro, Small and Medium Enterprises as Sources of Jobs

Manufacturing sceptics sometimes vaguely claim that millions of start-up enterprises with each employing five to ten individuals would open up job opportunities to hundreds of millions. But till date, they have provided no evidence showing that this process is under way. True, a few hundred, perhaps even a few thousand, startups have emerged in India recently. But taken together, even counting such successful startups as Flipkart, Ola, Paytm, OYO and Rivigo, they probably do not employ more than five million workers.

More importantly, it is not clear that such enterprises can be any more successful in creating well-paid jobs for workers at the lowest rung of the skill ladder than more conventional capital- and skilled-labour-intensive enterprises. The mass of Indian workforce has hardly any skills and is surely not employable in tech startups. Recognizing this, some manufacturing sceptics point to micro, small and medium enterprises (MSMEs) in services sectors as a never-to-dry-up well of jobs. But these commentators do not clarify if the bulk of these jobs will be in micro and small enterprises or medium size enterprises. If it is the former, how will they be any better at generating high-productivity jobs than the current own account enterprises and small establishment enterprises? All evidence shows that industries that are dominated by enterprises that begin small and stay small are almost certain to suffer from low productivity and low-wage employment. Enterprises that are highly productive and able to pay steadily rising wages grow bigger over time. They then define the industry within which other smaller enterprises must shape up to compete.

If the advocates of the hypothesis that services would serve as the primary engine of growth wish to make the case that jobs can still come from medium enterprises, they have not outlined how this will be achieved. All existing evidence shows that medium size enterprises are few and far between in India. So far, most services jobs in India at the low end of skill ladder have been of self-employment variety or in small enterprises.

Factors Favouring Manufacturing in India

Two factors make the current timing for the expansion of labour-intensive manufacturing opportune for India. First, wages in manufacturing in China are on average three times those in India. Due to demographic transition, the workforce in China has begun to shrink and will continue to do so in the next one to two decades. This would mean a further rise in manufacturing wages. This change is bound to shift China into higher value-added activities, including those in service sectors. Low-end manufacturing will move to other locations.

Second, despite some rapprochement between the United States and China recently, the trade war between them is likely to endure for some years to come. This is because some of the thorniest issues between them remain unresolved and Democrats share the view of the Trump administration on this subject. As such, even if the leadership changes, the stance of the United States is unlikely to change by much. At the same time, China has emerged as an aggressive, belligerent power in recent years and is unlikely to yield the concessions the United States seeks. This situation offers India opportunities to expand its trade with both the United States and China. Each will import less from the other, opening up opportunities for India.

Another aspect of the trade war is that it makes China a less attractive production base for multinationals supplying the United States market. Therefore, many export-oriented multinationals currently active in China are looking for alternative locations. Multinationals making new investments are also considering China less favourably than in the past. With its vast workforce, India can emerge as the new manufacturing hub, especially at the low end of the spectrum.

In response to high wages in China, some manufacturing multinationals are already moving out of China to other lower-wage locations. On the one hand, India can become the host to many of these multinationals while on the other its small and medium domestic firms can capture the market from their Chinese counterparts. The latter too will find it difficult to compete in low-end manufacturing due to high wages and out-migration of multinationals, which are often buyers of their products.

Walking on Two Legs: Industry and Services

If the creation of well-paid jobs for those with limited skills is an objective, accelerated growth in manufacturing with special attention paid to labour-intensive products remains an important component of the strategy for economic transformation of India in the forthcoming decades. Yet, it would be too much to expect that India's path towards transformation would be approximately the same as that followed by Singapore, Taiwan and South Korea in the 1960s through the 1980s and China during the past three decades. The unusual success achieved in several capital- and skilled-labour-intensive sectors at a relatively low level of per-capita income already distinguishes India's path from that followed by these countries. Unlike them, India has also achieved substantial success in some of the key modern services such as information technology (IT), IT enabled services (ITES), telecommunications and financial services at its current low per-capita income. Accelerated growth in these modern services sectors has also helped spur faster growth in some of the traditional, non-traded services. For its level of per-capita income, India is also poised to achieve a high level of digitalization of the economy.

Therefore, even as India needs a course correction in favour of manufacturing, especially of the labour-intensive variety, it must simultaneously continue to build on its strength in services. In other words, as the Indian economy transforms, it must walk on two legs, manufacturing and services, with agriculture progressively modernizing and releasing workers. It must endeavour to create an ecosystem in which large-scale, high-productivity firms may emerge and capture the world markets in both manufacturing and services.

Concluding Remarks

If India is to succeed in creating a significantly larger volume of high-productivity jobs that offer decent incomes to workers, there is no escaping the traditional, well-trodden path of manufacturing-led growth. Those who argue that services can serve as the exclusive or even primary engine of growth for India have provided no roadmap of how such a growth process would create jobs paying decent wages to those exiting agriculture or currently employed in tiny enterprises at meagre wages. I have also offered arguments as to why the path through manufacturing is not closed by any means. Despite episodes of increased protection, the world economy is more open today than during the years when South Korea, Taiwan and China transformed their economies. Likewise, the threat from automation—what I sometimes call Robophobia—is greatly exaggerated. In many labour-intensive manufacturing activities, automation is not even as yet technologically feasible. And in some activities in which it is technologically feasible, it will take a few decades for it to become commercially viable.

My bottom-line conclusion is that having already achieved some degree of success in some key services sectors, India must promote a healthy atmosphere for the growth of both manufacturing and services. To the extent that the policy regime in India has been particularly unfriendly to the growth of labour-intensive manufacturing, special attention must be paid to the removal of bottlenecks in this area. Armed with these conclusions, we may now turn to a detailed discussion of reforms aimed at facilitating the rapid growth of manufacturing and services.

PART III

THE ROAD TO REFORMS

6

REFORMS FOR EXPORT-LED AND MANUFACTURING-FED GROWTH

EVIDENCE SHOWS THAT THE bulk of India's non-agricultural workforce is stuck in low-productivity enterprises that either employ no hired workers on a regular basis or employ a few at subsistence level of wages. Specifically, according to the latest available NSO survey, unincorporated enterprises employed 111.3 million workers. Of these, 62.1 per cent were in OAEs that employed no hired workers on a regular basis and the remaining 37.9 per cent in establishment enterprises that employed one or more hired workers. The average annual wage in the latter was ₹103,744. If spread over a family of five, this amount would allow an expenditure of just ₹56.85 per person per day in 2015/16 rupees. If converted at the average market exchange rate prevailing during the year, the expenditure would amount to just 87 cents in the United States dollar.

India needs to create jobs that pay better wages to those at the bottom rung of the skill ladder in a much larger volume than is the case currently. Experience around the world shows that these jobs will have to come from manufacturing and services. Evidence also points to the fact that the key factor behind India's failure to create well-paid jobs in satisfactory numbers for those with no or limited skills has been the near absence of large- and medium-sized firms in labour-intensive sectors. Therefore, before we can identify policy reforms that would help create a larger number of well-paid jobs, we ask the question why large-scale enterprises have failed to emerge in labour-intensive sectors in India.

Missing Large-scale Enterprises in Labour-intensive Sectors

The answer to this question has three parts. First, until as late as 2000, India maintained an effective ban on the entry of medium and large enterprises in labour-intensive sectors. As a result, even though this ban has now been fully lifted, its historical legacy is a mass of small firms. Firms that have operated in these sectors for decades feel secure in operating at the same old small scale. Second, decades of exclusion of medium and large firms and business houses from these sectors and their experience with highly restrictive labour laws have hardwired them to keep away from unskilled-labour-intensive sectors. They habitually operate exclusively in capital- and skilled-labour-intensive sectors. Finally, despite the lifting of the ban on entry of medium and large firms in labour-intensive sectors, the policy regime remains less than friendly to large firms. Consider each of these factors in greater detail.

Prime Minister Nehru's original conception was that light manufactures should be left exclusively for production by small household enterprises, which could operate with small amounts of capital per worker, thereby freeing the bulk of available capital for heavier industries, which required some minimum scale to be viable. Initially, this policy was enforced by denial of investment licences, required for all investments beyond a relatively low threshold, in light manufactures. Later, Prime Minister Indira Gandhi formalized the policy via the Small-Scale Industry (SSI) reservation list, which explicitly reserved light manufactures for small-scale enterprises. By the late 1980s, this list had become more than 800 items long.

Although the government began trimming the SSI reservation list in 1996, the policy remained effective on most products until at least the year 2000, when SSI sectors were opened to large-scale enterprises that exported 50 per cent or more of their output. In principle, this change can be viewed as having ended the SSI reservation, but given the history of inward orientation in India, especially in light manufactures, few large-scale enterprises that could export 50 per cent of their output emerged. Subsequently, in several steps, the SSI list itself was trimmed, with the last twenty items removed from it in as late as 2015. Though the SSI reservation has thus been ended, the mass of inherited firms in light manufactures remains small. The vast majority of entrepreneurs currently active in this sector are those who entered it with limited ambitions.

It was expected that once the SSI reservation was ended, new, ambitious entrepreneurs would enter light manufactures to take advantage of the abundant workforce of India. But that expectation remained unfulfilled. The reason is to be found in the second factor noted above. Past SSI reservations had denied large firms and big business houses entry into these sectors. This exclusion created a culture among large entrepreneurs within which manufacturing of products such as apparel and footwear came to be shunned. This culture received a fillip from yet another policy initiative of the Indira Gandhi government. Beginning in the early 1970s, new investments by large firms and business houses, defined as those with assets worth ₹200 million or more, were confined by law to a set of highly capital-intensive 'core' industries. Initially, the list of these core industries contained only nine narrowly defined items. Though it was expanded subsequently, it remained highly restrictive. Over time, as the assets of other firms crossed the ₹200-million threshold, more and more of them came under the purview of the regulation.

Another factor contributing to the aversion towards labour-intensive sectors on the part of large firms and big business houses was the experience of textile firms in Mumbai and Kanpur during the 1980s. In those days, textiles were among the most labour-intensive products. India's labour laws, especially the Industrial Disputes Act, gave a disproportionately high level of protection to workers over entrepreneurs. An amendment to this law in the early 1980s further strengthened this protection by effectively making it impossible to terminate workers in firms with 100 or more of them. Armed with this protection, worker unions in textile mills in Mumbai and Kanpur went on strike one after another to seek superior terms of employment. Mounting losses due to this shutdown eventually led to the exit of nearly all textile mills. That experience left permanent scars on the psyche of Indian entrepreneurs.

Judicial interventions, which asymmetrically favoured workers, further contributed to the aversion towards labour-intensive activities among Indian entrepreneurs. In any dispute between workers and management, the judiciary would almost always rule against management, regardless of the merits of the case. This experience left entrepreneurs worried that they had no effective tool of disciplining errant and defiant workers. The problem seemed insurmountable in activities requiring a large number of workers. They began exhibiting a strong preference for capital- and skilled-labour-intensive manufacturing sectors. And even within these sectors, they often came to lean heavily in favour of the most capital-intensive technology.

The third and final factor, which continues to discourage the large-scale entry into light manufactures of even those entrepreneurs not hardwired to operate exclusively in capital- and skilled-labour-intensive sectors, relates to the numerous remaining policy and procedure-related barriers. Within this category, restrictive labour laws, to which I have already alluded, stand out. Under the Indian Constitution, labour is a concurrent subject, which means that both the central and state governments can legislate in this area. Consequently, laws with which an enterprise must abide have proliferated. There are more than forty central laws that apply to all states. In addition, each state has its own laws. Some of the laws even contradict one another, a situation that prompted a wit to quip that India cannot enforce 100 per cent of its laws without violating 20 per cent of them!

As already hinted, one highly restrictive labour law is the central Industrial Disputes Act (IDA). One of the provisions in this act effectively outlaws the termination of a regular worker under any circumstances by an enterprise employing 100 or more regular workers. Introduced in the early 1980s, it remains in effect. With permission from the central government, some states have been able to raise the threshold number of workers triggering the law to 300 but this too remains a low threshold. In modern times, when firms in China employ hundreds of thousands of workers to maximize the benefits of scale economies, firms need to acquire a scale going into at least tens of thousands of workers to be competitive. Recently, the central government has sought a halfway solution to the problem by allowing firms to hire workers on fixed terms. But this is less than ideal, since fixed-term employees do not develop loyalty to their enterprises and enterprises hesitate to invest in skilling them. Another provision in the IDA makes it extremely difficult to assign a worker a task different from the one for which he was hired. In a world in which technology changes rapidly, such inflexibility becomes very costly.

Today, demands for ever-rising minimum wages have emerged as another threat to the hiring of workers. Larger formal-sector enterprises must abide by minimum wage laws. But in labour-intensive activities such as apparel and footwear, competition in the global marketplace is intense and profit margins low. As a result, in an environment in which capital- and skilled-labour-intensive enterprises with high profit margins dominate and minimum wages are set keeping them in mind, they greatly undermine the viability of formal enterprises in labour-intensive sectors.

Procuring land in a suitable location at a reasonable price has also turned into a serious constraint on the entry of large-scale enterprises. With no definitive land titles in India, it is difficult for an entrepreneur to purchase contiguous pieces of land that are free of disputes and form a large total area. The holdout problem, whereby individual landowners try to extract exorbitant prices, knowing that the large areas sought by the buyer cannot be assembled without the purchase of their pieces of land, adds to this difficulty. The only alternative in such situations is for the government to acquire land on behalf of the entrepreneur. Unfortunately, this is a difficult task under the Land Acquisition Act in India, making both the central and state governments averse to doing it.

Finally, India also has myriad policy and procedural restrictions on the movement of goods, both within the country and at the border. These barriers make the cost of exporting and importing products particularly onerous relative to other competing countries. In view of the fact that large enterprises exploit scale economies effectively only by exporting their product and must also import many of their inputs to meet global quality standards for what they sell, these logistics barriers further discourage their entry.

The First Step: A Change of Mindset

If the government sincerely wishes to expand high-productivity jobs for those at the bottom rung of the skill ladder, it will need to make a concerted effort. Marginal changes here and there or subsidy packages without a sea change in policies will simply not do. The fancy capital-intensive, hi-tech and high-end products, on which the government's flagship scheme Make in India has focused the bulk of its efforts so far, must give way to the less flashy but employment-friendly sectors. Glorification of micro enterprises as fountainheads of job creation must stop. They do employ a large number of workers but the low-wage jobs and subsistence-level employment they provide are nothing to celebrate. To the extent that the government can offer rewards, they must go to enterprises that move up in size, from micro to small, small to medium and medium to large. The aim of the policy should be to ensure that approximately half of the jobs move to firms with fifty or more workers in no more than fifteen years. Achieving this goal requires reforms in multiple areas.

A Clear Focus on Export Expansion

Exports, made possible by good policies and not subsidies, are a good measure of the competitiveness of a country's products. Rapidly expanding exports testify to rapidly rising productivity. For a country like India, which has an extremely large pool of workers but with limited skills at best, the surest way to achieve rapid export expansion is to shift its production basket towards labour-intensive products in both manufacturing and services. The experiences of South Korea, Taiwan and Singapore during the 1960s to 1980s, and of China more recently, illustrate the success of this approach. As in India, the production structure in China did not reflect its abundance of labour relative to capital until 1980. But as the 1980s progressed, it rapidly reoriented its production structure towards labour-intensive products, which it came to export in large volumes. India needs to reorient its production structure in a similar manner so as to use its vast pool of workers effectively. My recent book, *Free Trade and Prosperity*, comprehensively shows the critical importance of free trade to the success of all those countries that have achieved rapid transformation in the post-Second-World-War era.[39]

Export markets are also critical to the growth of large firms. All evidence shows that productivity and scale of firms are positively correlated with export performance. For instance, firms in the apparel sector in China, Vietnam and Bangladesh, which have performed

39 Panagariya, 2019a

better than India in exports, are on average larger than those in India. Even the size of the average exporting firm in these countries is larger than in India. Therefore, it is critical that India adopts policies that expand trade. India should expand and export products in which it is more cost effective. In case of products where the opposite is true, it should give way to imports.

The timing could not be more opportune for India to make a success of export-oriented strategy. Existing large-scale firms in labour-intensive sectors are predominantly located in China. This is evidenced by the fact that it exported $186.6 billion worth of clothing and accessories, $56.2 billion worth of footwear and $782.2 worth of electrical and electronic products in 2014. Keqiao and Shenzhen on the southeast Chinese coast are known as textiles and electronic hardware cities, respectively. With wages in China having seen a significant rise in the last two decades and this trend predicted to continue in the forthcoming decade on account of its shrinking labour force, China is already exiting the export markets in these products. India can fill the gap. Furthermore, with high and rising wages and the trade war with the United States predicted to continue, many multinational firms currently located in China are looking for low-wage locations around the world. With its vast pool of labour supply, India has the potential to become that location.

A major advantage of attracting the existing established firms is that they bring their own capital, technology, management practices and links to the world markets. They create well-paid jobs and also promise to serve as catalysts to the entry of local firms in similar activities. But foreign multinational firms will not move to India only because of abundant labour supply. They also require an ecosystem that is friendly to manufacturing and export activities.

Achieving genuine success in turning India into the same factory of manufactures for the world over the next two decades that China has been during the previous two decades would require both a complete change of mindset and focused reforms. In the following paragraphs, I outline the major steps that are necessary to help India become a hub of labour-intensive manufacturing. I begin with a critique of import substitution. In 1991, India had steadily moved away from this policy and embraced greater export orientation. But sadly, the policy has made a comeback recently.

Avoid Falling into the Import Substitution Trap

After almost three decades of reforms aimed at unshackling the Indian economy, including trade liberalization, Indian policymakers have not been able to fully shed their love affair with import substitution. Nothing illustrates this better than a series of tariff hikes by the government during 2018 and 2019. Until about 2007, India had systematically lowered its tariffs. While liberalization did not progress further thereafter, there was no major reversal of it either. But, after a long pause, tariffs have begun to rise again.

This return to protectionism can be traced to at least four factors. First, despite a considerable shift in thinking in the post-reform era, India has not been able to fully free itself of socialist ideas. Many within the current ruling dispensation do not fully appreciate the damage protectionism had done to the Indian economy during the first four decades following Independence. Equally, they lack appreciation for the key role that outward-oriented policies have played in the sustained rapid growth that India has experienced in recent years. Many within the top bureaucracy, who have never come to terms with India's turn away from socialism, readily reinforce these convictions of their political bosses.

The second reason, which complements the first, is that the success of trade liberalization in India has led to a considerable expansion of imports as a proportion of the GDP. At its peak, this proportion had reached 31 per cent in 2012/13 and, despite a decline in recent years, stood at a hefty 24 per cent in 2018/19. The large share of imports in the GDP means that there is now a large scope for import substitution. Under pressure to make a success of Prime Minister Narendra Modi's Make in India programme, many ministries find it convenient to restrict the entry of imports to make way for domestic production. To some degree, the situation is similar to that in South Korea in the early 1970s when its success in expanding trade and consequent expansion of imports as a proportion of the GDP led it to turn to import substitution policies.

Third, India has a large surplus on the invisibles account due to remittances, as also an overall current account deficit. The mirror image of these balances is a very large deficit on the merchandise trade account. This large deficit adds to the temptation for restricting merchandise imports and replacing them by domestic output. Unfortunately, restrictions on imports to counteract trade deficit find approval in many respectable circles.

Finally, higher inflation in India relative to its trading partners combined with a relatively stable nominal exchange rate has led to a loss of competitiveness of many Indian products compared to foreign products. In turn, this situation has led to demands by the Indian industry for increased protection. The government, which is favourably inclined towards import substitution in the first place, has readily obliged the domestic industry.

If India is to relaunch itself into the 8 per cent-plus growth trajectory, however, policymakers must disabuse themselves of the import substitution ideology. This policy encourages the manufacture of items that are costly to produce at home and discourages the making of products that are cheaper to produce. Trade liberalization reverses this pattern of specialization by expanding the output of products that the country produces cheaply and contracting those that it produces at higher cost relative to its trading partners. Many devotees of import substitution erroneously believe that the policy allows the country to boost its GDP by replacing imports by domestic output. They fail to understand that such increase is accompanied by a larger loss in GDP through a decline in the output of export items.

To understand this subtle fact, think of the extreme case in which a country bans imports altogether. This policy would surely allow it to replace all imports by domestic production. But with no imports, why would the country export anything? The only reason to export is to earn foreign exchange that can be used to import products that are cheaper abroad. Therefore, extreme import substitution would lead to complete autarky, thus eliminating all gains from trade. That is more or less what India experienced during the first four decades following Independence.

The extreme I have posed is not an exception but only a dramatic illustration of the rule. In international trade theory, there is a powerful proposition that goes by the name of the Lerner Symmetry Theorem, so named because it was first propounded by economist Abbe Lerner in a paper published in a leading British journal in 1936. According to this remarkable theorem, the effect of an across-the-board 10 per cent import duty is identical to that of an across-the-board 10 per cent export tax. Both interventions reduce imports as well as exports and lead to a loss of the gains from trade.

While the precise logic behind the Lerner Symmetry Theorem is somewhat involved, its essence can be explained in simple terms. The initial reduction in imports through increased tariffs lowers the demand for foreign currency. This fact leads to a reduction in the price of foreign currency in terms of domestic currency from, say, ₹70 per dollar to ₹65 per dollar. A cheaper foreign currency in turn partially reverses the initial tariff-induced reduction in imports. Simultaneously, it lowers the profitability of exports and hence the quantum of exports. Eventually, the country finds itself with reduced imports on a net basis and an equivalent reduction in exports with the gains from trade reduced accordingly. It is thus an illusion that import substitution can make a net addition to the income. The sooner policymakers disabuse themselves of this illusion, the better for India.

Drop Insistence on a Strong Rupee

Alongside import substitution, a strong rupee has also gained currency in the present government. A strong, or what economists call overvalued, currency may make a country feel proud but it has a devastating effect on the competitiveness of its products vis-à-vis its foreign counterparts. A simple example will help explain this important point.

Consider a strong rupee exchange rate of ₹70 per dollar and a weak rupee exchange rate of ₹80 per dollar. Suppose an imported computer costs $1,000 while a domestically produced computer costs ₹75,000. Under a strong rupee rate, the imported computer would sell for ₹70,000 in the Indian market, outcompeting the domestically produced computer. Under the weak rupee rate, the imported computer would sell for ₹80,000, with the domestically produced computer outselling it.

A similar argument applies to exportable goods. Suppose a particular variety of shirt sells for $10 in foreign market. Then a shirt costing ₹750 to produce in India will fail to compete in the foreign market under the strong rupee rate, because it would fetch only ₹700 in Indian currency. But under the weak rupee rate, it will be able to compete because it will bring ₹800 to the exporter.

Inflation is often higher in developing countries than in the developed countries to which they sell the bulk of their exports. This means that over time, costs of production in terms of domestic currency rises faster in developing than in developed countries. Therefore, if the nominal exchange rate is fixed, products of developing countries become less and less competitive relative to those of developed countries. A nominal depreciation of the rupee, which weakens the domestic currency, corrects this differential in cost increases and restores the competitiveness of domestic goods.

When the domestic currency is allowed to remain strong in the face of higher inflation at home and domestic products lose competitiveness, producers of goods that compete with imported goods clamour for protection. Democratic governments often end up bowing to such clamour, as has happened in India in recent years. During the five years following 2013/14, depreciation of Indian rupee failed to keep pace with its higher inflation, making Indian goods 10 to 15 per cent more expensive in comparison to many imports. As a result, the domestic industry has demanded and got increased tariff protection in many sectors.

Using tariffs instead of exchange rate depreciation to restore the competitiveness of goods competing against imports has two disadvantages. First, exports will still continue to suffer from reduced competitiveness. In principle, exports too can be protected through export subsidies but they violate World Trade Organization (WTO) rules. Second, tariffs are very inefficient instruments of protection. They undermine the growth of trade and deprive the country of the gains that accrue with it.

During the decade following 1991, when India became progressively more open, it allowed the rupee to depreciate by a large margin. Between 1991/92 and 2003/04, the average tariff in India fell from 113 per cent to approximately 30 per cent. Yet, Indian goods remained competitive, with the current account (exports minus imports) showing a surplus from 2001/02 to 2003/04. This was because the rupee depreciated from ₹20 per dollar to ₹46 per dollar over the same time. The depreciation helped exports while also compensating producers of goods competing against imports that had been subject to large cuts in tariffs.

India needs to pay particular attention to the value of the rupee vis-à-vis the Chinese yuan. When the yuan depreciates vis-à-vis the dollar and the rupee does not, Indian goods lose competitiveness against Chinese goods. This has indeed happened in recent years. The result has been a massive expansion of imports from China by India without a parallel expansion of India's exports to China. Given the importance of China in India's trade, the India–China exchange rate is of special importance for India.

Rationalize Tariffs

Tariffs in India remain high and their structure complex. In many cases, tariffs on inputs are higher than those on outputs, leading to negative protection to the latter. In some cases, tariffs are imposed on items that India does not even produce domestically. Such tariffs hurt the buyers of the items, whether they are final consumers or firms using them as input, without benefiting anyone. India's last major effort to compress tariffs in 2007 brought the top tariff down from 12 to 10 per cent (with the exception of some tariff peaks applying to sectors such as textiles, apparel and automobiles, which remained significantly higher than the 10 per cent ceiling).

It is now time to resume liberalization and rationalize the structure of tariffs. If the exchange rate is managed prudently at the same time, such rationalization and liberalization can be accomplished while making Indian goods more competitive relative to foreign goods. With this in mind, India should set a goal of adopting a uniform across-the-board tariff of 7 per cent on all industrial products within three years. This will entail raising the tariffs that are currently below 7 per cent (except a handful that are bound below 7 per cent under India's commitments to the WTO and therefore cannot be raised) while reducing the higher rates.

A uniform tariff across all products has several advantages over the current highly variegated structure. It will end the existing tariff inversion whereby tariffs on many inputs are levied at higher rates than final products. It will also result in minimal distortion across import-competing sectors, though distortion vis-à-vis exports will remain as long as the tariff rate is positive.

But above all, once the government has committed to a uniform tariff across all imports, demands for higher and higher tariffs by industry lobbies would gradually subside. The reason is that once each lobby sees that an increase in its tariff would automatically raise the tariff on all other imports, its incentive to lobby will greatly diminish.

Symmetrically, commitment to a uniform tariff will also strengthen the hand of the government vis-à-vis lobbies seeking higher tariffs. The government would be in a position to diffuse the pressure for a higher tariff from a specific industry lobby by arguing that if it concedes to such demand, it has to raise the tariff on all other products, which is harmful to the economy.[40]

A remaining question is why the recommended tariff rate is 7 per cent and not higher or lower. This choice is based on the revenue consideration. It will ensure that the tariff revenue would not fall below its current level and may indeed rise. The recommendation is not meant to be a rigid number and may be fixed at a slightly lower or higher level than 7 per cent, as long as it results in some overall liberalization of the regime.

An Alternative Tariff Reform

If the recommendation of a uniform 7 per cent tariff is seen as too radical and lacking political acceptance, an alternative would be to bring all tariffs exceeding 10 per cent to the 10 per cent level. Such tariff compression will be in line with India's past approach. India needs to pay particular attention to tariff reductions in two areas: textiles and clothing, and the auto sector.

In textiles and clothing, nearly all tariffs range from 20 to 25 per cent. This is an area in which India should have the ambition to become the world's largest exporter and should not depend on protection. More importantly, the largest market in apparel globally is in garments made from manmade fibre. So far, India's exports of apparel are not only small in relation to its size, they are concentrated in garments made of cotton fibre.

---

40 Panagariya and Rodrik, 1993, offer a formal model showing how commitment to a uniform tariff can lead to a less distortionary tariff within a political-economy model.

An important reason for India's poor performance in garments made of manmade fibre is that it subjects the imports of this fibre to a tariff of 20 per cent and those of fabric made from it to 25 per cent tariff. Because GST is levied on tariff-inclusive prices, the effective custom duty ends up being even higher than these rates. In addition, India slaps anti-dumping duties on many items falling under the category of manmade fibre or fabric made from manmade fibre. This fact makes domestic producers of garments made of manmade fibre uncompetitive vis-à-vis their foreign counterparts. This single fact has prevented India from exploiting its comparative advantage in apparel made from manmade fibre, arguably the largest potential source of good jobs for workers with no or limited skills.

India has provided its auto sector an even higher level of tariff protection. According to the 2018 tariff schedule submitted by India to the WTO, the applied tariff rate on vehicles meant for ten or more passengers is 40 per cent and on those for fewer than ten workers is 125 per cent. These tariffs have produced a highly inefficient auto industry, with the result that India's share in the world passenger car exports remains less than 1 per cent. The industry produces cars that are of lower quality than their foreign counterparts and often sells them at one and a half times the price charged by the latter. With the industry having been protected by prohibitive trade barriers and the consumer having been punished for the entire seventy-plus years since Independence, it is time that the government subjects it to genuine competition.

Reimburse All Indirect Taxes to Exporters

The third area of border measures requiring correction concerns indirect taxes paid by exporters along the value chain. These must be reimbursed expeditiously in totality. Such reimbursement is fully consistent with the WTO rules. Currently, petroleum products are not integrated into GST. As a result, taxes paid on them by exporters are not reimbursed. Similarly, duty drawbacks on imported inputs, which are fully WTO-legal, end up being partial in some cases. There are also inordinate delays in reimbursements of indirect taxes and duties paid on inputs, which blocks the working capital of exporters.

Free Trade Agreements

Light manufactures, especially apparel and footwear, remain subject to high custom duties in most of the export markets of India. Some of India's competitors such as Bangladesh and Vietnam have duty-free access in the large European Union (EU) market. The only way India can improve its access to these markets and be at par with competing countries is by creating free-trade agreements (FTAs). Two such FTAs, already under negotiation, could prove especially helpful: the Regional Comprehensive Economic Partnership (RCEP) agreement with the major Asian countries and that with the EU consisting of twenty-eight European countries. Although India found the deal offered by other RCEP countries unsatisfactory and recently chose not to enter into an agreement with them, with additional concessions, it will be to its advantage to be a member of this arrangement. In the forthcoming years, the RCEP market in apparel, footwear and other light manufactures will be huge, so that establishing duty-free access to it can bring vast gains for India. Likewise, the EU is already a large market for Indian apparel exports. Duty-free access to it can potentially lead to a substantial expansion of India's exports.

These FTAs can also prove to be highly effective instruments to bring multinationals currently leaving China to Indian shores. The FTAs will give these multinationals duty-free access to the European and RCEP markets. They would also allow them to import their inputs duty-free from these countries. Such a change could be transformational in terms of creating good jobs and reshaping the ecosystem for manufacturing activity in India.

Trade Facilitation

India also needs to implement trade facilitation in all its aspects. This is a very substantial area of reforms involving many logistical details. I will not venture into all details here but will briefly mention the key areas. A report by a committee of the Economic Advisory Council to the Prime Minister (EAC-PM) provides a substantially more detailed set of recommendations.[41]

The cost of moving goods in and out of ports remains significantly higher in India than in competitor countries. The EAC-PM committee report points out that the average time to clear imports across Indian ports varies from six to thirteen days and that to clear exports ranges from 3.5 to six days. It also notes that port logistics costs at Indian ports average 15 to 16 per cent of the total consignment value compared with 8 per cent in developed countries. These costs make exports and imports costlier compared to domestic sales and discourage trade. Both time and financial costs also exhibit high variability across Indian ports, undermining the predictability of delivery costs. Delays in getting imported inputs used in exports can have an adverse impact on the ability to meet export orders on time. Likewise, failure to deliver exports of certain products at the precise designated time due to lack of predictability of clearance time at ports can be fatal to the renewal of orders. Retail stores in the United States and European countries have limited space for inventory. As a result, they require just-in-time delivery for products such as apparel, which have well-defined seasons for sales.

There are similar issues relating to transport links between the point of production and ports. Historically, the inward orientation of the economy, forced by poor policy choices in the past, has meant that production agglomerations have developed keeping in mind domestic markets, which are often far away from the coast and hence ports. The

---

41 Economic Advisory Council to the Prime Minister, 2018

problem is exacerbated by the fact that India is a large country with a wide geographical spread. The combined effect of these factors has been poor connectivity between production centres and ports. Efforts to build transport links have taken the form of megaprojects such as the Delhi–Mumbai industrial corridor, which have progressed at snail's pace. Consequently, the time taken in and cost incurred on moving goods to and from the ports have remained high. According to the EAC-PM committee report, time taken in moving goods on the same route shows fluctuations of 15 to 20 per cent around the mean time.

Autonomous Employment Zones

Perhaps the most important initiative India can take today to better integrate itself with the global supply chains and become the world's manufacturing hub is through the launch of Autonomous Employment Zones (AEZs) of which two or three may be located near the coast in Gujarat and Andhra Pradesh to take advantage of the deep dredge ports in these states. These zones would be along the lines of Shenzhen in China. Unlike the Special Economic Zones (SEZs) with which India experimented during the past one and a half decades with mixed results, AEZs would be spread over large areas in excess of 500 square kilometres, with the early ones located close to a deep dredge port. They will also be far fewer in number—no more than half a dozen, perhaps only two or three, in the beginning—than SEZs. Since suitable unused land areas of this size are unlikely to be available, especially near the coast, the zones may include existing habitations and establishments.

The key feature of AEZs would be to define the boundaries of the zone and then give virtually all powers to frame the rules of economic engagement, including labour and land laws and administration of customs, within the zone to the local administration. The zones will offer a highly flexible environment with respect to labour and land laws, allowing rapid reallocation of these factors from one activity to another. They will also allow exporters to import inputs with minimum friction, process them and export. But there will be no export requirement for firms locating in the zones.

In the initial phase, say during the first ten years, the government may provide a waiver on either GST or corporate profit tax to any single employer employing 10,000 workers or more. This will incentivize the early entrants to the zones who must function within an area that would still be developing. Later entrants would be entering a well-developed area and therefore would not require a similar benefit. The government must proactively court multinationals currently active in China and other countries, especially in labour-intensive manufacturing, in the early phase of the zone.

The government's other contributions to the zones may be limited to building first-rate infrastructure and dormitory housing, which migrant workers can rent. When seen in the national context, the resources needed for building infrastructure and dormitory housing in AEZs are relatively small. They can be drawn out of the general pool of resources devoted to infrastructure and urban housing.

Once success is demonstrated in a handful of AEZs, more of them may be considered. What is important, however, is that the numbers are kept in proportion to available resources to build such zones. A key flaw of many government initiatives in India is that they are multiplied too rapidly, which spreads limited resources too thinly to produce any successes.

Tax Simplification and Tax Predictability

India also needs to reform and simplify its tax laws. Complex tax laws with their myriad exemptions create uncertainty for investors. The high frequency of changes in the laws and high propensity of the government to engage in tax disputes add to this uncertainty. India needs to clear the existing stock of disputes and take measures that would discourage the creation of frivolous tax disputes in the future.

Unjust taxes can render profitable investments unprofitable and drive away future investors. The introduction of retrospective taxation during the second term of the UPA government had a chilling effect on investors. The relevant law still remains on the books and may be invoked by a future government. Therefore, it is best to repeal it.

The GST is an important step in the direction of simplification and transparency. But it too has been subject to considerable uncertainty during its short life, with tax rates on many items being revised. The necessary adjustments to the rate should be done relatively fast and then maintained. It will be best to quickly move the system to two rates of 12 and 18 per cent with no exception, other than zero-rated items.

The government has insisted on maintaining the 28 per cent tax rate on grounds of taxing luxury items at a punishing rate. But it is unwise to pursue the equality objective through every instrument on which the government can lay its hands. Instead, it is best to choose the tax system that minimizes loss of efficiency and pursue equality objective principally through expenditures targeted at favoured groups. Extremely high tax rates may even undermine the revenue objective by discouraging the purchase of highly taxed items.

Finally, historically, India has also maintained extra-high tax rates on corporate profits. In the early years of reforms, some rationalization of this tax was done but that process was not taken to its logical end. Indeed, the effective rate saw a rise through the imposition of a surcharge on the tax. Luckily, the government has recently taken a big step by knocking down the corporate profit tax for domestic companies to 22 per cent, with the effective rate inclusive of surcharge amounting to 25.2 per cent. For new firms starting production before 2023, the government has reduced the effective tax rate to 17 per cent. Alongside, it has ended all exemptions and incentives. This is a reform worthy of applause not only for its lower rate but also for ending exemptions and incentives. Similar reforms must also be undertaken in the area of personal taxation to incentivize work by professionals and minimize evasion through bribery.

Labour Market Reforms

Labour market rigidities have asymmetrically hurt the manufacturing sector. This has manifested itself in a much more tepid response of manufacturing, relative to services to product-market liberalization on which the reforms have focused till date. As Table 6.1 shows, during the first three decades of development ending in 1979/80, services grew slower than industry. During the transition decade of the 1980s, they almost caught up with the latter. But following the launch of the reforms in 1991, which principally focused on product-market liberalization, growth in services came to decisively outpace the growth in industry.

Table 6.1: Average Annual Growth in Broad Sectors by Decades, 1951/52 to 1916/17

Period	Agriculture	Industry	Services	GDP at Factor Cost
1951/52 to 1959/60	2.7	5.8	4.2	3.6
1960/61 to 1969/70	2.5	6.2	5.2	4.1
1970/71 to 1979/80	1.3	4.3	3.9	2.9
1980/81 to 1989/90	4.4	6.4	6.3	5.7
1990/91 to 1999/2000	3.2	5.8	7.2	5.8
2000/2001 to 2009/10	2.5	7.3	8.8	7.3
2010/11 to 2016/17	3.7	7.1	7.9	7.0

Source: Author's calculations from the CSO-estimated data

In India, manufacturing firms can choose to stay small with fewer than ten workers (twenty, if not using power) or become larger. If they choose the former, they can escape most of the myriad labour laws. They do not have to offer formal employment contracts and benefits such as paid leave, sick leave, pension and medical insurance. They can terminate workers without notice and need not pay severance pay. The only major labour law that applies to firms with seven or more workers is the Trade Union Act, 1926, under which seven or more workers can form a trade union. Most Indian firms choose to hire fewer than ten workers, often fewer than seven.

Firms choosing to hire ten (twenty if not using power) or more workers must register under the Factories Act, 1948, and accept obligations that become increasingly demanding with rising size of the workforce. The Factories Act itself limits the maximum hours of work per week to forty-eight and overtime hours per quarter to 100. It also bans the employment of women for more than nine hours per day and forbids them from working from 7 p.m. to 6 a.m. At 150 workers, a lunchroom must be provided; at 250 workers, there should be a canteen on factory premises; and at thirty women employees, a daycare centre must be made available.

Several other laws add to the requirements to be satisfied by larger firms. At ten workers, firms must offer health insurance under the Employee State Insurance Act, 1948. At twenty workers, they must establish a pension fund for the workers under the Employees' Provident Funds and Miscellaneous Provisions Act, 1952. At fifty workers, the Industrial Disputes Act, 1947, makes assignment of a worker from one task to another excessively difficult. At 100 workers, under the same act, termination of a worker, though possible in theory, is impossible in practice.

Each of these laws has many more requirements than those mentioned above. And there are numerous other labour laws that I choose not to list. The central government alone has enacted over forty labour laws which larger enterprises in all states must abide by.[42]

---

42 A partial list of these other pieces of legislation includes the Minimum Wages Act, 1948; the Payment of Bonus Act, 1965; the Payment of

In addition, each state has its own labour laws. Though the central government laws have been amended over time, the original dates of their passage indicate that many of them had been already in place under the British rule and the vast majority of them were already in place by the 1950s.

Therefore, historically, India has had a very high level of protection for labour in the formal sector. Even in the 1960s, when the Licence Permit Raj regulated investment allocations with a heavy hand of the state, labour legislation was at par with developed countries. Though some leading scholars recognized the deleterious effects of such inflexibility in the labour markets at an early stage of development, little was done to get the right balance between the rights of employees and employers. P. C. Mahalanobis, who is regarded as the architect of India's Second Five Year Plan and was revered by leading economists of his time as 'The Professor', expressed his concern in a 1969 article (p. 1121) in these terms:

> However, it seems to me that in certain respects, welfare measures tend to be implemented in India ahead of economic growth, for example, in labour laws which are probably the most highly protective of labour interests, in the narrowest sense, in the whole world. There is practically no link between output and remuneration; hiring and firing are highly restricted. It is extremely difficult to maintain an economic level of productivity, or improve productivity. At early stages of development in all countries there has been a real conflict between welfare measure and economic growth. Japan is an outstanding example; the concept of minimum wages was introduced only about 10 or 12 years ago when per capita income had reached the level of $250 or $300 per year; and minimum wages were fixed

---

Gratuity Act, 1972; the Workmen's Compensation Act, 1923; the Industrial Employment (Standing Order) Act, 1946; and the Contract Labour (Regulation and Abolition) Act, 1970.

> more or less at actual average levels. In India with a per capita income of only about $70, the present form of protection of organized labour, which constitutes, including their families, about 5 or 6 per cent of the whole population, would operate as an obstacle to growth and would also increase inequalities. It is a serious problem not only in India but in other under-developed countries.[43]

The need for making labour laws more liberal had thus been identified even in the 1960s. Yet, the populist government of the day did exactly the opposite, making them yet more stringent. An amendment to the Industrial Disputes Act introduced in 1976 and strengthened in 1982 made it mandatory for an enterprise with 100 or more workers to seek permission from the labour department with jurisdiction over it before terminating a worker. By convention, such permission is never granted. Therefore, the effect of the amendment is to ban termination of workers by enterprises with 100 or more regular employees.

There is an acute need to both rationalize and liberalize India's labour laws. In this respect, the current effort to demarcate the existing over-forty central labour laws into four codes covering wages, industrial relations, social security and welfare, and safety and work conditions is a welcome move. These four codes must carry uniform definitions of terms such as worker, wages, industrial disputes and retrenchment and be consistent with each other. But they should not just be collections of different existing laws in the relevant areas with definitional inconsistencies removed. They must also be vehicles for rewriting labour laws to make them flexible. In this respect, the Code on Wages, 2019, which brings together all existing central laws on wages into a single law and has already been enacted, falls short. Rather than provide for a single minimum wage in any given region, it retains the existing provisions for multiple minimum wages depending on the level of skill of the worker. It also calls upon the central government

43 Mahalanobis, 1969

to fix separate minimum wages for railways and mines. If the code on industrial relations follows the same approach as the code on wages and organizes existing laws into a single code without liberalizing them, the cause of reform would hardly progress.

The new codes must seek a better balance between the rights of employees and employers. They must ensure that protection to those having regular employment is not kept at such a high level that firms are discouraged from hiring workers in the first place. Giving employers the right to terminate workers with a generous severance pay is crucial. Employers need workers as much as workers need employers. But when an occasional worker persistently violates discipline, refuses to perform his duties and vitiates the work environment, employers need the powers to rectify the situation.

The right to lay off workers is also needed for firms to have the option to exit. No investment is without risk. Therefore, for any entrepreneur seeking to enter into a labour-intensive sector on a large scale, the right to lay off workers with a reasonable severance pay is essential. Anyone who fears that once he hires a large workforce, he will have to pay the wages of those workers even if the venture turns unprofitable, will not take such a risk. The option to exit is a pre-condition for entry.

It is important to appreciate that the power to lay off workers may not mean much to employers in highly capital-intensive sectors. In such sectors, labour costs are a tiny part of the total cost. According to the managing director of a leading two-wheeler manufacturing enterprise, wage and salary bill for his entire workforce from himself down to the watchman is just 4 per cent of the total sales.[44] Therefore,

44 This was stated by Rajiv Bajaj, managing director of Bajaj Auto, in a live interview on TV channel CNBC-TV18 on 22 August 2019. The interview can be found at https://www.cnbctv18.com/auto/automobile-slowdown-rajiv-bajaj-says-industry-must-look-at-its-shortcomings-before-asking-for-stimulus-4220291.htm (last accessed on 26 August 2019).

it is possible for such employers to give golden handshakes to workers when they need to trim the workforce. This is the reason why, when asked if they find Indian labour laws burdensome, large-scale entrepreneurs in India, who are predominantly engaged in capital-intensive manufacturing, invariably reply in the negative, arguing that they are able to get around them. Employers in labour-intensive sectors such as apparel and footwear, where labour costs constitute a disproportionately large part of the total cost, do not have this luxury. They have had to get around the onerous laws by simply staying small.

These arguments apply equally to minimum wage laws. On the surface, setting the minimum wage at a relatively high level seems an attractive proposition. What could be so bad about ensuring that workers receive a decent wage? The problem once again is that the wages employers in labour-intensive sectors can pay to remain competitive in the global marketplace are significantly lower than what those operating in the capital-intensive sector can afford to pay. With formal sector employers predominantly in capital-intensive sectors, it is tempting to fix the minimum wage keeping their capacity to pay in mind. But those minimum wages can readily render unprofitable employers in sectors in which labour costs are proportionately large.

Another important aspect of minimum wages is that the cost of living varies across regions and between rural and urban areas. Therefore, appropriate minimum wages would be different according to region, and the rural versus urban character of the area. One option is to anchor the minimum wage in poverty lines that vary across states and between rural and urban areas within each state according to the cost of living differences.

Finally, setting different minimum wages for different levels of skills, as India does, goes against both ethical and economic principles. Ethically, the philosophy behind the minimum wage is to set a base-level wage sufficient to ensure a certain socially accepted minimum living standard. How can such a minimum standard vary according to the level of skill of the worker? What sense does it make to say that higher the skill level of the worker, higher the minimum acceptable living standard for her? Because a socially acceptable minimum living standard cannot vary according to skill level, the minimum wage in nearly all countries other than India is set to target unskilled workers.

Good economics says that once the minimum wage for those at the lowest rung of the skill ladder has been set, we should let market forces do the remainder of the work. For instance, when the demand for a product using a certain type of engineer declines, the salaries of those engineers must be allowed to decline as well. If the minimum wage for those engineers interferes with such a decline, it will only make that sector prematurely unprofitable and force it to shrink through layoffs of engineers.

Enterprises also need the flexibility to assign workers from one task to another. With technological change, enterprises must often reinvent themselves to survive in the highly competitive marketplace. If they cannot reassign workers to tasks other than those for which they were originally hired, as is the case currently, their production costs rise unduly. The difficulty of exit under such circumstances makes matters worse still.

Before leaving the subject of labour laws, let me point out that the Indian government has made some progress towards making life easier for enterprises. It has introduced digital filing of compliances under various central labour laws with enforcement done through random inspections. This change has helped ameliorate the excesses of the inspector raj that have existed historically. The government has also permitted hiring of workers on fixed terms, which allows some flexibility in right-sizing workforce. Some states have also exempted firms with workforces of up to 300 workers (instead of 100 workers) from the ban on the termination of workers. While these are steps in the right direction, much more needs to be done to create a transparent labour-market regime that balances the rights of the workers and those of employers.

Land Market Reforms

Setting up a large-scale firm requires a large-sized piece of land. Land ownership in India is fragmented and, with no definitive titles in existence, often in dispute. This fact makes the task of assembling a large piece of land through purchases of numerous small pieces a difficult as well as costly task. With low profit margins in labour-intensive sectors, the high cost of land can quickly make an otherwise profitable enterprise unprofitable.

There are only two viable alternatives under such circumstances. First, the government can step in and acquire land for the enterprise under the Land Acquisition Act, 2013. Unfortunately, this law makes acquisition of land by the government for private enterprises extremely difficult and costly. The law needs to be amended to make such acquisition at a reasonable cost possible. The enterprise may still be asked to purchase the bulk of the land but where ownership is in dispute or other encumbrances exist, the government needs to intervene.

Second, to some extent, the enterprise can reduce its need for land by building the production facility vertically upwards. Modern apparel factories can be and are built on multiple floors. This option requires flexible floor space index (FSI) rules. FSI is the ratio of floor space area permitted in a building to the area of the plot on which the building stands. Again, cities and states in India have tended to be stingy in setting the FSI, often keeping it below two, which means that maximally, only twice as much floor space as the area of the plot on which the building stands can be built. With such low FSI, it is not feasible to build large-scale factories on limited land area.

Logistics Sector

I have already touched upon transportation in the context of trade facilitation. But this important factor needs to be considered in a broader context. Insofar as locations of sources of inputs and destinations of final products are different from the locations of production activity, delivered costs depend on infrastructure. Closely associated with transportation are the other components of the logistics sector: storage, handling, inventory and packaging. All these activities require development in India. A vibrant logistics sector is critical to the smooth functioning of supply chains. Today, with the development of e-commerce, it is possible for even individual customers to order products from almost any location. This makes the role of a well-functioning logistics sector even more critical.

Rivigo, a start-up that began operations in 2014, is bringing about a major change in this sector. Breaking away from the model of small fleets of trucks, which dominates the Indian scene, it has built a fleet of several thousand trucks. Its relay-trucking model has cut delivery time by a significant magnitude by keeping trucks running 24x7 while allowing truck drivers to return to their homes the same day. It is also doing innovative advances in storage and handling. This model needs to be replicated on a larger scale.

Potentially, railways could play a significantly greater role in low-cost speedy transportation. In principle, costs of transportation ought to be lower on railways than by road. But, saddled with bureaucratic inefficiencies, which result in delays in delivery, they have progressively lost ground to roadways. Today, roads not only account for a much larger proportion of freight than they did two decades ago, but also for a much higher proportion of passengers.

Concluding Remarks

Numerous reforms are required to help with the emergence of medium- and large-scale firms in labour-intensive sectors, especially within manufacturing. Because large firms must operate in the global marketplace, exporting a part of their output while also relying on many of their inputs on imports, the recommended reforms are partially aimed at bringing down the costs directly associated with exports and imports. But lowering these costs alone is not sufficient to ensure the emergence of large- and medium-scale firms. There also remain serious constraints related to labour and land markets and uncertainty of taxation that asymmetrically work against these firms. These constraints must also be addressed.

A necessary accompaniment to industrialization is urbanization. As manufacturing expands and creates attractive jobs, workers exit low-productivity employment in agriculture and migrate to them. In turn, this migration leads to the expansion of existing cities or creation of new cities. If cities are not prepared to accommodate these migrant workers, manufacturing growth may get choked. Therefore, it is critical that governments pay particular attention to managing urbanization as manufacturing growth proceeds. This, then, is the subject of the next chapter.

7

URBANIZATION: MAKING ROOM FOR MIGRANT WORKERS

RAPID GROWTH AND CREATION of formal-sector jobs in industry and services invariably results in greater urbanization.[45] This happens either because formal industry and services are concentrated in existing urban agglomerations and expand by drawing workers out of agriculture, or because their growth turns rural and semi-urban habitations into urban spaces. In China, Shanghai, which has grown rapidly on the back of migration from other regions during the last three decades, illustrates the former phenomenon; Shenzhen, which grew into a twelve-million-strong urban agglomeration out of a group of fishing villages with a population of just 300,000 in 1980, represents the latter. In either event, expansion of urban spaces is a necessary accompaniment to the creation of good jobs.

Consistent with the low level of growth in formal-sector jobs, urbanization has been slow in India. The share of urban population in the total population was just 17 per cent in 1951 and rose to barely

45 This chapter adapts and updates Chapter 7 of Panagariya, Chakraborty and Rao, 2014. The latter offers additional details on reforms at state and local levels in areas such as piped water supply, sewage and waste management.

31 per cent in 2011. This growth amounts to a paltry 2.3-percentage points per decade on an average. Some observers argue that this slow growth reflects the stricter definition of urbanization that India uses compared with other countries. Adjusting for this factor would raise the rate of urbanization to some degree but would not overturn the basic fact that urbanization in countries such as Brazil and China has been much faster and these countries are far more urbanized than India today.

In addition to slow growth in well-paid jobs in industry and services, two factors have contributed to the slow rate of urbanization in India. First, with accelerated growth providing larger revenues, the government has introduced benefits that are available only in rural areas. For example, guaranteed employment for a hundred days for one member of every household under the National Rural Employment Guarantee Scheme is available only in rural areas. Food subsidy coverage in rural areas far exceeds that in urban areas. Subsidies on water, electricity, seeds and fertilizer are also available only in rural areas. Direct revenue grants to local bodies mandated by the Finance Commission are available only to rural local bodies called gram panchayats, and not to municipalities in urban areas. These benefits have discouraged workers from migrating out of rural areas. They have also discouraged rural local bodies from agreeing to reclassification as urban settlements, even when such reclassification is warranted by economically relevant parameters.

Second, urban areas themselves have done a poor job of providing cheap rental housing for potential migrants, often leaving slums and footpaths as the only residential options. Low-fare public transportation is also often missing, which denies potential migrants the option to live in low-rent housing in the suburbs and commute to the city for work. This has made an already weak pull-effect of decent jobs for aspirant rural migrants weaker still.

Unlike China, where rural–urban migration has played a very important role, growth in urban population in India has been dominated by the natural growth of population. The other three contributors to urbanization—expansion of existing urban areas (urban sprawl), reclassification of previously rural into urban areas and rural–urban migration—have been much less important. The contribution of the natural growth of population to urban growth was a hefty 62.7 per cent during 1981–91 and 59.2 per cent in 1991–2001. It saw a significant decline but remained substantial at 44 per cent during 2001–11. While the bulk of the shift during 2001–11 represents the reclassification of previously rural into urban areas, migration also saw a small acceleration during this decade. From 22.6 and 21.1 per cent during the 1980s and 1990s, respectively, the contribution of migration rose to approximately 24 per cent during the 2000s.[46]

The urban population in India has come to increasingly concentrate in Class-I cities, defined as those with 100,000 or more people. The number of these cities rose from seventy-seven in 1951 to 468 in 2011, with their share in urban population rising from 45 to 70 per cent over the same period. Metropolitan cities, which have populations of one million or more, have risen from five in number in 1951 to fifty-three in 2011, with the corresponding shares in the total urban population rising from 18.9 to 42.6 per cent. Eighteen metropolitan cities have been added in the 2001–11 decade alone.

According to the Census 2011, India has three urban agglomerations whose populations individually exceed ten million—Greater Mumbai, Delhi and Kolkata, with populations of 18.4, 16.3 and 14.1 million respectively. Together, these agglomerations represented 12.9 per cent of the total urban population in 2011. Despite the fact that the population growth in these agglomerations saw a significant slowdown

---

46 Planning Commission 2011, Chart 1.5 for estimates relating to 1981–1991 and 1991–2001. Estimates relating to 2001–11 are from a presentation entitled 'India's Urban Demographic Transition' by the National Institute of Urban Affairs, available at http://www.urbanindia.nic.in/UDataResource/CensusResult_2011.pdf (last accessed on 11 May 2013).

in the 2000s compared to the 1990s, their combined population grew at an impressive 14.8 per cent during the former period. Two municipal corporations, Mumbai and Delhi, qualify as mega cities defined as cities with populations of ten million or more. In 2011, these cities were home to 12.4 and eleven million people, respectively.

Given the crucial role of cities and towns as centres of economic activity and engines of economic transformation, the importance of their orderly growth and well-functioning life in them can be scarcely overestimated. Unfortunately, however, grossly insufficient attention has been paid to either the development of new cities or maintenance and orderly expansion of the existing ones. Basic urban services such as housing, water, electricity, sewage, solid waste management and transportation are poorly supplied in much of urban India. Indeed, with the vast majority of Indians living in rural areas, democratic polity has resulted in a general neglect of cities, with their development largely governed by short-term responses to day-to-day pressures of life.

The Indian Constitution vests much of the power to govern cities and towns, including the power to enact laws for them, in the states. Though urban local bodies such as municipalities and municipal corporations must attend to the daily needs of the citizens, they lack the power to make rules, raise revenues to finance expenditures, design policies or do long-term planning in areas of local concern. The state government controls the budgets of local bodies while also wielding the power to make all major decisions. Although the 74th Constitutional Amendment Act of 1992 mandated setting up of elected municipalities as institutions of self-government, the devolution of real power has been, at best, limited.

Therefore, states have a crucial role in undertaking reforms related to urban India. In the following paragraphs, I discuss the problems and possible reforms in four key areas relating to cities: availability of space at affordable prices; transportation; provision of public goods such as clean piped water, clean air and a well-functioning sewage system and disposal of solid waste; and preponderance of slums.

Housing at Affordable Prices

The bigger Indian cities suffer from sprawl and acute shortage of space within a 10-or-15-kilometre radius around the city centre. Sprawl creates a distance between where people live and where they work, and burdens the government with large expenditures on urban infrastructure and transportation. If the government fails to provide adequate infrastructure, commuting becomes a nightmare for those working in the city centre and living on the periphery. The shortage of space in and around the city centre results in an extra-high cost of living and crowding out of all but the wealthiest residents and most profitable businesses.

A comparison of Mumbai and Shanghai best illustrates this shortage. In 2009, Mumbai residents, on an average, had just 4.5 square metres of space per person. In 1984, Shanghai suffered even worse space shortage with only 3.65 square metres per person. But then the Shanghai municipality decided to make raising space availability its top priority. It decided to make liberal use of the only option available: permit taller and taller buildings. By 2010, the city could boast of having raised the available space to 34 square metres per person.[47]

There are seven supply-side factors and one demand-side factor constraining the availability of space in Indian cities that must be addressed.

Urban Land Ceilings and Regulation Act

The Urban Land Ceilings and Regulation Act (ULCRA), 1976, which gave the government the right to acquire vacant lots exceeding 500 to 2,000 square metres in size, depending on the size of the city, at the throwaway price of ₹10 per square metre, led to the disappearance of large plots from the market. Many plot owners tried to use loopholes

---

47 Bertraud, 2011

in the law to claim exemptions from the act. That led the government to take the matter to the court.

Although the central government and most states have repealed the ULCRA, many large pieces of land remain tied up in litigation. The government must find ways to quickly settle these disputes so that these pieces of land can become available and be put to appropriate commercial use. If possible, these plots of land could be auctioned at competitive prices and the proceeds placed in an escrow account. Those funds can then be transferred to the party that eventually wins ownership rights.

Land Owned by Public Sector Enterprises

Many public sector enterprises (PSEs) in India own much larger chunks of land than they need. Many of them were set up during the first three or four decades of Independence when land was plentiful. Therefore, states competed for those units with generous offers of land. For example, many ordnance factories today own land that is ten to twenty times of what they actually use.

Additionally, through investment licensing, the central government controlled the location of private manufacturing units. Once again, state governments coveted these units and were willing to offer large chunks of land to them. As a result, many private manufacturing units, which eventually became sick and were taken over by the government, also have large chunks of land. The government should systematically hive off extra land owned by these units and sell it to the highest bidder. In the case of units that are sick and must be closed down, the entire land should be placed back on the market for commercial use.

Land Owned by Other Public Entities

Central and state governments own substantial land that is unused or used in commercially unviable activities. For example, railways, civil aviation and defence ministries own substantial urban land that is either unused or is subject to encroachment. Auctioning this land would not only put it to better use but also generate valuable revenues for the government. Excuses of future need should not be permitted to come in the way of this process. Should the government need some of this land in the future, it can reacquire it using its powers under the Land Acquisition Act, 2013.

Land Acquisition Act, 2013

The Land Acquisition Act, 2013, has also contributed to high prices of land, since it mandates that the government pay a multiple of the market price for the land it acquires from private owners. This fact contributes to a higher cost of public projects, such as affordable housing. The act also makes it difficult for the government to acquire land for private industry. This would not have been a problem had land rights been clearly defined in India. But that is not the case and often parcels of land are subject to a variety of encumbrances. This makes purchasing large chunks of contiguous land extremely challenging for private buyers. The government needs to amend the act appropriately to remove these bottlenecks.

Land Conversion Rules

Stringent conversion rules further contribute to the shortage of urban land. Potentially, cities could expand to accommodate the migrant population by extending their boundaries on the periphery. But this is often a challenge because such land is classified as agricultural and requires conversion to non-agricultural use. The authority for the conversion is usually vested in state revenue departments, which are reluctant to grant it. State governments could overcome this bottleneck by transferring the powers to grant conversion to departments responsible for urbanization, and making the process of conversion transparent and flexible.

Flexibility is also required in the conversion of existing urban space from one use to another. Efficiency requires that as demand shifts, warehouses should be converted into residential spaces and residential spaces into office spaces or parking lots. In many Indian cities, such conversion can be a serious challenge.

Coastal Regulation Zones

For decades, rules defining Coastal Regulation Zones (CRZs) under the Environmental Protection Act, 1986, have obstructed the development of coastal areas within 500 metres of the coastline. Similar restrictions in island cities in other countries such as New York, Hong Kong and Singapore do not exist. Coastal land is highly valuable for building properties that can attract high-end tourism. It is also a source of high-value housing that can further help relieve the overall shortage of land. Though the stated objective has been the preservation of the coastline and associated ecology, in reality, these areas have been subject to encroachment and illegal occupation. A new CRZ notification, issued in 2018, has begun to relax the regulation but there is a need to go further in this direction.

Floor Space Index

Finally, in addition to the above challenges to the availability of land horizontally, Indian cities have also constrained themselves to expand the supply of floor space vertically. They are notorious for fixing the floor space index at very low levels. Other things being the same, a higher FSI allows taller buildings, which leads to the creation of more floor space on a given plot of land. When land is scarce, a high FSI also makes it possible to free up space for the construction of wide roads, an above-ground rail-based transit system and parks, without compromising on the availability of living and office space.

A related perverse feature of the policy in Indian cities has been that in complete contrast to the world's well-functioning cities, they fix FSI at lower levels in the central business district and at higher levels in the periphery. This creates a serious shortage of space in the central business district, which forces the cities to reserve it for commercial activities only. In turn, this pushes residential units to the periphery, leading to a heavy burden on transport systems and high human cost in terms of time spent on commuting between workplace and home.

According to experts, the FSI varies from 5 to 15 in the central business district and 0.5 or less in the periphery in most large cities of the world.[48] As technological improvements have made it possible to build safe taller structures, the FSI in most large cities in the central business districts has risen over time. A high FSI in the city centre allows for the development of a vibrant central business district in which businesses can interact efficiently without having to tightly fit into small spaces. As business activity expands, a rising FSI allows the central business district to accommodate more and more businesses without creating congestion. Cities with limited space such as New York, Singapore and Hong Kong have rebuilt their central business districts many times over by raising the FSI in response to increases in business activity.

Oddly, Indian cities have chosen to ignore this simple common sense principle and kept the FSI in the central business districts exceptionally low. The FSI in the island city area of Mumbai since 1991 stands at a paltry 1.33, down from 4.5 in 1964, when the FSI restriction was first introduced. In the suburbs, the FSI drops to 1, with exceptions made in small areas where it is allowed to rise to 4. The FSI in Delhi is 1.2 and in Pune and Maharashtra just 1.

48 Bertraud, 2011

Black Money and the Demand for Real Estate

An important demand-side factor reinforces the effect of the above supply-side factors on real-estate prices in India. Many wealthy Indians do not declare, or only partially declare, their income and wealth to tax authorities to evade taxes. The resulting black income and wealth cannot be parked in banks for fear of discovery by tax authorities. Until recently, the go-to investment for such wealth has been real estate. This flow of funds further contributes to high real-estate prices in urban India.

Luckily, recent actions by the government to combat corruption and black wealth have begun to ameliorate the effect of this factor on real-estate prices. For example, the demonetization of ₹500 and ₹1,000 notes in November 2016 had a significant dampening effect on real-estate prices immediately. The measure has also led sellers to begin insisting on payment via formal instruments such as bank cheques or electronic transfer instead of cash. If this trend holds up, fresh flows of black wealth into real estate will decline considerably.

Another factor contributing to an arrest of flows of illicit money into real estate is the tightening and improved enforcement of the Benami Transactions (Prohibition) Act, 1988, beginning in 2016. This is leading to further brakes on the flow of black money into real estate and greater transparency in transactions in this sector. Continued efforts by the government to enforce laws against black money are required to keep the effect of black wealth on real-estate prices in check.

Shortage of Rental Housing

Shortage of urban land, which makes urban housing overly expensive, displaces all but the wealthy from ownership of housing, especially in and around the central business district where many middle-class workers have jobs. These high prices also contribute to a shortage of rental housing. Sadly, given the difficulty of conversion of agricultural land into urban land, high land prices lead to a shortage of rental housing for middle-class and poor residents even on the periphery of Indian cities.

High housing prices and limited purchasing power of the middle class and poor sections of society lead to low rental yields, which refer to rental income as a proportion of the value of the property. Rental yields in Mumbai offer an extreme example of this phenomenon: already low at 6 per cent of the monthly instalment on mortgage loan in 2006, they fell to 3.5 per cent in 2009 and 1.5 per cent in 2011.[49] Today, they are perhaps lower still. Such low yields make investment in commercial rental property a losing business. Census data show that the share of rental housing in total housing fell from 54 per cent in 1961 to 28 per cent in 2011. The problem hits the migrant population the hardest, since it has no accumulated wealth to purchase dwellings outright. The outcome then is encroachment of publicly owned unoccupied land and creation of slums on it.

Apart from ultra-high land prices, the absence of market-friendly rental laws has also undermined the development of competitive rental markets in India. Traditionally, rental laws in Indian states have been overfriendly to tenants and neglectful of the interests of owners. They cap rents at low levels, eliminating the incentive to maintain rental units that exist and for investment in fresh units. With rental leases having no legal standing in most states, eviction of tenants can be a challenge. Worse yet, since India has no ownership titles for dwellings, owners are often afraid that tenants would claim ownership of their units. The result has been that a large number of units remain vacant despite a severe shortage of rental housing. According to the Census 2011, 11.09 million or 12.3 per cent of a total of ninety million units were lying vacant.

49 Ministry of Housing and Urban Poverty Alleviation, 2015, pp. 12–13

A handful of states including Delhi, Rajasthan and West Bengal have introduced reforms lifting rent controls above a threshold level of rent, with the threshold rising with the cost of living. Among these states, the law in Rajasthan best balances the rights of tenants and owners. This law was originally introduced in 2001 and applied only to divisional headquarters. It was amended in 2017 to apply to all cities. With the exception of units with rents below a threshold level, the law allows the potential tenant and owner full freedom to determine the rent. The threshold level for excluded units varies between ₹2,000 and ₹7,000 per month, depending on the city of location of the unit. The law also provides for eviction of the tenant upon failure to pay rent for four months. Laws in Delhi and West Bengal are less liberal, linking permitted rent to market value of the property, but they are steps in the right direction.

The introduction of liberal tenancy laws that protect ownership rights of the lessor and allow her to charge market rent would bring many currently empty dwelling units in Indian cities on the market. This would go some distance toward easing the housing problem in urban India. But solving the problem fully, especially creating low-rent housing for the poor, would require expansion of urban land, generous floor space index and brakes on the flow of black money into real estate so that land prices and, consequently, rental yields come to be better aligned to interest rates and house prices.

To avoid the creation of slums, it is also important to implement policies that will lead to the emergence of dormitory housing for migrant workers. Many states treat such housing as commercial hotels and subject them to water and electricity tariffs and property taxes at commercial rates. This leads to high rents on dormitory housing, pushing it out of the reach of most migrants, who then seek cheaper alternatives in slums. States that serve as substantial destinations for migrant workers should consider adopting more rational policies towards low-end dormitory housing.

Urban Transportation

Poorly functioning transportation networks contribute to inefficient use of valuable space. In the absence of transportation networks, workers must live close to their workplace. This leads to the use of a sizeable part of the scarce space in the city centre and around it for housing. Ceteris paribus, the outcome is creation of slums and small amount of space per individual in the city centre. The problem becomes progressively worse as development proceeds and the demand for office space in the city centre rises. In cities with low-priced public transportation networks such as New York City and London, workers are able to live in spacious homes in the suburbs and commute to work in the city centre.

Designing transportation systems for cities is a specialized field. Therefore, the following discussion is limited to some basic issues in urban transportation. I have divided it into two parts: transportation services for the existing urban population and using transportation as a tool for future urbanization. In the first case, transportation follows urbanization and in the second, it precedes and leads urbanization.

Transportation for the Existing City Population

In a nutshell, the urban transportation problem is two-fold: building a rapid transit system that connects distant points of urban agglomerations to the city centre and with each other; and providing last-mile connectivity, especially in and around the centre. Basic transportation services in and around the city centre have existed in most major cities for a long time. But rapid transit systems are of a more recent origin.

The rapid transit system has deployed both bus- and rail-based systems. A successful example of a bus-based rapid transit system is the Bus Rapid Transit System or BRTS in Ahmedabad. By the end of 2017, it had 89 kilometres of dedicated corridor and a daily ridership of 350,000 passengers. The most successful example of a rail-based system is the Delhi Metro. As of early 2019, it was 373 kilometres long, connected Delhi to its satellite cities and had a daily ridership of 2.5 million. While bus-based systems are significantly less costly, for major cities, it is rail-based systems that riders find more comfortable. At least the bigger cities in India such as Delhi, Mumbai, Kolkata, Chennai, Bengaluru and Hyderabad have opted for this system.

In-city transportation remains a challenge in most cities in India. Traffic jams and delays on roads are endemic. While the high volume of traffic and limited number of lanes is partially to blame, the lack of enforcement of traffic rules also makes a significant contribution to these delays. Drivers do not follow traffic rules, especially those relating to staying in and changing lanes, which slows down everyone. Stricter enforcement of traffic rules can yield significant gains in speeding up movement. This would also help cut carbon emissions, since movement in traffic punctuated by frequent and long waits ends up contributing substantial volumes to such emissions.

One further challenge of urban transportation in India is the design and maintenance of city roads. Roads are often pedestrian-unfriendly, narrow and poorly surfaced. Frequent and prolonged digging up of roads to resurface or repair them adds to delays. A contributory factor to the narrowness of roads is the highly restrictive FSI in most Indian cities. This has meant that every inch of available land is coveted for some use with space for public projects, mainly roads, becoming the main victim. Cities need to adopt more generous FSIs and use the increases in it to negotiate freeing of some horizontal land for road infrastructure. There is also a need for better planning and design of roads such that lane-width is standardized, provision is made for footpaths for pedestrians and utility ducts under footpaths are included in the initial design and construction. Better coordination between utilities providing electricity, water and cable services and those responsible for building city roads is also needed.

Transportation Network to Promote Urbanization

Transport infrastructure, in particular roads, can also play a critical role in promoting future urbanization. There are three major avenues towards accomplishing this objective. First, cities can build roads and related infrastructure on their outer peripheries in advance to attract industrial and commercial activity. In addition to catalysing industrialization and urbanization, such infrastructure may also help relieve congestion along major arteries passing through the city. An example of this approach is the 159-kilometre-long Hyderabad outer ring project. It has connected the existing townships around the city and created potential for growth and development of new satellite townships consisting of business parks and technology clusters along a growth corridor of 1 kilometre on each side of the road. The ring road also connects to various state and national highways, which allows pass-through traffic to avoid having to enter the city and avoid congestion.

The Delhi–Mumbai Industrial Corridor (DMIC) project illustrates the second approach towards catalysing industrial growth and urbanization. This is a far more ambitious approach and requires the cooperation of the central government and multiple state governments. The project involves the construction of a 1,483-kilometre-long dedicated freight corridor passing through Delhi, Haryana, Rajasthan, Uttar Pradesh, Gujarat and Maharashtra. In addition to the freight line, the DMIC project includes nine mega industrial zones of 200 to 250 square kilometres each, three ports, six airports and a six-lane intersection-free expressway connecting Delhi and Mumbai.[50] The main shortcoming of this approach is that it requires massive investment and any positive return to it may take decades to fructify. It is perhaps wiser to break up such projects into multiple smaller

50 For further details, visit the DMIC website, http://delhimumbaiindustrialcorridor.com/

projects and implement them in a way that returns to it do not have to wait till it is completed in its entirety.

Building all-weather rural roads that connect villages to nearby urban centres offers the third and final approach towards using transportation as a means to promote urbanization. Road connectivity allows village residents to exploit urban markets more fully, as buyers as well as sellers. Increased exposure to city life may eventually lead some village residents to begin locating their businesses and commercial activities in the cities and migrate to them.

Clean Piped Water, Clean Public Spaces and Clean Air

With the share of urban population predicted to increase significantly over the next decade, India needs to address three key problems associated with urban life. First, after more than seventy years of Independence, most Indian cities still lack a continuous supply of piped water. Second, poor management of waste, sewage and drainage mean that the threat of spread of communicable diseases remains omnipresent, becoming especially acute in the rainy season. Finally, with increased industrialization and growth in the use of fossil fuels that accompanies rising incomes, the air in most cities is polluted to dangerous levels, posing a serious threat to health, especially that of children.

There are four problems associated with piped water. First, not all households receive piped water. According to the Census 2011, only 71 per cent of urban households had their drinking water supply source located within the premises. Going by the findings of a 2012 NSO survey, a significant minority of these households had piped water coming to their yards or plots, but not the dwelling.[51]

Second, most households with water pipes in their homes do not receive a continuous supply of water. In most cases, local utilities

51 NSO 2014, Table 3.1, p. 17.

supply water for a few hours per day and on some days they may not supply it at all. As a result, households that can afford it keep water tanks that they fill during the hours that water is supplied. This means that even if local utilities supply properly treated water, it may get contaminated while stored in the tank.

Third, often water pressure in taps is low. This leads households to instal booster pumps, which is a socially wasteful use of resources, both due to unnecessary investment in equipment and energy consumption. Additionally, when a few residents instal booster pumps, water pressure for the remaining residents drops further, forcing them to instal booster pumps as well.

Finally, most urban households in India are leery of drinking water straight from the tap, due to the fear of its contaminated nature. The result is that households that can afford it get costly filtering and treatment devices installed in their kitchens to ensure that the water they drink and use in cooking is safe. Many choose to drink exclusively bottled water. Those unable to afford either filtering equipment or bottled water end up drinking tap water directly and risk becoming sick more frequently, for which they must later pay in terms of costs of medical treatment and lost workdays.

According to newspaper reports, the government has taken the bold decision to bring piped water to all households in rural and urban areas by the year 2024. This is an ambitious goal, but one that the present government is capable of achieving. What will also be necessary, however, is improving water governance to ensure that households receive uninterrupted water supply seven days a week. Supply interruptions result in the contamination of even well-treated water supply for two reasons. One, when water supply is interrupted, contaminants get into the water supply due to low pressure, backflows and physical faults in pipeline. And two, when water supply is intermittent, households resort to storage of water in tanks for use during hours when water is not supplied. Stored water in tanks is prone to contamination. Governance of water supply remains one of the most difficult problems and few developing countries have solved it satisfactorily in the early stages of development. As such, India is likely to continue to face major challenges in this field.

The level of cleanliness in public spaces in Indian cities remains poor along nearly all dimensions. The Swachh Bharat Mission (SBM), or Clean India Mission, has made a major push towards improving cleanliness in public spaces, with some success. But it remains work in progress. Achieving greater cleanliness would require work in three areas: sewage, drainage and waste management. According to the 2011 Census, 19.6 per cent of urban households lacked toilets within their premises and had to use public facilities. This proportion has perhaps fallen considerably in the wake of the SBM but continued progress in this area would still be required. Many public toilets lack water supply while many are not connected to the city's sewage system.

A related problem is that of the drainage systems in Indian cities. Only 44.5 per cent of the households are connected to closed drainage and another 37.3 per cent to open drainage. This still leaves 18.2 per cent of the households without any connection to drainage. Following the launch of the SBM, these indicators have likely improved but there can be little doubt that much progress remains to be made to make Indian cities healthy places to live.

Even when drainage and sewage systems exist in India, they are poorly maintained. With rising consumption levels, solid waste is rising and its poor management has the seriously harmful side-effect of clogging drainage systems. Solid waste littered in public spaces gets into drains during rains and blocks them. The result is that raw sewage often overflows into the open, creating unsanitary conditions on roads and pathways and around residential areas. With clogged drains, even minor rains result in the creation of standing bodies of water everywhere, bringing cities to a standstill. Cities such as Hyderabad and Mumbai have been well known for these problems.

Per capita solid waste in India remains low even in comparison to many developing countries. But this is changing rapidly, with rising incomes and consumption levels, and waste management is failing to keep pace. Often, households and businesses dump garbage at nearby dumpsites from which collection is infrequent. There has been at best limited efforts to instil civic sense in people, with the result that individuals often feel free to dispose small pieces of trash outside their homes, shops and businesses. As a result, piles of trash, which are an eyesore, are commonplace in Indian cities.

Solid waste management is almost entirely a local issue with municipalities and municipal corporations bearing the primary responsibility for it. Arguably, this is the most important function with which these bodies are entrusted. Unfortunately, few municipalities have enough finances, managerial capacity and technical knowhow to discharge the function effectively. Within the context of overall management of services in local jurisdictions, waste management also gets lower priority than water and sanitation.

The third cleanliness-related challenge in Indian cities is air pollution. Major Indian cities have come to be counted among the most polluted in the world. Air pollution is measured by the average annual concentration of particulate matter in micrograms per cubic metre of air. Particles whose concentration is commonly measured to gauge pollution are those smaller than 2.5 micrometres and those between 2.5 and 10 micrometres, which are referred to as PM 2.5 and PM 10, respectively. Particulates can penetrate deep into the lungs and bloodstream and cause permanent DNA mutations, heart attacks and respiratory diseases. Studies show that there is no safe level of particulates and even starting from low levels, increases in them can raise the risk of lung cancer by a proportionately large amount. The smaller PM 2.5 particulates are particularly deadly.

According to the latest available data compiled by WHO and released in 2018, going by the annual mean PM 2.5 concentrations, nine out of the ten most polluted cities in the world are in India. Arranged from the most to the least polluted, these cities are Kanpur, Faridabad, Gaya, Varanasi, Patna, Delhi, Lucknow, Agra and Gurgaon.

Another four cities appear among cities ranked between 11 and 20. According to declining pollution levels, they are: Muzaffarpur, Jaipur, Patiala and Jodhpur.

The four biggest sources of air pollution in India are industries, transportation, construction and stubble burning. Each of these factors is directly related to economic growth. Industrialization is an essential element in rapid growth. Rising incomes lead to increased demand for both personal and business transportation. Enhanced construction activity is both the source and consequence of growth. Finally, with growth, cities expand their boundaries and the distance between them and the countryside, where farming takes place, declines. In countries with rising population and incomes, the need for agricultural production rises as well. Both factors work towards making cities more vulnerable to pollutants released by stubble burning, which is the lowest-cost means to preparing the farmland for the next crop.

Technical solutions to the problems of clean water, clean public spaces and clean air have been widely discussed and we need not go into them in detail here. The real challenge is efficient management and governance. The challenge is multiplied by the fact that within the Indian federal system, city administration is principally under the jurisdiction of the state and, to a lesser degree, municipal governments. The central government can at best play the role of a catalyst for change. For instance, the central government has decided to bring piped water to every household in the next five years. While it may successfully lay down the pipelines connecting water sources to individual households, maintenance of water reservoirs, pipelines, continuous flow of water and water quality will remain the responsibilities of state and possibly municipal governments.[52]

52 For further details on what needs to be done at state and municipal levels, see Panagariya, Chakraborty and Rao, 2014, Chapter 7.

Slums: Rehabilitation and Redevelopment

Urban slums have been a feature of all major cities during the early phase of urbanization. A quick search on the Internet yields photographs and descriptions of 19th-century slums in London, Paris and New York that would make many modern-day slums in the developing countries look like palaces by comparison. Indian cities are no exception. A sizeable proportion of most of the major Indian cities lives in slums.

The Census 2011 divides slums into three categories called notified, registered and identified. Slums in the first category are areas that state, union territory or local governments have notified as slums. Those in the second category are areas that these same entities have recognized but not notified as slums. The identified slums are compact areas 'of at least 300 population or about 60–70 households of poorly built congested tenements, in unhygienic environment usually with inadequate infrastructure and lacking in proper sanitary and drinking water facilities.'[53] The Census data we report below include slums in all three categories.

Often slums begin to form in a city with migrant workers hired to work on industrial or construction projects locating themselves in temporary dwellings on nearby empty land, often owned by the government. Once a few workers have located themselves in these temporary settlements, their relatives and friends looking for employment in the city join. Over time, small settlements grow into slums. In a democratic country, a sufficiently long stay in the dwellings leads to the conferment of voting rights that impart considerable political clout to slum dwellers. Of course, slums need not always acquire permanence. If the land on which they are located becomes valuable, its owner, usually a government entity, decides to reclaim it.

53 See Chandramouli, undated

In such situations, slum residents must relocate, a process that can be complicated and painful for both the government and the residents.

As per the Census 2011, 63 per cent of 4,041 statutory towns have one or more slums.[54] One-fifth of these slums are in Maharashtra alone. India-wide, 13.8 million households representing 17.4 per cent of all urban households and consisting of sixty-four million people live in slums. Among the original fifteen largest states, Andhra Pradesh and Madhya Pradesh are the most intensive and Gujarat and Kerala the least intensive in slums. Mumbai has a gigantic 41.3 per cent of its households living in slums (Table 7.1).

Table 7.1: Proportion of Urban Households in Major Cities and States

City, State or Country	Per Cent of Urban Households in Slums
INDIA	17.4
States with Highest Proportions of Urban Households in Slums	
Andhra Pradesh	35.7
Chhattisgarh	31.9
Madhya Pradesh	28.3
Orissa	23.1
West Bengal	21.9
States with Lowest Proportion of Urban Households in Slums	
Gujarat	6.7
Jharkhand	5.3
Assam	4.8

54 Statutory towns are places with municipalities, municipal corporations, cantonment boards or notified town area committees.

City, State or Country	Per Cent of Urban Households in Slums
Kerala	1.5
Five Largest Metros by Population	
Greater Mumbai (Municipal Corp.)	41.3
Kolkata (Municipal Corp.)	29.6
Chennai (Municipal Corp.)	28.5
Delhi (Municipal Corp)	14.6
Bangalore (Municipal Corp.)	8.5
Million-plus Cities with Highest Proportion of Urban Households in Slums	
1. Greater Visakhapatnam (Municipal Corp.)	44.1
2. Jabalpur (Cantonment Board)	43.3
3. Greater Mumbai (Municipal Corp.)	41.3
4. Vijayawada (Municipal Corp.)	40.6
5. Meerut (Municipal Corp.)	40
6. Raipur (Municipal Corp.)	39
7. Nagpur (Municipal Corp.)	34.3
8. Greater Hyderabad (Municipal Corp.)	31.9
9. Kota (Municipal Corp.)	31.8
10. Agra (Municipal Corp.)	29.8

Source: Author's construction from slides 15, 17 and 18 in Chandramouli, 2013

Going by the Census 2011 data, differences between the averages of slum and non-slum urban populations in terms of living conditions do not appear large. In Table 7.2, we show the distribution of slum households and all urban households across types of census houses, by the number of rooms in the house and ownership. The differences between the two populations do not appear alarmingly large. The most glaring difference is that almost 45 per cent of slum households live in dwellings of one room compared with 32 per cent for urban population as a whole.

Table 7.2: Percentage of Distribution of Households in Slums and Urban Population by House Type and Ownership, 2011

House Type and Ownership Status	**Urban**	**Slum**
Percentage of Households by Type of Census House		
Permanent	84.3	77.7
Semi-permanent	11.6	16
Temporary	3.2	5.3
Any other	0.9	1
Percentage of Households by Number of Rooms		
No exclusive room	3.1	4.4
One room	32.1	44.8
Two room	30.6	29.5
Three room	18.4	12.3
Four room	9.3	5.4
Five rooms and above	6.5	3.5
Percentage of Households by Ownership Status		
Owned	69.2	70.2
Rented	27.5	26.3
Others	3.3	3.5

Source: Author's construction from slides 22, 25 and 28 in Chandramouli, 2013

Next, consider the distribution of slum and all urban households according to basic amenities such as the sources of drinking water and lighting availability and type of drainage and toilet facilities. I have showed the main indicators as per the Census 2011 in Table 7.3. With respect to drinking water, the main difference is that proportionately far fewer slum households have a water tap on premises. The access to electricity for lighting is remarkably similar. The availability of drainage is also similar, with the difference that slums have greater exposure to open drains. Even the access to banking is not alarmingly different. The key area of significant difference with serious health implications is the access to proper toilets. Here, slum dwellers lag by a good 15 percentage points.

Table 7.3: Percentage of Households in Slums and Urban Population as a Whole with Access to Basic Amenities, 2011

Amenity	**Urban**	**Slum**
Source of drinking water		
1. Tap	70.6	74
From treated source	62	65.3
From untreated source	8.6	8.7
2. Well	6.2	3
3. Hand pump	11.9	12.7
4. Tube well / Borehole	8.9	7.6
5. Other sources	2.5	2.8
Location of Drinking Water Source		
1. Within premises	71.2	56.7
2. Outside premises	28.8	43.3
Source of Lighting		
1. Electricity	92.7	90.5

Amenity	Urban	Slum
2. Kerosene	6.5	8.2
3. Solar	0.2	0.3
4. Other oil	0.1	0.2
5. Any other	0.2	0.2
6. No lighting	0.3	0.5
Drainage connectivity		
1. Closed drainage	44.5	36.9
2. Open drainage	37.3	44.3
3. No drainage	18.2	18.8
Type of Latrine Facility—India		
1. Latrine within the premises	81.4	66
(a) Water closet	72.6	57.7
(b) Pit latrine	7.1	6.2
(c) Other latrine	1.7	2.2
2. No latrine within premises	18.6	34
(a) Public latrine	6	15.1
(b) Open	12.6	18.9
Availing Banking Services		
1. Availing	67.8	53.2
2. Not availing	32.2	46.8

Source: Author's construction from slides 29, 31, 33, 36, 37 and 40 in Chandramouli, 2013

Finally, let me turn to the distribution of households in slums and the general urban population across some basic assets. Table 7.4 provides the relevant data from Census 2011. The pattern previously observed carries over to these assets. Slum dwellers lag behind their non-slum counterparts, but not dramatically so. Every tenth slum household (as opposed to every fifth urban household) has a computer. Some even own a car, jeep or van. Every fifth slum household has a scooter, motorcycle or moped.

Table 7.4: Percentage of Households in Slums and Urban Population as a Whole Owning Various Assets, 2011

Asset	Urban	Slum
1. Radio/Transistor	25.3	18.7
2. Television	76.7	69.6
3. Computer	18.7	10.4
– With Internet	8.3	3.3
– Without Internet	10.4	7.1
4. Telephone	82	72.7
– Landline only	5.9	4.4
– Mobile only	64.3	63.5
– Both	11.7	4.8
5. Bicycle	41.9	40.2
6. Scooter/Motorcycle/Moped	35.2	22
7. Car/Jeep/Van	9.7	3.6
8. None of the specified assets	7	10.7

Source: Author's construction from slides 42 and 44 in Chandramouli, 2013

This bright picture of slums must be tempered by the recognition of potentially large quality differences. A permanent house need not mean a well-built house. Counting rooms may be misleading because they may differ in size and the quality of walls and floor. Electricity brought into the house through an exposed wire is not the same as that brought through proper wiring and available to run various appliances, including air conditioners. A television may be small and black-and-white, and bought used for as little as ₹300 or may be a large modern one selling for over ₹30,000. The same goes for laptops, computers and motorcycles and cars.

Even more important, slums are characterized by generally poor availability of most public services. Streets are poorly lit, road infrastructure is not well built and maintained, and connectivity to sewage is often missing. Streets and alleys are narrow and dingy. When combined with poor access to toilet facilities and infrequent collection of solid waste, these features make the environment in slums unhygienic.

The policy question that nearly all of the state governments must confront is what they can do to improve the lot of slum dwellers and the city life at large. Before considering the policy options, it is perhaps useful to explain the complexity of the problem and the limits of what policy can and cannot do. Three points in particular are worthy of mention.

First, it is unrealistic to think that city, state and central governments can end the slums anytime soon. As of 2011, sixty-four million people constituting 17.4 per cent of the country's urban population lived in slums. Moreover, the slum population is concentrated in certain cities so that the proportions in many cities are much higher. The top ten million-plus cities have 30 per cent or more of the households living in slums. Moving nearly one-third of the households to alternative housing within a short period is not a minor task in a country where local governments are often dysfunctional.

Second, slums are not merely places of residence but also centres of economic activity. This is particularly true of larger slums in which households sell the goods and services they produce to each other as well as to outsiders, including customers abroad. In these cases, moving slum dwellers to alternate locations may involve the loss of their livelihood, further complicating such movement.

Finally, if the Indian economy grows at the rate of 7 per cent per year or higher over the next two to three decades, as is highly likely, there is bound to be massive rural–urban migration. Moreover, such migration will be concentrated in the larger cities including some new ones that will form in the forthcoming decades. As long as migrants are poor and transportation costly, preventing the formation of new slums near the workplace is going to be a losing battle.

This is not unlike the immigration problem in the United States. Conferment of citizenship on illegal migrants is often viewed as a solution to the problem of illegal migrants. But before the system is able to make a decision and process the existing illegal migrants, more of them arrive from a border that remains porous despite tougher enforcement.

Given these facts, governments at various levels need to take a long-term approach to the eventual elimination of slums. The objective should be to reduce the incidence of slums on the margins through their replacement by proper housing and steps to minimize the formation of new slums. The policy needs to be multi-pronged and adaptable to the specific circumstances of each slum. With these observations as the context, in the following paragraphs, I have briefly summarized various elements of the policy.

First, the measures discussed earlier to relieve land shortages must form an integral part of the overall policy package. Land shortages created by such measures as the ULCRA of 1976, complex laws governing the conversion of land from one usage to another and low FSI on the one hand and building material shortages created by the Licence Permit Raj in such critical industries as cement and steel on the other have created a shortage of urban housing and encouraged the proliferation of illegal slums. Rental laws and rent controls, which afflicted almost all major cities until recently and remain unduly tilted in favour of tenants despite reforms during the last decade, have worked in the same direction. State governments must take all steps necessary to relieve land shortages and pave the way for reasonably priced housing supply to emerge.

Second, a well-functioning transportation system, including a rapid transit service, also forms an important part of the policy to discourage the formation and growth of slums as well as to phase out slums through rehabilitation. As their incomes rise, slum dwellers themselves would want to move out to better neighbourhoods where they can rear their children in healthier surroundings. But this is only possible if they can find affordable housing in locations from where they can commute to work. A well-functioning transportation system can speed up such transition. The government's proactive efforts to rehabilitate slum dwellers in alternative locations have a greater chance of success as well if the city has a good transportation system.

Third, it is essential that the ability of local governments to deliver basic public services such as water, sewage, electricity, solid waste removal, road connectivity and street lights is greatly enhanced. If these services cannot be adequately supplied, any attempts at rehabilitation either through redevelopment of slums for in-situ housing or distant locations cannot succeed. Any alternative housing must have multiple floors and without adequate provision of water, sewage and electricity, such housing cannot be made to function satisfactorily. If water pressure is low, residents must instal pumps, which is costly. If electricity is not supplied with regularity, lifts will not function and residents on the upper floors will be subject to undue hardships. And, of course, proper sewage is an essential key to improving the quality of life of the slum dwellers. Additionally, the concerned government departments also have to be able to build the basic infrastructure consisting of roads and streetlights for residential developments.

Finally, a proactive policy of rehabilitation from and redevelopment of slums is required. When a slum is located on land that cannot be used for housing for reasons of safety or because it must be used for another public project, rehabilitation of slum dwellers is the only option. For instance, when the Gujarat government decided to undertake the Sabarmati Riverfront Development Project, it had no choice but to move slum dwellers along the riverbanks and rehabilitate them in alternative locations. Similar issues may also arise on safety grounds when the slum is located too close to a road or railway line. Sometimes, even when slum land can be used for housing, some residents and the government may find rehabilitation more attractive.

The overwhelming experience, however, has been that as long as slum land is available for housing, rehabilitation in situ works better. Dwellers do not want to move away from their workplaces and they predominantly work near the slums in which they live. As a result, the efforts during the last two decades have focused on how best to redevelop slum housing. The dominant model in the largest slum in India, Dharavi, has been to build taller buildings, which allows some land to be reclaimed while allowing the builder to recover costs as well through the sale of some units in the open market. The effort began in the mid-1990s but success so far has been at best partial because of the inability of the system to make effective provision of basic amenities such as water supply, drainage and sanitation. There have also been issues with the cost of running lifts in buildings with several floors.

Slum redevelopment will remain a work in progress for some time to come. One thing the governments may try is to focus first on smaller slums where the scale and complexity are less challenging than in a gigantic slum like Dharavi. Additionally, a greater focus on relieving land shortage, raising the floor space index in general, building transportation infrastructure including rapid transit systems and improving the ability of the local governments to effectively deliver water, electricity and sanitation may go some distance toward offering slum dwellers alternative options.

Concluding Remarks

The growth of industry and services on the one hand and urbanization on the other are intimately linked. Urban centres are often homes to growth in industrial and service enterprises. At the same time, growth in industry and services promotes urbanization. In part, this happens through migration of rural workers to industry and services located in urban centres. But it also happens through conversion of previously rural areas into urban, when industrial activity begins to concentrate in rural areas, as has been the case with Shenzhen in China, which consisted of fishing villages in the late 1970s but has become one of the most vibrant urban centres in the world today.

Given this crucial importance of urbanization in the transition of an economy from an agrarian and rural structure to a modern industrial one, I have discussed policies conducive to healthy growth of urban centres in this chapter. I have identified four intimately linked components of urban development: availability of land; provision of water supply, sanitation and solid waste management; transportation; and rehabilitation and redevelopment of slums. In order for urbanization to proceed smoothly and for urban residents to have healthy lives, economic policy and reforms must be aimed at progress in each of these four areas. Because of interconnections among these components, progress in one area can make progress in another easier. By the same token, bottlenecks in one area can create bottlenecks in another.

States can work on many fronts to alleviate land shortages. These include the repeal of the Urban Land Ceilings Act in both letter and spirit; raising the FSI; provision of legal titles to property; rental laws that balance the rights of the tenants and landlords; and reform of laws governing the conversion of land and property from one use to another. Of particular importance for the local and state administration is to understand the importance of a significantly higher floor space index than currently, administered transparently on a uniform basis within a given region rather than its ad hoc 'sale' to builders selectively. Equally important is to allow rapid conversion of land and property from one use to another. Efficient use of space requires that warehouses and apartment buildings can be converted into office buildings, shops and parking lots as the demand shifts. Likewise, transparent laws must exist for the conversion of agricultural land on the periphery of a city into living and office space.

Transportation infrastructure complements the measures necessary to alleviate land shortages in an essential way. Conversely, the transportation network can expand more rapidly as land shortages are alleviated. A well-functioning rapid transit system means that workers can reside outside the city and avail of cheaper rents and a cleaner environment. For this reason, as cities grow and the demand for offices in the city centre grows, the need for a rapid transit system grows. We have described two successful experiments in this area from which other cities can learn: the rail-based Delhi Metro and the Bus Rapid Transit System in Ahmedabad.

As many as sixty-four million individuals, constituting 17.4 per cent of the urban population, live in slums in India, as per the 2011 Census. Growth of slums in the early stages of development has been a feature of virtually all major cities in the world including New York, London and Paris. A comparison of various assets and amenities between slum dwellers and the rest of the urban population also suggests that the former have access to better lives overall than the average rural resident in India. Surveys also show that few slum dwellers want to return to their places of origin.

Nevertheless, slums remain highly deficient in many respects. Access to sewage is poor, leading slum dwellers to resort to open defecation. Access to electricity exists but often through exposed wiring. Public services such as roads and streetlights outside living spaces are poorly supplied as well. All these factors point to the need for rehabilitation and redevelopment of slums. In the chapter, I have made several suggestions based on the experience till date.

There also remain complex issues relating to water supply, sanitation, drainage, solid waste disposal, and air pollution. Indian cities are very far behind in each of these areas. Availability of 24x7 piped-water supply remains a rarity; sanitation and drainage are poor, with mild rains leading to the flooding of roads and streets; and solid waste disposal is in its infancy. There are important governance issues surrounding each of these services. These problems are often local while all the decision-making authority rests at the level of the state. Without the states cooperating with local bodies and at least partially devolving financial and administrative powers to them, arriving at satisfactory solutions will remain a challenge.

In the ultimate analysis, industrialization and urbanization cannot proceed smoothly without well-functioning financial markets. Medium and large firms, which are critical to rapid manufacturing growth, must necessarily operate in the formal sector and depend on a vibrant financial sector for investment resources. Likewise, as the urban population prospers, its need for finance for purchases of house, automobile and other durable goods rises. Government agencies and local urban bodies also depend on capital markets for financial resources. While India has achieved considerable progress in building its financial sector since the launch of the reforms in 1991, a lot more remains to be done. Accordingly, the next two chapters focus on this important sector.

8

INVESTING PRODUCTIVELY: THE SECURITIES MARKET

CAPITAL IS USUALLY SCARCER in developing countries compared to developed ones. As such, the opportunity cost of its misallocation is higher in the former than in the latter. For this reason alone, it may be argued that financial markets are at least as important in developing as developed countries. Yet, they tend to be neglected in the former, especially in the early stages of development.

Reinforcing the scarcity factor is the large variation in the rates of return on investments in different enterprises within the same narrowly defined sectors in these countries. Units with very high and very low returns coexist within a sector. Therefore, governments cannot promote high-return investments without simultaneously promoting low-return ones when they protect or subsidize entire sectors.

What is required, instead, is assignment of priority at the level of the enterprise: within each sector, support must be provided to enterprises and projects with high returns. But this is possible on an economy-wide basis only if financial markets, which can separate projects and enterprises with high return from those with low return, are well developed. In competitive financial markets, lenders can only survive by lending on high-return, low-risk projects. Therefore, they have a vested interest in developing expertise in evaluating projects and selecting those yielding high returns. Governments cannot perform this task.

The Financial System: An Overview

The subject of financial markets is extremely wide, technical and specialized. Therefore, I will not spell out detailed reforms in all areas of financial markets. Instead, I have picked and chosen some key areas while only flagging others. To help the reader understand this technical subject in as simple terms as possible, I have devoted the first half of this chapter to an overview of the financial system. In the second half, I have discussed capital markets. I take up the banking sector, the backbone of the financial system, in the next chapter.

The financial system consists of a set of markets, organizations and individuals that engage in borrowing or lending funds via different instruments including bank credit, stocks, bonds, commercial paper and instruments derived from them. It also includes regulatory institutions that define and implement the rules governing the transactions. The basic function of the financial system is to channel the surplus funds of one set of units in the economy to another set of units facing a deficit of funds. Actors in the former category are called savers or lenders and those in the latter category are spenders or borrowers.

Figure 8.1 provides a schematic chart to describe the financial system. Because the chart has been kept deliberately simple, it does not contain all the details. But it provides a useful reference point to introduce the main components of the financial system. In principle, lenders can include households whose current income exceeds their current expenditure; businesses that may generate more profits than they invest in their own enterprises; government entities, which spend less than their revenues; and foreign entities having funds they wish to lend to entities in the financial system under consideration. Symmetrically, borrowers include households whose current income falls short of expenditures; businesses that want to invest or spend more than they earn in profits; government entities that runs a fiscal deficit; and foreign entities that want to borrow from the given financial system. Several aspects of the financial system deserve elaboration.

Figure 8.1: A Schematic Representation of the Financial System

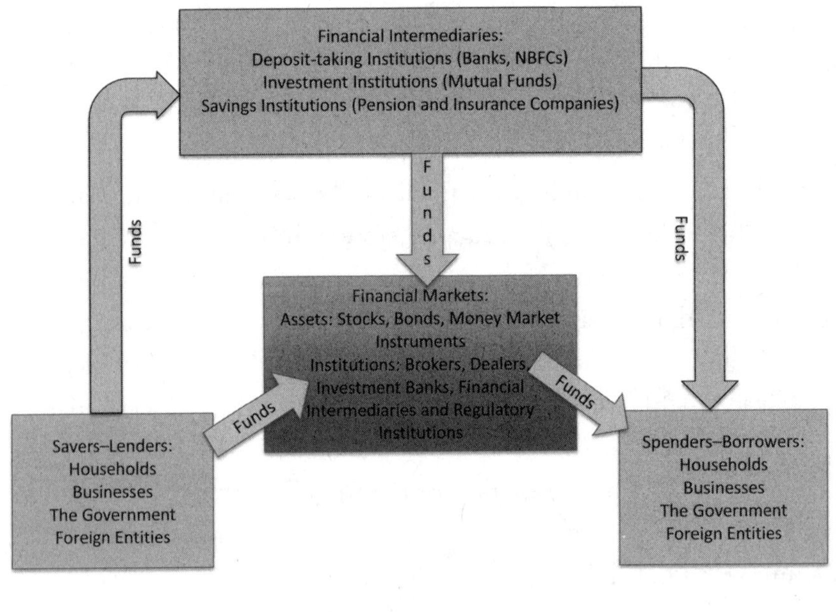

Source: Author's construction

Direct and Indirect Channels of Transmission of Funds from Savers to Borrowers

Savers have two broad avenues to channel their excess funds to borrowers: an indirect channel and a direct one. The indirect channel requires financial intermediation by a set of institutions, which take the funds from savers and channel them to borrowers either as loans or as investments in securities issued by the latter. These institutions include deposit-taking institutions such as commercial banks and non-bank finance companies (NBFCs), investment institutions such as mutual funds and savings institutions such as pension and insurance funds. When savers opt for the direct channel, they invest directly in the securities issued by borrowers.

Debt and Equity Instruments

Instruments that borrowers issue and in which savers or financial institutions invest can be classified into two categories: debt and equity. The most common debt instruments are bonds and mortgages. The borrower issues a bond at a certain price, which is also its face value. The bond pays an annual return as percentage of the face value and has a maturity date. At maturity, the bond is redeemed at face value. The holder of the bond has no claim on the assets of the issuer of the bond. Therefore, the annual return on the bond reflects the prevailing interest rate and the risk of default associated with the issuer of the bond. The greater the risk that the issuer might default at or before maturity, the higher the return she must offer to persuade the purchaser of the bond to invest in it.

Bonds fall in two broad categories, those publicly traded and those sold as private placements. The former are bought and sold in the financial markets while the latter are not. In India, so far, the market for publicly traded bonds issued by corporations has been thin. The bulk of bonds issued by corporations have been issued as private placements. When interest rates rise, new public issues of bonds must offer commensurately higher rates of return. This means that the prices of existing traded bonds, which were issued when interest rates were lower, would fall to ensure that the implicit return on those bonds matches the new, higher interest rate. Bonds with maturity periods of one year or less are called short-term bonds and those with maturity periods of ten years or more are called long-term bonds. Bonds with maturity periods of more than one year and less than ten years are intermediate-term bonds.

In India, the central and state governments are the issuers of the vast majority of publicly traded bonds. The governments issue these bonds to finance their fiscal deficits. Bonds are also issued by a host of other public sector entities, including all-India financial institutions such as the National Bank for Agricultural and Rural Development (NABARD) and the Small Industries Development Bank of India (SIDBI) as well as public sector enterprises such as the Oil and Natural Gas Corporation (ONGC) and Steel Authority of India Limited (SAIL). In the private sector, NBFCs account for a significant proportion of bonds.

The second broad form of instrument through which savers can transmit their funds to borrowers directly is equity, commonly referred to as a share or stock. A stock effectively gives its buyer a share in the ownership of the borrower's enterprise. Once again, stocks fall into two broad categories: private equity and public issues. The latter can be bought and sold on the market. If the enterprise that issued the stock performs well in terms of profitability or its future promise, the price of its stock rises. Unlike bonds, stocks do not promise an annual return but the enterprise issuing it may occasionally choose to distribute a part of its profit to its stockholders in the form of dividend. Stocks do not have a maturity date and therefore can be bought and sold indefinitely. Only if a company goes bankrupt does its stock get withdrawn from the market with the stockholders receiving their share as per the terms of bankruptcy.

Primary and Secondary Markets

Markets in securities—stocks and bonds—can be divided into primary and secondary. In the primary markets, borrowers issue and sell new securities. This generally requires the services of investment banks. Once securities have been issued publicly, they become tradable in secondary markets. Most of the secondary trades happen in stock exchanges and nowadays can be carried out through the Internet. An alternative to stock exchanges is over-the-counter market, which represents a dealer network. Stocks and derivatives not listed on any stock exchange may trade on these over-the-counter markets. There is generally less transparency in these markets.

Financial Institutions

Financial institutions are many and varied and do not always lend themselves to an all-inclusive classification. The high frequency of innovation in financial markets makes such classification yet more difficult. At the risk of oversimplification, these institutions may be divided into brokers, dealers, stock markets, investment banks and financial intermediaries. The first four of these institutions help connect savers directly to borrowers with securities serving as the conduit while the last ones do so indirectly by collecting the funds from savers by offering them a specified return and lending those funds to borrowers as credit or through purchases of securities.

Brokers only assist their clients in buying and selling securities. They earn their income by charging their clients a fee or commission on the transactions. They do not buy or sell securities for themselves in the hope of making profits through purchases at lower prices and sales at higher prices. Unlike brokers, dealers buy and sell securities for themselves. Rather than rely on commissions, they earn profits by buying the securities cheap and selling them dear.

Stock markets and commodity exchanges offer centralized facilities for purchase and sales of shares in ownership of companies and commodities, respectively. Examples of commodities traded on commodity exchanges include gold, silver, cotton, coffee, corn and oil. India has four permanent stock exchanges and three permanent commodity derivatives exchanges. The stock exchanges are: Bombay Stock Exchange (BSE), National Stock Exchange (NSE), Calcutta

Stock Exchange and Magadh Stock Exchange. Commodity derivatives exchanges include Commodity Exchange, Multi Commodity Exchange of India, and National Commodity and Derivatives Exchange.[55] Founded in 1875, the BSE is Asia's oldest stock exchange. The BSE and NSE together account for more than 95 per cent of shares traded in India.

Investment banks such as J.P. Morgan, Kotak Investment Banking and Credit Suisse provide a variety of investment services. The most notable of these services is handling of all aspects of sales of newly issued bonds and stocks of enterprises. At the initial stage, this involves advice on whether to raise the necessary funds through debt, equity or a combination thereof and preparation of necessary papers to fulfil regulatory requirements. At later stages, the bank advises on pricing of the securities, buys certain proportion of them at a specified price and helps brings other potential buyers of securities on board. Investment banks also conduct research to predict market trends and identify securities that would yield high returns and those that would do poorly in the future. They use this research to advise their clients with respect to purchase and sale of securities in the secondary market. They offer broker services and help manage the portfolios of pension and insurance funds and wealth of individuals and families.

Functions of Financial Markets

Financial markets serve many functions. First and foremost, they channel savings to productive investments. Savers themselves do not know how their funds can be invested to bring high returns. Financial intermediaries such as commercial banks, mutual funds, NBFCs and pension and insurance funds help bridge this important gap. Price movements in securities markets and analyses by investment banks

---

55 https://www.sebi.gov.in/stock-exchanges.html (last accessed on 19 January 2019)

allow savers to directly invest in profitable enterprises. From the viewpoint of enterprises, by presenting credible business plans to intermediaries, they are able to obtain the necessary finance.

Financial markets also help diversify risk. Borrowers are able to transfer risk of business partially to financial intermediaries or savers who offer them funds. Intermediaries who lend funds to many borrowers diversify risk by investing in enterprises with wide range of risk-return combinations. Savers investing directly can similarly diversify risk by investing in diversified portfolios of securities.

Financial markets also offer liquidity to owners of assets. In a well-developed financial market, there are many buyers and sellers. This allows asset holders to sell their assets at short notice and convert them into cash should they need it. In a similar vein, credible borrowers are also able to raise funds from the market by selling stocks or bonds.

Finally, financial markets serve the critical function of coordination and provision of information. In the absence of financial markets, savers and lenders lack information on borrowers. Financial markets help bridge this gap. Partly, this information is conveyed by the performance of securities issued by different enterprises. But financial institutions such as investment banks also collect, analyse and disseminate such information to markets.

Regulation

Regulation and regulatory institutions constitute an integral part of the financial system. There are four key regulatory institutions that actively regulate financial markets in India: the Reserve Bank of India (RBI), the Securities and Exchange Board of India (SEBI), the Insurance Regulatory and Development Authority of India (IRDAI), and the Pension Fund Regulatory and Development Authority (PFRDA). Mention may also be made of the Insolvency and Bankruptcy Board of India (IBBI). Strictly speaking, this is not a financial regulatory institution but bankruptcies of companies with which it deals have important implications for the working of financial institutions. Finally, the Financial Stability and Development Council, a non-statutory body chaired by the finance minister, performs the function of coordinating across different regulatory agencies. The council is also charged with helping strengthen and institutionalize financial stability mechanisms and promoting financial sector development.

The RBI is, first and foremost, the regulator of all deposit-taking institutions and as such has the responsibility to ensure the security of hundreds of millions of customers who hold deposits in banks and other institutions. It also regulates the foreign exchange market and the payments system and manages the debts of central and state governments. Additionally, it serves as the banker of the central and state governments.

SEBI is the regulator of markets for all securities including stocks, bonds and their derivatives. It frames and implements rules for new issues of stocks. It registers and regulates the working of stockbrokers, sub-brokers, share transfer agents, merchant brokers, bankers to stock issues, underwriters, portfolio managers, investment advisers, foreign institutional investors, credit rating agencies and all other entities associated with securities markets. It also registers and regulates the venture capital funds and collective investment schemes including mutual funds. Its mandate further includes regulation of depositories, which serve as custodians of securities. Finally, SEBI conducts inquiries and audits of stock exchanges and regulates takeover of the companies.

SEBI also regulates trade in commodity derivatives. The Forward Markets Commission had performed this function until recently. But beginning in September 2015, it was transferred to the newly created Commodity Derivatives Market Regulation Department within SEBI. SEBI sets the policy on trading, clearing and settlement operations relating to commodity derivatives; approves new commodity-based products; registers and regulates stock exchanges hosting trading in commodity derivatives; and handles investor grievances and complaints relating to commodity derivatives trades.

The IRDAI regulates all aspects of the insurance market in India. It registers and regulates all insurance companies. It also issues licences to insurance agents. It controls and regulates rates and terms and conditions offered by insurance companies to policyholders. It adjudicates disputes between insurance companies and others in the insurance business. Above all, the IRDAI protects the interests of policyholders by ensuring speedy settlement of legitimate claims and preventing fraud and other malpractices.

The PFRDA regulates the National Pension Scheme and pension schemes to which the PFRDA Act applies. It registers and regulates intermediaries for the purpose of collection, management, recordkeeping, and distribution of accumulations. It also approves schemes, terms and conditions, and norms for the management of corpus of pension funds. Finally, the PFRDA settles disputes among intermediaries and between intermediaries and subscribers.

Sources of Commercial Flows in India

Table 8.1 shows different sources of financial flows to the commercial sector for every other year beginning in 2007/08. According to the broad pattern that emerges, approximately half of the fund flows are associated with commercial banks. The bulk of these flows takes the form of credit. For instance, in 2017/18, 43.1 per cent of the total flows took the form of bank credit and 6.5 per cent that of investments in financial instruments by commercial banks. Of the remaining commercial fund flows, approximately 30 per cent come from non-bank domestic sources including private and public placements by non-financial entities in the forms of stocks and bonds, credit by housing finance companies, and investments in instruments issued by entities such as NBFCs and four All-India Financial Institutions, namely, NABARD, NHB, SIDBI, and Exim Bank. Approximately 20 per cent of the flows come from foreign sources, most notably, direct foreign investment.

Table 8.1: Sources of Financial Flows to the Commercial Sector

Source	2007/08	2009/10	2011/12	2013/14	2015/16	2017/18
Commercial Banks (Credit Plus Investments in Securities)	44.1	45.0	55.7	54.0	55.4	49.6
Non-bank Domestic Sources	25.3	34.3	25.3	30.4	27.0	32.1
Foreign Sources	30.6	20.7	19.0	15.6	17.6	18.3
Total Resources (in trillion rupees)	10.09	10.64	12.16	14.13	13.99	18.47

Source: Author's calculations using data from the RBI *Handbook of Statistics on Indian Economy*, Table 68

Table 8.2 provides further details on domestic fund flows to non-bank instruments and entities. It divides them into seven categories and, as in Table 8.1, shows the share of each category in the total fund flows for every other year beginning with 2007/08. The first two of the instruments are public issues and private placements by non-financial entities in private and public sector combined. Funds flowing directly to financial institutions in the private as well as public sector are covered by other categories in the table. A key feature of the flows to non-financial institutions is that private placements are significantly larger than public issues. In spite of all the attention that stock markets receive, public issues as a source of new funds remain relatively small.

Table 8.2: Detailed Breakdown of Shares of Non-Bank Domestic Sources of Commercial Flows in the Total Commercial Flows

Source	2007/08	2009/10	2011/12	2013/14	2015/16	2017/18
Public issues by non-financial entities	5.1	3.0	1.2	1.4	2.7	2.4
Gross private placements by non-financial entities	6.8	13.3	4.6	9.3	8.1	7.9
Net issuance of CPs (commercial paper) subscribed by non-banks	1.1	2.5	0.3	1.0	3.7	-1.4
Net credit by housing finance companies	4.1	2.7	4.4	5.2	8.5	10.8
Total gross accommodation by four RBI-regulated AIFIs*	2.2	3.2	3.9	3.1	3.4	5.1
Large non-deposit-taking NBFCs (net of bank credit)	3.6	5.7	7.5	8.0	-2.0	5.2
LIC investment in corporate debt, infrastructure and Social Sector	2.4	4.0	3.4	2.5	2.6	2.0
Total (as per cent of total commercial flows)	25.3	34.3	25.3	30.4	27.0	32.1

*AIFI stands for All India Financial Institutions. The four AIFI are NABARD, NHB, SIDBI and EXIM Bank

Source: Author's calculations using data from the *RBI Handbook of Statistics on Indian Economy*, Table 68

Resources flowing directly from savers to housing finance companies have emerged as a major item in commercial flows in recent years. From 5 per cent or less, they have increased to 8 to 10 per cent of the total commercial flows. It is likely that the Real Estate Regulation and Development Act, 2016, has accelerated the growth of larger real-estate companies that raise funds directly from the market. Another form of domestic entities raising substantial funds from the market in recent years is non-deposit-taking NBFCs. To some degree, these NBFCs have filled the void created by slower growth in bank credit due to rapid rise in the non-performing assets of commercial banks.

Equity and Debt Markets

As in most other countries, bank credit remains by far the largest single source of commercial funds in India. How banks allocate these resources among borrowers has a major impact on the productivity and growth of the country. At the same time, because banks are deposit-taking institutions, they are the key entities helping individuals and households earn a competitive return with minimal or no risk of default. As such, they play an important role in encouraging savings by individuals and households that do not intend to engage in their own business activity. From the viewpoint of resource allocation as well as resource mobilization, it is important that the banking sector be stable, secure and vibrant. Keeping this in view, I devote the next chapter entirely to issues in banking reforms.

Presently, I focus on the securities market. Banks offer individual savers a secure return. On average, this return is lower than what banks charge their borrowers and the latter themselves earn on their investments. Sometimes, banks may do a poor job of allocating their resources among borrowers in which case their earnings are poor and they pay depositors poor interest rates as well. Additionally, large banks may profit from exercising some degree of monopoly power over both savers and borrowers thereby creating a large spread between deposit rates and lending rates. The existence of a transparent and competitive securities market, which offers individual savers the opportunity to lend directly to investors, can help counter these factors. In principle, securities market allows savers to share in the high returns that investors earn (with concomitant risk of such investments) while subjecting banks to competition for their funds.

Securities serve another important function. Valuations of companies on the stock market and the performance of bonds they issue offer valuable corporation-specific information to banks. Banks can use this information in their evaluation of future loans to these companies. The likely result is a lower risk of default on loans and fewer non-performing assets on the books of the banks. The fear of fall in valuation in the stock and bond markets can also serve as a check on corporations in terms of meeting their payments to the banks. A vibrant securities market thus confers many economic benefits.

After reforms were launched in 1991, they reached the equity sector of securities market rather quickly. As a result, today, India has a thriving equity market. Beginning in mid-2000s, India also recognized the importance of the debt market and undertook a series of reforms. These reforms have yielded splendid results with debt markets quickly outdoing equity markets in terms of new issues. In terms of the total size, equity markets remain significantly larger, however.

Data on new issues show private placements dominating in both equity and debt markets. What is most striking, however, is that private placements in the debt segment have outdone equity placements in public and private placements taken together. Figure 8.2, which depicts public and private placements in equity and debt segments from 2010/11 to 2017/18, makes the point.

Figure 8.2: Public and Private Placements in Equity and Debt Markets, 2010/11 to 2017/18

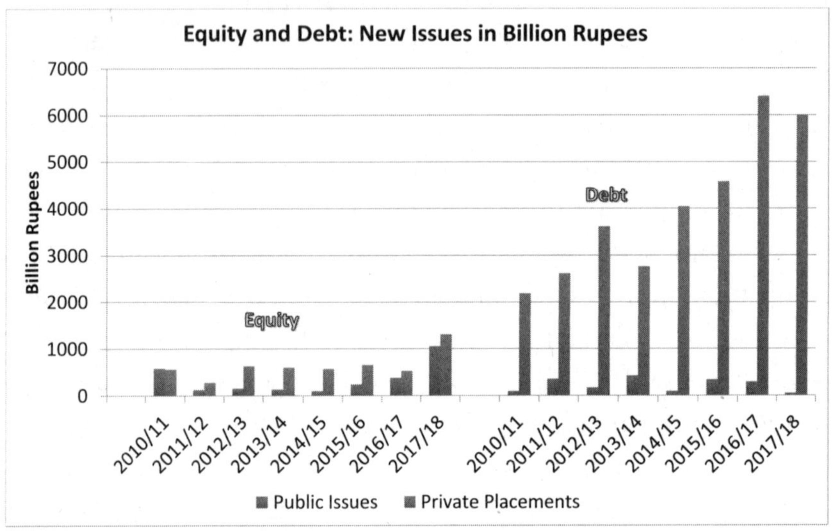

Source: Author's construction based on SEBI data

Given that reforms and development efforts targeting equity markets preceded those aimed at debt markets by more than a decade, in term of overall depth, they are significantly more developed than the latter. This is particularly true of publicly traded equities despite their low levels of new issues. The market capitalization of the Bombay Stock Exchange (BSE) as of 31 March 2018 amounted to 84.8 per cent of the GDP in 2017/18. In absolute value, it was in excess of $2 trillion. Forbes has ranked BSE tenth by market capitalization as of April 2018.[56] Since the daily trade volumes at both BSE and NSE are large, publicly traded equity shares are substantially more liquid than their debt counterparts.

56 https://www.forbes.com/pictures/eddk45iglh/the-worlds-biggest-stock-exchanges/#394c58436d2b (Last accessed on 25 January 2019)

Deepen the Corporate Debt Market

Unlike equity shares, whose life is as long as that of the company issuing it, debt is retired at maturity. In a country like India, the maturity period of nearly all corporate debt instruments is five years or less. As a result, building and deepening corporate debt market takes much longer than equity markets. For this reason and in view of the short history of the efforts to develop corporate debt market in India, it remains small and shallow compared to some other countries, where the market has had a longer history of development.

At the end of June 2018, outstanding corporate debt in India was ₹28.4 trillion. It amounted to 16.6 per cent of the GDP in 2017/18. In comparison, outstanding corporate debt at the end of June 2018 as a proportion of the GDP in 2017 stood at 114.4 per cent in the United Kingdom, 64.7 per cent in Japan, 107.4 per cent in the United States, 57 per cent in China, 59.7 per cent in Malaysia and 60.3 per cent in Chile.[57] India still has some distance to go in terms of the development of corporate debt market.

Indian policymakers recognize this fact as reflected in the appointment of several committees on this subject beginning in the mid-2000s. Of particular importance is the H.R. Khan Committee, which submitted its report in August 2016. This committee made several specific recommendations, which the government has largely implemented. Some of the acceleration in the issuance of debt instruments by corporations to raise funds in 2017/18 and 2018/19

---

57 These percentages have been calculated by taking the data on outstanding corporate debt of financial and non-financial corporations from the Bank of International Settlement and the nominal GDP data from the International Monetary Fund. The former can be found at https://www.bis.org/statistics/secstats.htm and the latter at https://en.wikipedia.org/wiki/List_of_countries_by_GDP_(nominal) (both accessed on 24 January 2019).

can be attributed to the implementation of the Khan Committee recommendations.

There remains scope for further reforms in this area on both the demand and supply sides of the market. A 24 October 2018 speech by SEBI chairman Ajay Tyagi offers some excellent suggestions.[58] Consider, first, the demand side. In comparison to equity instruments, corporate bonds form far more complex instruments. Credit rating of a bond majorly depends on the overall creditworthiness of the issuer. In deciding ratings, ratings agencies consider issuer's assets, debt, income, expenses, financial history and track record of payments on bonds previously issued. Nevertheless, risk-return matrix of a specific bond additionally depends on whether or not it is secured, its liquidity, tax benefits associated with it, and whether some form of sovereign support backs it. Because bonds have a specified life, market conditions during that period can seriously impact their riskiness. This is less of a problem with equity shares, since they have indefinite life, and if held long enough, their value may recover from slump at some future time.

These complexities, combined with the thinness of public issues of corporate bonds, have meant that so far institutional investors have been the near exclusive customers of corporate bonds in India. Shares in outstanding corporate bonds currently amount to 30 per cent for non-financial corporations, 25 per cent for banks and other financial institutions, 20 per cent for mutual funds, 15 per cent for trusts and 7 per cent for foreign portfolio investors. The share of retail investors in the total outstanding corporate bonds is a paltry 3 per cent.

---

58 https://www.sebi.gov.in/media/speeches/oct-2018/chairman-s-speech-at-the-crisil-s-5th-annual-seminar-on-expanding-india-s-corporate-bond-market-bonds-of-growth-assessing-the-supply-demand-matri-x-october-24-2018_40787.html (last accessed on 27 January 2018). In the remainder of this section, I draw heavily on this speech.

Several steps can be taken to enhance the demand for corporate debt. First, strengthening the participation of retail customers in the bond market is likely to remain an uphill task in the short term. But the benefits of investment in these assets can still be brought to them through increased participation of pension, provident and insurance funds. The current investment norms set by regulators on these funds are highly restrictive. Allowing these funds to invest higher proportions of their total investments in corporate bonds would boost demand for corporate debt while also bringing the benefits of higher returns to subscribers of these funds. Currently, these bonds are issued nearly exclusively by entities with AA or higher rating. Therefore, the risk of investment in these bonds is minimal.

Second, the market for long-maturity bonds is currently non-existent in India. Nearly all of the existing corporate bonds have a maturity of five or fewer years. When projects begin to yield full returns in five or fewer years, which is true for the vast majority of corporate projects, this maturity period works fine. But most infrastructure projects take much longer to complete. For these, bonds of longer maturity are required. Unfortunately, potential issuers of infrastructure bonds are unable to rise above BBB ratings on their own.

Given that banks are typically unwilling to offer loans with maturity in excess of five years, the corporate bond market would seem to be a natural source of funds for infrastructure companies. Here too, allowing large pension, provident and insurance funds to invest small proportions of their portfolios could help break the ice. Subscribers to these funds need to be able to earn decent returns to support themselves upon retirement and being relatively large the funds are best positioned to diversify risk. In most countries, these funds are an important source of finance for infrastructure companies.

Taking into account the public good nature of infrastructure, the government can also help boost the ratings of longer-term bonds issued by infrastructure companies through its credit enhancement fund, announced in the 2016/17 Budget. Such a fund can either insure or provide collateral for long-range infrastructure bonds. Given India's generally conservative approach to regulation, only truly creditworthy companies will get access to this fund. As such the risk that the fund will actually be used to repay lenders is minimal.

In this context, it is important to note that the idea of credit enhancement has been widely prevalent in developed countries for five decades. Credit enhancement through third-party guarantees or insurance plays an important role when the underlying sector has strong potential but companies within the sector are unable to obtain high ratings on their issues on their own. The private market in India is not sufficiently developed to provide such insurance or third-party guarantee.

Third, under the current practice, banks get to show their loans at book value on their balance sheets. In contrast, corporate bonds are marked to market. Any loss of creditworthiness of the issuer immediately reflects in the value of the bonds. Other things held constant, this factor makes loans a more attractive instrument of investment than corporate bonds (and equity) for banks. Removal of this asymmetry through periodic assessments of loans by the regulator would help boost the demand for bonds.

Finally, the number of billionaires in dollar terms now exceeds 130 and their number will continue to rise at a fast pace in the decades to come. Likewise, small corporations with surplus funds have been growing in number as the economy grows bigger. Potentially, corporate bonds could be attractive investment instruments for these entities. But inability to borrow against these bonds while loans against investments in equity shares are routinely available places them at a disadvantage. Allowing the high net-worth individual (HNI) and small corporations to borrow against bonds would remove this asymmetry.

While it is demand-side factors that are most constraining, some supply-side measures may also be taken to accelerate the development of bond markets. First, limiting the exposure of banks to large corporations, as envisaged in the RBI exposure framework, would cap the access of corporations to bank credit and nudge them towards the bond market. Second, the announcement in the 2018/19 Budget requiring large corporations to eventually raise 25 per cent of their funds from bond market would exert some supply-side pressure in the market. How precisely will SEBI operationalize this mandate remains to be seen, however. Finally, moving to a system of 'on tap' bond issuance by corporations may encourage them to rely more on bonds than bank credit.

Concluding Remarks

The importance of well-functioning financial markets for growth and development cannot be overemphasized. High- and low-productivity enterprises coexist within the same sector in disproportionately large volumes in developing countries. As a result, any policy initiatives at the level of the sector end up promoting both high- and low-productivity activities in that sector. Well-developed and well-functioning financial markets can overcome this problem by directing finance to high-productivity activities regardless of the sector.

Security markets, especially in the debt sector, remain work in progress in India. Though equity markets have deepened, new issues as a source of funds still remain small. The debt market has had a late start in India. Though it has seen a high growth in recent years, the total corporate debt remains only 16.6 per cent of the GDP. Until new issues of equity and debt take off in a big way, bank credit will remain the most important source of investment funds. Indeed, a well-functioning banking sector, which is the backbone of the financial system of any country, is also critical to the growth of the securities market. Therefore, it is urgent for India to take actions necessary to grow its banking sector and make it competitive, secure and efficient. This is the subject I consider in the next chapter.

9

INVESTING PRODUCTIVELY: THE BANKING SECTOR

THE BANKING SECTOR IS the backbone of the financial sector of an economy. Even in advanced economies with highly developed capital markets, banks remain the most critical component of this sector. In part, banks enjoy this key position because individuals and households are risk-averse and prefer to keep their savings predominantly in instruments that would be subject to minimal or no risk of default while also earning them a reasonable return. Indeed, even governments and corporates often choose to park significant volumes of funds in banks.

In addition to taking deposits, banks serve several other important functions. They play the important role of facilitating transactions between buyers and sellers. Until the recent arrival of digital wallets and similar platforms, banks were the only entities clearing non-cash transactions among households, businesses and governments. Even after the arrival of digital technologies, they remain the key platform for clearing transactions at low cost through transfers from one bank account to another. Banks also intermediate nearly all legitimate foreign currency transactions between residents of two or more countries.

A more challenging function of banks is investing the collected funds into activities that maximize returns on them, taking into account risks associated with the investments. Ultimately, whether or not the banking system of a country makes a significant contribution to growth and prosperity depends on the lending choices it makes. Bank staff must have the ability to distinguish between high- and low-return projects for a given level of risk and between high- and low-risk projects for a given return.

When banks end up investing funds predominantly in projects of dubious quality, which either yield low returns or carry an unduly high risk of default, the banking system undermines growth. Indeed, the persistence of investments in such projects can undermine the banking system itself. When borrowers begin to fail in meeting their payments, either depositors suffer or the government has to bail them out at taxpayers' expense. The central bank must regulate banks in an effective manner to guard against such outcomes. It must ensure that banks refrain from engaging in fraudulent practices while maintaining a healthy risk-return mix on the funds they lend.

In India, banks have generally done a poor job of selecting high-return, low-risk projects. As a result, there have been two major episodes of large accumulations of non-performing assets (NPAs) following the 1991 liberalization of the banking sector. In both episodes, the government had to come to the rescue of the banks and infuse substantial equity in them at the expense of the taxpayer. Currently, NPAs amount to more than 10 per cent of the total loans by the banks. Underlying these large recurrent accumulations of NPAs are serious governance issues that future reforms must address.

Before turning to these reforms, it is necessary to understand the developments that led to the current weaknesses in the banking sector. In turn, this requires tracing the history of banking. To keep the focus on reforms, I relegate a detailed account of the early history to an annexe and concentrate here on developments since the launch of economic reforms in 1991. All we need to note here about the early history is that at the time of Independence, all banks in India were private. But in 1955, with a desire to expand bank branch network rapidly to rural areas and bring formal credit to agriculture, the government decided to nationalize the largest bank at the time, the Imperial Bank, renaming it the State Bank of India (SBI). Later in 1969, political considerations led the government to nationalize all fourteen banks with deposits of ₹500 million or more. A final round of nationalization using the same criterion brought another six banks into the public sector in 1980.

Two key policies that the government pursued during the post-nationalization phase were aggressive bank branch expansion in rural areas and promotion of 'priority sector lending', under which up to 40 per cent of credit was required to be made available to favoured sectors such as agriculture, exports, and small and medium firms. Throughout the period, the government kept a tight control on interest rates and credit allocation across various sectors. It also deployed a high cash reserve ratio and statutory liquidity ratio to keep its borrowing costs low.

Reforms and the First Bout of NPAs: 1991–2002

The government ownership of all major banks with a minuscule role by private banks, aggressive bank branch expansion, tight controls on credit and interest rates, and financial repression came at a high cost.[59] True, the government had some success in promoting what it considered to be social objectives. But efficiency took a heavy toll. As an acknowledgement of the failure of at least one of its policies, in 1990, a year ahead of the launch of the liberalizing reforms, it discontinued its branch expansion policy.

India entered the 1990s with a fragile economy. The banking sector was no exception. The RBI had introduced a 'health code'

---

59 Evidence in this regard is summarized in my book, *India: The Emerging Giant*, 2008, Chapter 11.

system in 1985, which required banks to classify each loan into one of eight categories based on its performance. Classification in one of the bottom four categories meant that the loan was non-performing. Based on this classification, 14.5 per cent of total outstanding advances were classified as non-performing at the end of March 1992.

In April 1992, this classification was replaced by a more demanding one that required banks to classify each loan into one of four categories: standard, sub-standard, doubtful and loss. Loans classified into any of the last three categories were considered non-performing. The classification was based on objective criteria and on the length of time for which the payment of principal and interest was overdue. The criteria introduced in 1992 placed non-performing assets at 23.2 per cent of the total outstanding advances at the end of March 1993.

The criteria defining healthy loans were tightened over time. In 1995, assets with unpaid interest or principal for 180 days were classified as non-performing. By 2004, this threshold was revised to the international norm of ninety days. This year onward, an asset remaining as an NPA up to one year or less had to be classified as sub-standard and an asset remaining an NPA for longer than a year as doubtful. Assets considered substantially uncollectible had to be classified as loss assets. Banks were to make provision to the extent of 10 per cent for sub-standard assets, 20 to 50 per cent for secured portion of doubtful assets and 100 per cent for unsecured doubtful assets and all loss assets.

A key objective of the financial sector reforms during the 1990s was restoration of the health of banks. With liberalization gaining acceptance, the government was able to take several measures that helped restore profitability of banks while also bringing down NPAs. Four such measures are worthy of note.

First, beginning in 1993/94, the government infused funds into banks to recapitalize them. By the end of 1997/98, its capital contribution to nationalized banks had reached ₹200.5 billion. In addition, it provided ₹15.3 billion to two banks to write off losses. Second, the government allowed its stake in public sector banks to be diluted as long as it remained no less than 51 per cent. The dilution allowed the banks to mobilize equity funds from the market. By the end of March 1998, nine public sector banks had raised ₹60.2 billion. Third, the RBI reduced the SLR from the peak rate of 38.5 per cent in February 1992 to 25 per cent by October 1997 and the cash reserve requirement from 15 per cent in October 1992 to 9.5 per cent in November 1997. These relaxations went a long way towards rolling back financial repression and releasing funds for credit expansion. Finally, the government freed up all but a small number of deposit and lending interest rates and did away with credit controls except in priority sector lending. This reform allowed banks to better align interest rates and loan amounts towards profitability.

Alongside these measures, the government also introduced tighter prudential norms with respect to income recognition, asset classification and provisioning, and capital adequacy criteria. Banks were advised not to take interest on NPAs to income account. NPAs were defined using objective criteria and new and higher provisioning norms were specified. Finally, the capital to risk-weighted assets ratio (CRAR) system was introduced for banks in a phased manner. These measures helped turn around the balance sheets of the banks. From -1.1 per cent in 1992/93, the return on assets rose to 0.8 per cent in 1997/98. The number of loss-making public sector banks fell significantly over the period.

For the first time since the nationalization of fourteen banks in 1969, the government also allowed entry to new private banks. It announced the norms of entry in January 1993 and by 1998, ten new private banks had begun operations. The government also liberalized the entry of foreign banks, with twenty-two new foreign banks being set up by 1998. The policy for branch expansion, both domestic and foreign, was liberalized. By the end of March 1998, the share of new private banks in total banking assets had risen to 3.2 per cent and of foreign banks to 8.2 per cent. Competition from new domestic private banks as well as foreign banks helped improve service conditions in public sector banks and old private sector banks.

In the post-reforms era, the government also tried to create avenues for recovery of NPAs. The first step in this direction was the passage of the Recovery of Debts Due to Banks and Financial Institutions Act, 1993. The act provided for the establishment of Debt Recovery Tribunals (DRT) and Debt Recovery Appellate Tribunals (DRAT). In the following years, twenty-nine DRTs and five DRATs were established.

The pace of recovery under the DRT–DRAT process was painfully slow. Therefore, the government set up asset reconstruction companies (ARCs). To provide legal underpinning to ARCs, it enacted the Securitization and Reconstruction of Financial Assets and Enforcement Security Interest (SARFAESI) Act, 2002. The act provided for enforcement of security interest for recovery of dues with the intervention of courts. It also permitted banks and financial institutions to seize the assets of defaulting borrowers or sell their bank accounts to ARCs. A third avenue had previously existed for the recovery of small loans in the form of Lok Adalats organized by civil courts.

Unfortunately, the three avenues still proved inadequate for recoveries. As mentioned, the DRT–DRAT process was extremely slow. SARFAESI gave banks leverage by empowering them to take over the assets of defaulting borrowers, but they had no expertise in either working the acquired assets productively or liquidating them for recovery. Public sector banks also did not want to sell the accounts of defaulting borrowers to ARCs at less than face value for fear of being investigated by vigilance agencies. Some recoveries were made under all three processes but recovery rates in these cases were invariably low.

Recapitalization by the government, provision of dilution of government equity up to 51 per cent and some increase in profitability due to accelerated economic growth helped reduce NPAs from 23.2 per cent at the end of March 1993 to 16 per cent at the end of 1998. Though the government did not undertake any significant recapitalization after 1998, NPAs continued to decline approximately at the rate of 2 percentage points each year with non-performing loans as a proportion of total advances declining to 2.7 per cent by the end of March 2007. Unfortunately, however, even as NPAs and other indicators suggested the emergence of a healthy and competitive banking sector, the seeds of the next NPA crisis were being sown.

Rapid Expansion of Credit: 2003–2013

Economic reforms under Prime Ministers Narasimha Rao (1991–96) and Atal Bihari Vajpayee (1998–2004) launched India into a high-growth trajectory. In 2003/04, the economy grew approximately 8 per cent, with this growth momentum sustained for nearly a decade. Expectations of high returns in a burgeoning economy led entrepreneurs and business houses to line up for bank credit. From the rapid expansion that followed for several years, it would seem that banks successfully accommodated this growth in credit demand.

Figure 9.1: Total Outstanding Advances of Broad Groups of Banks at the End of the Fiscal Year: 2004/05 to 2017/18

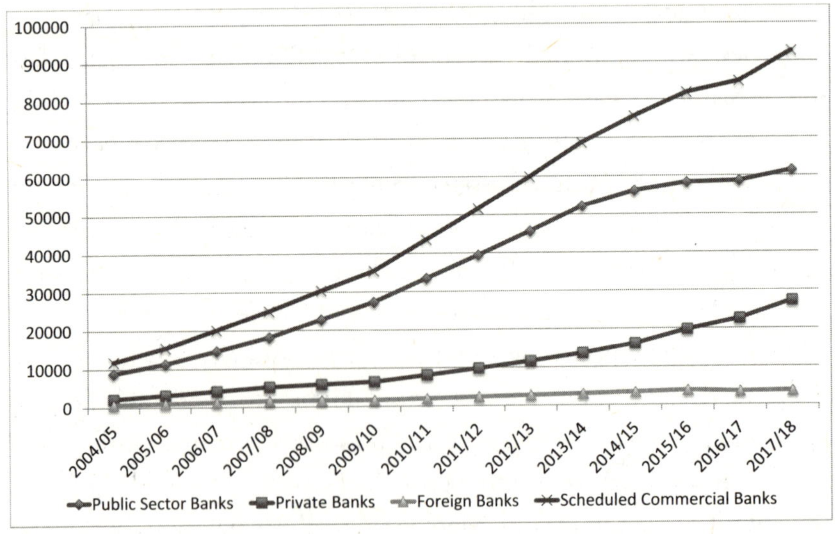

Source: Author's construction based on RBI data at https://dbie.rbi.org.in/DBIE/dbie.rbi?site=publications#!4 (last accessed on 15 March 2019)

Figure 9.1 shows the total outstanding advances of public, private, foreign and all scheduled commercial banks at the end of fiscal years 2004/05 to 2017/18. Total outstanding advances of all scheduled commercial banks (SCBs) rose from ₹11.9 trillion at the end of 2004/05 to ₹68.7 trillion at the end of 2013/14. Indian banks, both public and private, drove this growth in credit. Foreign banks also contributed, but in a limited way. Credit growth slowed down considerably beginning in 2014/15.

Table 9.1: Growth in Credit by Broad Groups of Banks: 2005/06 to 2017/18

Fiscal Year	Public Sector Banks	Private Banks	Foreign Banks	Scheduled Commercial Banks
2005/06	28.0	40.6	28.4	30.5
2006/07	29.2	32.3	29.3	29.8
2007/08	24.2	25.2	27.5	24.6
2008/09	25.5	11.2	4.0	21.1
2009/10	19.7	10.1	-1.4	16.7
2010/11	22.4	26.0	19.1	22.9
2011/12	17.8	20.9	17.7	18.4
2012/13	15.7	18.1	14.6	16.1
2013/14	14.4	17.4	11.4	14.8
2014/15	7.7	18.2	12.4	10.0
2015/16	3.8	22.7	11.9	8.2
2016/17	0.7	14.5	-8.7	3.6
2017/18	4.7	20.6	5.6	9.4

Source: Author's calculations using the RBI data at https://dbie.rbi.org.in/DBIE/dbie.rbi?site=publications#!4 (accessed on 15 March 2019)

Table 9.1 shows annual growth in credit of each broad group of banks. Three observations may be made on the basis of these growth rates. First, overall credit by SCBs grew very rapidly till at least 2011/12 and maintained a healthy pace till 2013/14. But after that year, credit expansion rapidly decelerated, with its growth dropping to just 3.6 per cent in 2016/17.

Second, public and private sector banks behaved similarly until 2013/14 but differently subsequently. Credit expansion by public sector banks from 2014/15 onwards suffered a serious setback while private sector credit expansion maintained its healthy pace. Foreign banks, which are impacted a lot more by what goes on in the global economy, showed a different pattern. They saw a sharp decline in their credit during 2008/09 and 2009/10 due to the global financial crisis and again after interest rates rose in 2016 in the United States.

Finally, overall growth in credit remains heavily tied to growth in credit by public sector banks. This reflects the disproportionately large volume of deposits held by these banks. Because public sector banks are backed by an implicit guarantee by the government, they continue to receive deposits even when they perform poorly.

NPAs Masquerade as Restructured Loans

The progressive weakening of the banking system was accompanied by rapid growth in credit from 2005/06 to 2013/14. It would have seemed that the adoption of international standards in prudential regulation would have protected the banking sector against renewed fragility. It turned out, however, that the government and the RBI failed in implementing international best practice in regulation in one important respect: treatment of restructured loans. The international best practice is to treat restructured loans as sub-standard. For a long time, the RBI chose to treat them as standard. The regime regulating NPAs was thus effectively subverted. Governance problems associated with the ownership of the vast majority of banking assets by public sector banks, most notably undue government interference in the grant of credit by these banks, added to this subversion.

Restructuring of loans involves adjustment to one or more out of payable amount, payment period, amount of instalment and interest rate. The earliest directives on restructuring in India were issued in the 1970s in the context of flood-affected borrowers and rehabilitation of sick enterprises. Later, in 1985, the government issued more detailed guidelines for the identification of sick units and parameters determining their viability for purposes of loan restructuring.

In 1992, when the government introduced the system of classification of loans into standard, sub-standard, doubtful and loss categories, it also adopted the practice of classifying loans restructured after commencement of production by a unit as sub-standard for two years. Upon satisfactory performance by the borrower over these two years, the loans could be reclassified as standard. In 1999, the regulation was weakened with reclassification of restructured loans into the standard category permitted after one year of satisfactory performance. A further weakening took place in 2001 when the RBI issued revised guidelines permitting restructured standard and sub-standard loans to retain their respective classifications, provided they were fully secured.

Until 2001, formal mechanisms for restructuring and subsequent classification of loans were available only on loans extended to enterprises by a single bank. They did not accommodate restructuring of large loans advanced by multiple banks. In 2001, the RBI took steps to fill this gap by putting in place a Corporate Debt Restructuring (CDR) framework for standard and sub-standard accounts. This framework initially applied to loans extended by two or more banks and adding to ₹200 million. It provided for coordinated restructuring of viable standard and sub-standard corporate loans and allowed them to retain their respective classifications. Later, in 2003, the facility was extended to doubtful accounts and in 2005 it was broadened to include all consortium loans worth ₹100 million or more.

In 2005, the RBI also issued guidelines for restructuring of debt for small and medium enterprises (SMEs). Different sets of guidelines were issued for non-corporate and corporate SMEs enjoying banking facilities from a single bank as also for corporate SMEs with outstanding loans up to ₹100 million from a group of banks. Therefore, by 2005, a formal loan restructuring mechanism became available to all enterprises, whether corporate or non-corporate, and whether the loan was extended by one bank or a group of banks.

In 2008, all restructuring guidelines were aligned towards those applying under CDR. These guidelines allowed banks to restructure accounts of viable entities classified as standard, sub-standard and doubtful. They also provided that accounts with standard asset classification, other than those relating to Commercial Real Estate (CRE), Capital Market Exposure (CME) and personal loans, could retain their classification upon restructuring as long as they satisfied certain conditions.

Both the borrower and the lender found it profitable to restructure a loan that faced the prospect of turning into an NPA. For the borrower, restructuring offered the opportunity to renegotiate the terms of loans and continue business as usual without any loss of reputation that might follow his loan being classified as NPA. For the lender, restructuring came with a substantially reduced provisioning requirement. While the provisioning requirement for a loan falling into the sub-standard category was 15 per cent, the requirement for a restructured standard loan until November 2012 was only 2 per cent. Even in November 2012, it was raised merely to 2.75 per cent. A further hike to 5 per cent on 1 April 2013 still left provisioning for restructured standard loans well below the 15 per cent-level for sub-standard loans.

These small tweaks to rules were done on the recommendation of a Working Group of the RBI, which had been tasked with offering advice on desirable changes in the restructuring regime in the light of international best practices. As late as July 2012, contrary to the prevailing international practice of downgrading restructured loans, the Working Group recommended permitting them to retain their original classification, as long as certain conditions were satisfied. The report stated,

> The WG [Working Group] has observed that internationally accounts are generally treated as impaired/downgraded on restructuring. The WG examined the consequences of aligning our restructuring guidelines with this best practice but felt that doing so immediately might act as a disincentive to banks to restructure viable accounts which would severely impact the viable accounts facing temporary challenge and may result in higher provisioning requirement for banks on account of increase in the non-performing assets.[60]

Figure 9.2: NPAs and Restructured Standard Loans of Scheduled Commercial Banks, 2004/05–2017/18

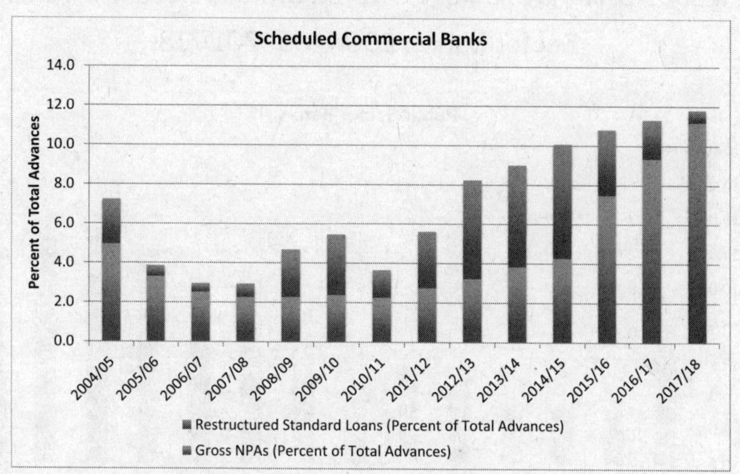

Source: Author's construction using RBI data[61]

60 Reserve Bank of India, 2012, *Report of the Working Group to review the existing prudential guidelines on restructuring of advances by banks/financial institutions*, p. 74, at https://www.rbi.org.in/Scripts/PublicationReportDetails.aspx?UrlPage=&ID=676 (last accessed on 17 March 2019).

61 https://dbie.rbi.org.in/DBIE/dbie.rbi?site=publications#!4 (last accessed on 15 March 2019).

Figure 9.2 shows the evolution of NPAs and restructured standard loans of all scheduled commercial banks taken together from 2004/05 to 2017/18. Between 2004/05 and 2007/08, NPAs saw a decline with restructured loans staying at relatively low levels. This was the period during which the banking system was still coming out of the first round of NPAs that had carried over from the 1990s and early 2000s. The decline in NPAs as proportion of advances was substantially driven by the rapid expansion of advances, which grew 30 per cent in 2005/06 and 2006/07 and 25 per cent in 2007/08 (Table 9.1). But beginning in 2008/09, the year of the global financial crisis, restructured standard loans began to rise at a fast pace. By 2014/15, they had increased to nearly 5.8 per cent from 0.4 per cent in 2006/07 while NPAs rose to only 4.3 per cent from 2.5 per cent over the same period.

Figure 9.3: NPAs and Restructured Standard Loans in Public Sector Banks, 2004/05–2017/18

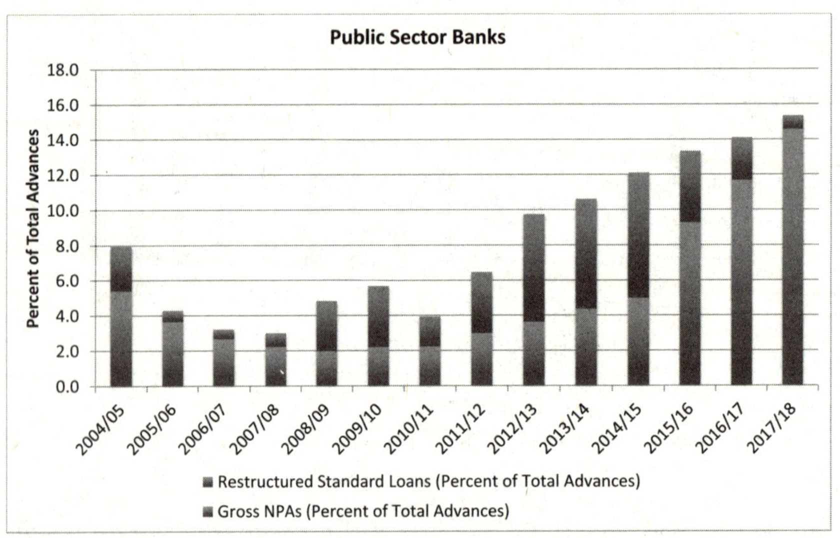

Source: See Figure 9.2

Disaggregated data shows that though the rising proportion of restructured standard loans characterized all three major groups of banks—public, private and foreign—the expansion was heavily concentrated in public sector banks. Figure 9.3 provides the evolution of NPAs and restructured standard loans in these latter. Restructured standard loans in public sector banks rose from 0.6 per cent of total advances in 2006/07 to 7.1 per cent in 2014/15. With these banks accounting for two-thirds or a higher fraction of outstanding advances throughout the period, their health had a determining effect on the health of the banking system as a whole.

The performance of private and foreign banks, depicted in Figures 9.4 and 9.5 respectively, was significantly superior as far as NPAs and restructured standard loans are concerned. Even at their peak in 2014/15, restructured standard loans amounted to only 2.3 per cent of total advances in private banks. In foreign banks, the peak had been reached in 2008/09, the year of the global financial crisis. Their restructured loans that year amounted to only 1.1 per cent of total advances. Indeed, their NPAs at 4.3 per cent that year were significantly higher.

Figure 9.4: NPAs and Restructured Standard Loans of Private Banks, 2004/05–2017/18

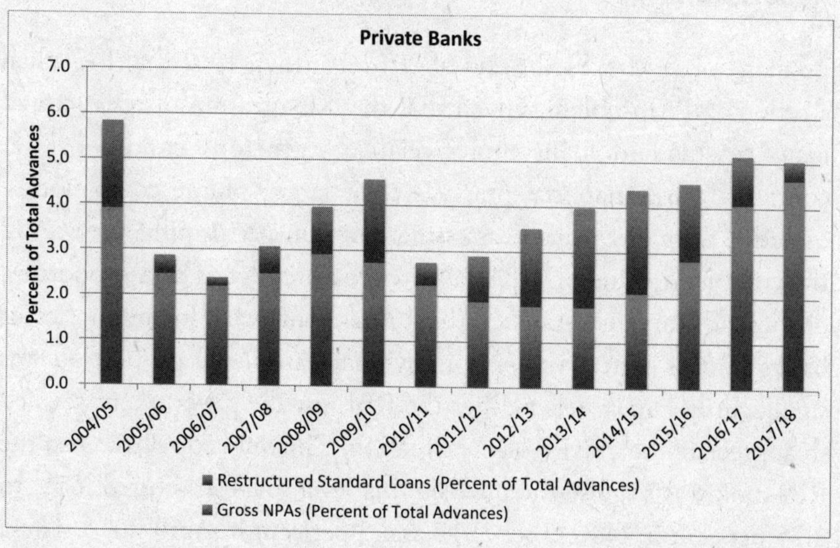

Source: See Figure 9.2

Figure 9.5: NPAs and Restructured Standard Loans of Foreign Banks, 2004/05–2017/18

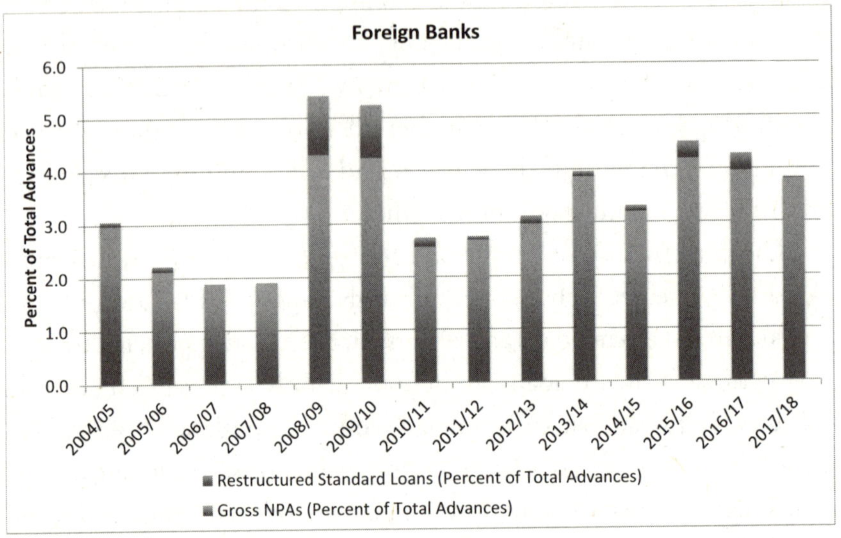

Source: See Figure 9.2

Much-delayed Recognition but No Effort Towards Resolution

To many observers, by the end of 2012/13 it was clear that India had a serious NPA problem. Given that the classification of restructured loans as standard loans under relatively generous conditions was contrary to international practice, their large volume could not be excluded from any realistic assessment of non-performing assets. And the combined value of NPAs and restructured loans as a proportion of total advances had crossed the 10 per cent mark for public sector banks by this time. For some individual banks, the proportion was significantly larger. Yet, neither the RBI nor the government seemed to appreciate the gravity of the situation. The only corrective step the RBI took was to raise the provisioning level for restructured loans to 2.75 per cent in November 2012 and 5 per cent in April 2013. These measures amounted to no more than Band-Aid solutions.

It was not until 1 April 2015 that the RBI finally recognized that lenders and borrowers were abusing the CDR by representing many bad loans as those with temporary problems, which would go away if given breathing space through restructuring. At that juncture, it adopted the international best practice of downgrading restructured loans to sub-standard category. By this time, the NPAs plus restructured loans of public sector banks had reached 13.5 per cent, though NPAs by themselves amounted to 5 per cent only.

While aligning the CDR with international best practice, the RBI also offered borrowers several new restructuring avenues to escape the classification of their loans as NPAs. In June 2015, it introduced a Strategic Debt Restructuring (SDR) scheme under which it provided for the conversion of a part of the loan to an ailing company into equity. Under the scheme, lender banks had to become majority owners with the right to replace management to turn around the asset. Though they were not allowed to sell partial equity, they could recover dues by selling the company in its entirety to a new promoter. The scheme gave banks relaxation on several RBI regulations and allowed loans to be reported as standard assets. In case of failure to sell the company to a new promoter in eighteen months, the relaxations were withdrawn and loans downgraded to sub-standard category.

On 13 June 2016, the RBI introduced the Scheme for Sustainable Structuring of Stressed Assets (S4A). Under the scheme, the concerned company's debt was divided into sustainable and unsustainable components. As long as the sustainable component accounted for 50 per cent or more of the loan and could be serviced under original terms, the unsustainable component could be converted into equity or optionally convertible debentures with clearly spelt-out terms. Banks could sell this stake to a new owner.

A third RBI initiative, introduced in July 2014, was the scheme for Flexible Structuring of Long Term Loans to Infrastructure and Core Sector Industries. Commonly known as the 5:25 scheme, it was intended to resolve lending problems in the infrastructure sector, where projects take twenty to twenty-five years to complete. Banks normally do not lend beyond ten- to twelve-year terms, creating a mismatch between what is needed and what is available. The 5:25 scheme allowed lenders to offer loans with terms extending till twenty to twenty-five years by refinancing outstanding amounts every five to seven years. The scheme did not permit any haircuts, however, which meant that banks had to protect the net present value of the loans refinanced.

In 2014, the RBI also attempted to create a mechanism to coordinate restructuring when multiple lenders were involved. It issued guidelines for the creation of a Joint Lenders' Forum (JLF) that would recognize stressed assets early and formulate a Corrective Action Plan (CAP) with the consent of the majority of JLF members within forty-five days. Later, in 2015, the RBI also directed banks to set up an empowered group that would be tasked with the approval of the restructuring package.

Predictably, these schemes failed to produce any major successes and were principally used by borrowers and lenders to delay downgrading of loans to non-performing status. The measure that made a major difference was the ending of CDR, which finally began to bring bad loans into the open. At the end of 2015/16, just a year after the CDR facility was ended, the NPAs of public sector banks zoomed 5 percentage points to reach 9.3 per cent and restructured loans fell from 8.5 per cent to 6.7 per cent. This shift continued in the following years with public-sector-bank NPAs rising to 14.6 per cent and restructured loans declining to 4.2 per cent at the end of 2017/18.

No progress took place, however, on cleaning up the NPAs. Defaulting borrowers had a vested interest in maintaining the status quo, since it allowed them continued ownership of their assets. The CEOs of public sector banks were reluctant to initiate action towards a resolution that would lead to partial and not full recovery for the fear that this may bring accusations of corruption or future investigation by vigilance agencies. They preferred to postpone any action until their term was over and pass the buck to the successor. This remained true even after the Insolvency and Bankruptcy Code, 2016—that provided a clear, time-bound pathway to resolution of loans in default—had become operational.

Given this situation, any progress towards cleaning NPAs required intervention by the RBI and the Department of Financial Services (DFS) in the finance ministry. Unfortunately, neither the RBI nor the DFS exhibited any interest in the task during 2014 to 2016. The RBI remained preoccupied with the introduction of different methods of restructuring loans and carrying out stress tests on them and the DFS with its Indradhanush initiative, which consisted of quick-fix solutions such as the replacement of the appointments board of public sector banks by the Bank Boards Bureau, cosmetic governance reforms and recapitalization of banks by the relatively small amount of ₹700 billion spread over a period of four years.

Collapse of Credit and Action at Last

By early 2017, the evidence became compelling that rapidly accumulating NPAs were choking credit growth. As Table 9.1 shows, the credit growth of public sector banks, which accounted for two-thirds of total credit, dropped to just 0.7 per cent in 2016/17. The figure for all scheduled commercial banks fell to 3.6 per cent the same year. These growth rates compared with substantially higher growth of credit of 14.5 per cent for private sector banks, which enjoyed substantially lower levels of NPAs.[62]

Very likely, it was this breakdown in credit growth that finally led the government to move decisively to tackle NPAs. In May 2017, it

62 The credit growth of foreign banks during 2016/17 was negative but its cause was rooted in interest rate increases in the United States.

enacted an ordinance amending the Banking Regulation Act, 1949. The ordinance empowered the government to authorize the RBI to issue direction to banks to initiate the insolvency resolution process in cases involving defaults. It also empowered the RBI to appoint committees with authority to advise banks on the resolution of stressed assets. The first part of the amendment helped ensure that banks would have the backing of the government and the RBI in the initiation of bankruptcy proceedings against politically connected and powerful defaulters. The second part of the amendment gave them the cover of RBI-appointed committees against potential charges of corruption on grounds such as excessive haircuts taken. Soon after the enactment of the ordinance, in October 2017, the government also announced its decision to raise the amount to be infused into public sector banks from ₹700 billion to ₹2.1 trillion. The period of this infusion was pegged at two years.

Armed with the ordinance, the government moved swiftly to authorize the RBI to issue direction to the banks to initiate insolvency proceedings against defaulting borrowers. The RBI moved equally fast and immediately directed banks to begin proceedings under the IBC in respect of all accounts with outstanding amount of ₹50 billion or more. Numbering twelve in all, these accounts had an outstanding amount of ₹3.45 trillion and represented a quarter of all NPAs at the time. The liquidation value of these accounts was assessed at ₹732.2 billion.[63]

IBC Process Yields Impressive Outcomes

In its early stages, the IBC process has led to impressive outcomes with many large accounts reaching resolution faster than ever before

---

63 Unless otherwise mentioned, data and information in the remainder of this section has been taken from the *RBI Report on Trends and Progress in Banking 2017–18* and the *Quarterly Newsletter October–December 2018, Volume 9*, published by the Insolvency and Bankruptcy Board of India.

and yielding significantly higher recovery rates. This has been the case despite the fact that the IBC process itself is relatively new and has been going through the usual teething pains. By 31 December 2018, resolution plans for four of the twelve accounts had been approved. In another case, liquidation order had been passed. The four accounts approved for restructuring had more than 920 billion rupees due on them jointly. Recovery rate on them at 51 per cent was considerably higher than their estimated liquidation value.

Table 9.2: Status of Corporate Insolvency Resolution Process as of 31 December 2018

Status of CIRPs	**Number of CIRPs**
Admitted	1484
Closed on Appeal / Review/ Settled	142
Closed by Withdrawal under Section 12A	63
Closed by Resolution	79
Closed by Liquidation	302
Ongoing CIRP	898
> 270 Days	275
> 180 Days < 270 Days	166
> 90 Days < 180 Days	202
< 90 Days	255

Source: Insolvency and Bankruptcy Board of India, 2018, Table 4

Table 9.2 provides a summary of timeline of all cases admitted under the Corporate Insolvency Resolution Process (CIRP) of IBC as of 31 December 2018. Of the total 1,484 cases admitted, 586 or 39.5 per cent had already reached closure by this date. Another 623 cases or 42 per cent had been under resolution for less than 270 days. Cases exceeding 270 days of specified ceiling for resolution numbered 275 or 18.5 per cent of the total. Compared to India's past history, this is a significant jump in the speed of resolution of bankruptcy cases. Given that the National Company Law Tribunal, which conducts proceedings, remains understaffed, these numbers bode well for the future of bankruptcy cases in India.

One criticism of the IBC process has been that it has led to liquidation in a disproportionately large number of cases. According to Table 9.2, a hefty 51.5 per cent of the total cases reaching closure resulted in liquidation. The criticism misses the fact, however, that 227 out of 302 or 75.2 per cent cases culminating in liquidation had been with the Bureau of Industrial and Financial Restructuring earlier and had lost much of their economic value before they were brought into the IBC process.

Reduced delays in resolution have also translated into increased recovery rates. Under alternative channels such as Lok Adalat, the Debt Recovery Tribunal (DRT) and SARFAESI, which are subject to long delays, recovery rates have been much lower. Table 9.3 provides recovery rates associated with these alternative avenues to bankruptcy for financial years 2016/17 and 2017/18. In aggregate, recovery rates from the three channels have averaged less than 15 per cent. The recovery rate under SARFAESI has been significantly higher than under the other two processes and has also seen an improvement in 2017/18. The reason for this latter fact may be an amendment to the SARFAESI Act providing for three months of imprisonment in case the borrower did not give asset details and for the lender to get possession of mortgaged property within thirty days. In comparison, based on realizations by twenty-one financial creditors during 2017/18, the recovery rate under IBC has been 49.6 per cent.

Table 9.3: Recovery in Cases under Channels Existing Prior to the IBC

Amounts Involved or Recovered	Lok Adalats	DRTs	SARFAESI	Total
2016/17				
Amount Involved (Billion Rupees)	361	1008	1414	2783
Amount Recovered (Billion Rupees)	23	103	259	385
Recovery Rate*	6.3	10.2	18.3	13.8
2017/18				
Amount Involved (Billion Rupees)	457	1,333	1,067	2857
Amount Recovered (Billion Rupees)	18	72	265	355
Recovery Rate*	4.0	5.4	24.8	12.4

*Amount recovered as per cent of amount involved

Source: Reserve Bank of India 2018, Table IV.15, p. 64

Though cleaning of NPAs remains work in progress, there is no doubt that the IBC–RBI process has turned a new leaf in this area. If this process continues with the RBI leading the way, banks should see a steady improvement in the quality of their assets. This improvement would also lead to a return to healthy credit growth.

Combating the Creation of New NPAs

A final question concerns the creation of new NPAs. Even if the current bout of NPAs passes, how can India be sure that the same history will not be repeated? In February 2018, the RBI issued a circular specifying a number of measures aimed at early detection of NPAs and their resolution in a time-bound manner. Unfortunately, the Supreme Court struck this circular in April 2019 on the ground that it violated the laws under which it had been issued. Subsequently, in June 2019, the RBI issued a new circular, which aims to achieve the objectives of the February 2018 circular but is significantly weaker than the latter.

During the short time it was in force, the experience with the February 2018 circular was very encouraging. Therefore, it is worthwhile to consider its main provisions. It withdrew the existing restructuring plans such as CDR, SDR and S4A and mandated that banks must report a loan as being in default if the borrower misses her payment even for a day. It required the banks to report the account as a Special Mention Account. If the account remained in default for ninety days or longer, it was classified as non-performing. All lenders associated with an account in default were required to put in place a board-approved resolution plan (RP).

In the case of accounts with an aggregate exposure of lenders equalling or exceeding ₹20 billion, the circular applied additional regulations. Resolution plans in such cases had to be implemented within 180 days of the first day of default. If this was not done, lenders had to compulsorily file an insolvency application under IBC within fifteen days of the expiry of the 180-day deadline. If the RP was implemented within the180-day period, the account had to remain free of default at all points during the 'specified period'. The specified period, in turn, was the longer of the following two: (i) One year from the commencement of the first payment of interest and principal; and (ii) Period from the date of implementation of RP until the date on which 20 per cent of the outstanding principal debt and interest capitalization as per the RP was paid.

The circular strengthened the IBC regime by making the process of resolution of accounts in default automatic and time-bound in the case of loans worth ₹20 billion or more. It required that banks either demonstrate the sustainability of loans in default by implementing a resolution plan that keeps the borrower out of default during the specified period or compulsorily file an insolvency application. The provision meant that borrowers and lenders could not let an account remain in default indefinitely.

The episode of default by Jet Airways illustrates the power of the circular. A story in the *Economic Times* describes the episode thus:

> Indian bankers were never this powerful … A resolution plan for a failed airline, with debt of more than ₹8,000 crore [80 billion], is in place in less than three months from the day of default. This would have been impossible without the new rules — the Reserve Bank of India's (RBI) February 12 order on the treatment of defaults, and the December 2016 bankruptcy laws.[64]

The story goes on to contrast this experience with that of Essar Steel, whose promoters managed to delay a takeover of their company for two years after defaulting on a loan as large as ₹400 billion under the old rules.

The revised RBI circular of June 2019 retains many features of the February 2018 circular but it does away with the requirement of compulsory filing for bankruptcy in the event of lenders failing to implement a resolution plan for accounts amounting to ₹20 billion or more. Instead, it provides for additional provisioning if lenders fail to implement a resolution plan in 180 days. This change represents a vast improvement over the situation prevailing prior to 1 April 2015 when the RBI did away with the CDR. But it is a step back from the RBI circular of February 2018.

64 Rangan, 2019

The Case for Privatization of Public Sector Banks

The decision to nationalize the larger banks in 1969 was wholly political. Prime Minister Indira Gandhi faced an existential threat from her rivals who controlled the organizational wing of the Congress party. Morarji Desai, the finance minister, was one of them. To break loose of the organizational wing, Gandhi needed to sack Desai and take full charge of the government. Opposition to bank nationalization by Desai gave her the necessary excuse to sack him. She took charge of the finance ministry and issued an ordinance nationalizing all banks with deposits worth ₹500 million or more. The decision led the organizational wing of the Congress party to separate from Gandhi. But with nationalization proving highly popular, Gandhi came out victorious. Her faction of the Congress eventually scored a resounding victory in the parliamentary elections in 1971.

Although many commentators have hailed bank nationalization as an important step towards bringing banking to the masses and improving access of the common man to credit, the reality remains that on balance, the measure has been costly on many dimensions. My conviction is that it is now time for the government to return public sector banks back to the private sector. This conviction is based on a number of factors.

Efficiency

First, there is overwhelming evidence that public sector banks have performed less efficiently than their private sector counterparts. Much of the earlier evidence gathered by economists has been discussed in my 2008 book, *India: The Emerging Giant*. Here, it suffices to present four key indicators of efficiency: credit deposit ratio, return on assets, wages as a proportion of income and asset shares.

Figures 9.6 to 9.9 depict the relative levels of these indicators in public, private and foreign banks from 2004/05 to 2017/18. Across all four indicators and all years shown, private banks unambiguously outperform public sector banks. Broadly, foreign banks also perform better than the latter. If exceptions arise with respect to foreign banks, they are related to events in the global economy, such as the global financial crisis of 2008 and shifts in interest rates abroad in 2016 and subsequently, especially in the United States, due to greater integration of these banks in the global economy.

According to Figure 9.6, the credit–deposit ratio in private sector banks has been consistently higher than that in public sector banks. The gap between the ratios of the two sets of banks has seen a sharp rise in recent years. In all likelihood, this rise in gap has originated in the significantly faster accumulation of NPAs in public sector banks. What is remarkable, however, is that even during the years that public sector credit expanded rapidly without due diligence, private sector banks maintained a higher credit-deposit ratio and yet did not suffer as high a conversion of their loans into NPAs as public sector banks in subsequent years. Foreign banks also outperformed public sector banks in terms of credit–deposit ratio except in 2009/10, the year immediately following the global financial crisis.

Figure 9.6: Credit–Deposit Ratio in Public, Private and Foreign Banks: 2004/05–2017/18

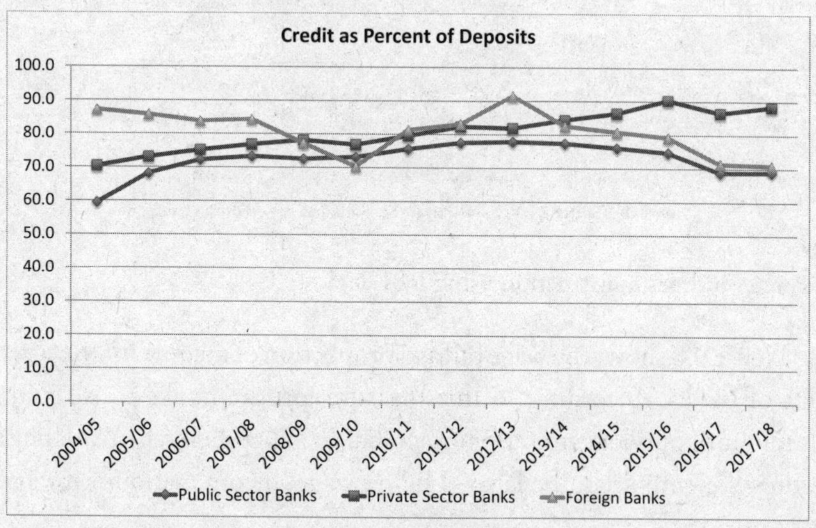

Source: Author's construction using RBI data

Figure 9.7 shows the return on assets in the three sets of banks. This is the single-most important measure of performance of banks and the contrast between public sector banks on the one hand and private and foreign banks on the other according to the return on assets could not be sharper. Not only is the return in private banks higher than in public sector banks for every single year shown, during 2009/10 to 2014/15, the former saw the return rising while the latter experienced a decline in it. During the last three years shown, the return turned negative in public sector banks. Foreign banks have outperformed even private banks in all but three of the years shown.

Figure 9.7: Return on Assets in Public, Private and Foreign Banks, 2004/05 to 2017/18

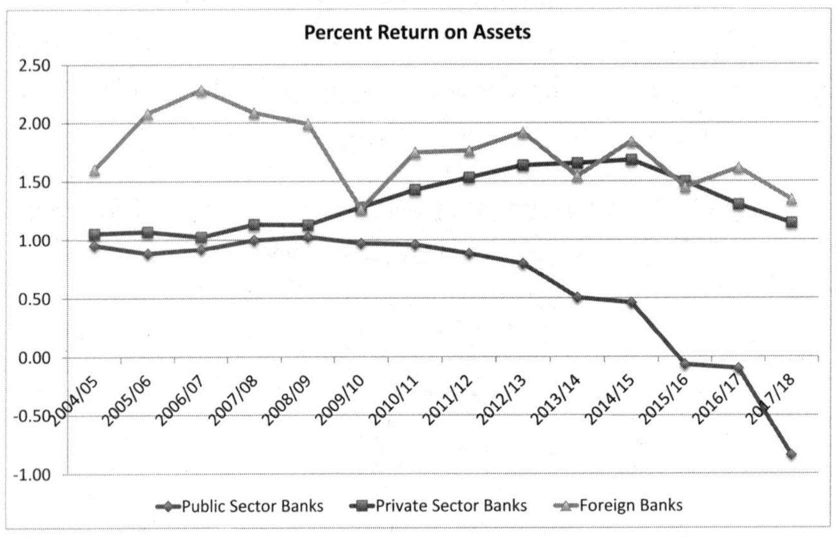

Source: Author's construction using RBI data

Figure 9.8 shows the wage bill as a proportion of income for the three sets of banks. According to this measure, private banks consistently outdo both public sector and foreign banks. They generally use labour more efficiently than the latter. Higher wage–income ratio for foreign banks is not surprising, given that their wages are partially linked to international wages. What is surprising is that during the last five years shown, the wage–income ratio in public sector banks has exceeded even that in foreign banks.

Figure 9.9 depicts shifts in asset shares of the three sets of banks. Better performance of private sector banks has resulted in a progressive shift in relative shares in their favour. From around 90 per cent in the early 1990s, the share of public sector banks in the total assets of scheduled commercial banks had already fallen to 80.2 per cent as on 31 March 2000. This share further fell to 71.9 per cent by 31 March 2009 and then to 66.0 per cent by 31 March 2018. The trend has continued despite large infusions of capital by the government in public sector banks on different occasions.

Figure 9.8: Wage Bill as Percentage of Income in Public, Private and Foreign Banks: 2004/05–2017/18

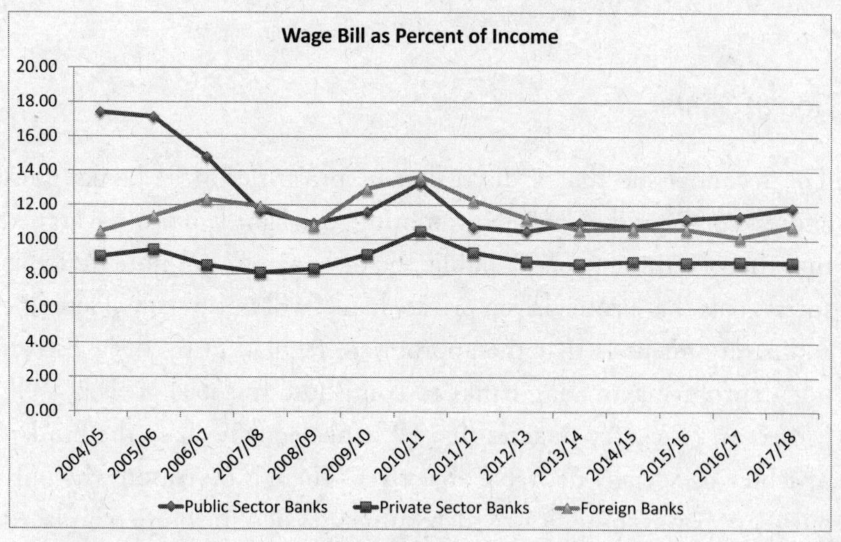

Source: Author's construction using RBI data

Figure 9.9: Percentage of Shares of Bank Groups in the Total Assets of Scheduled Commercial Banks

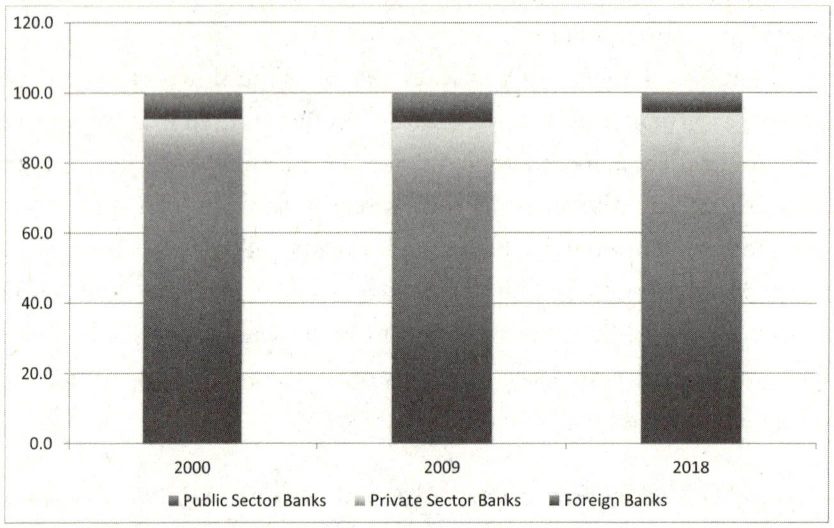

Source: Author's construction using RBI data

Social Goals

The second issue that a discussion of privatization of banks must address concerns their role in promoting social goals. It is often argued that the government needs public sector banks to promote desirable social goals that profit-driven private banks will not pursue. Here, the counterargument is that the appropriate regulation by the RBI can nudge profit-maximizing banks to contribute to social goals as well. Moreover, efficiency dictates that all banks equally share the burden of achieving socially desirable objectives. There is no reason why only one set of banks should carry such burden. When the burden is placed only on one set of banks—public sector banks—it creates a distortion in the system. Moreover, it necessitates offsetting action to compensate these banks in some form. This adds to the initial distortion.

In one important area, priority sector lending, experience shows that it is entirely possible to have a common regime for public and private sector banks to promote social objectives. This can be seen in Figure 9.10, which depicts the share of priority sector advance in the total advances of different bank groups. While it is true that the share has been higher for public sector banks during many of the years shown, private and foreign banks have also delivered satisfactory outcomes. Indeed, in some years, private banks have allocated larger share of their advances to priority sectors than public sector banks.

Regulation by the RBI can be used to promote other social goals as well. For example, the burden of expansion of rural banking can be placed equally on all banks through appropriate incentives. Expansion of bank accounts to promote financial inclusion can be similarly spread over all banks. In a similar vein, a non-discriminatory regime can be devised to incentivize speedy digitization of transactions should that be viewed as a desirable social goal.

Figure 9.10: Share of Priority Sector Advances in the Total Advances of Different Bank Groups: 2004/05–2017/18

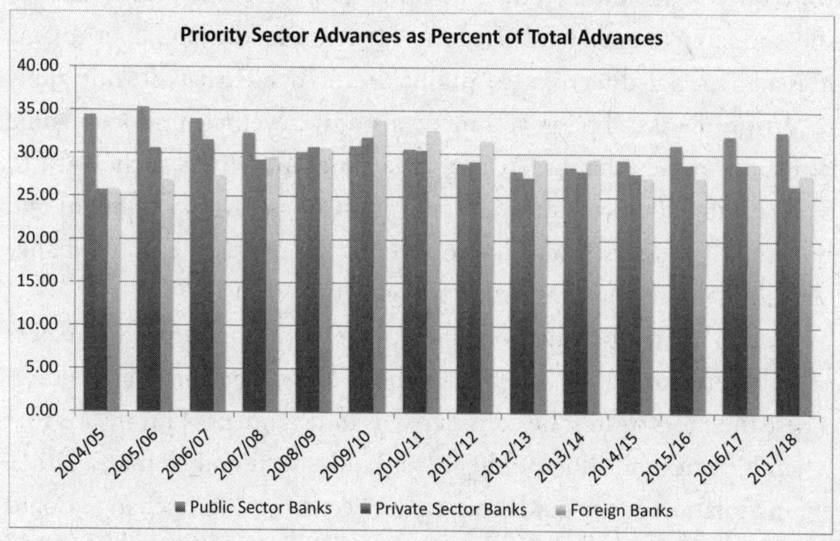

Source: Author's construction using RBI data

Governance

Finally, it is issues related to governance that offer the most compelling cases for privatization of public sector banks. A number of factors are worth highlighting.

First, the government ownership has led to a regulatory regime that is not ownership-neutral. The RBI can remove directors or management of private banks but not public sector banks. It can force a merger or trigger liquidation of a private bank, but not a public sector bank. It has the legal authority to hold boards of private and foreign banks accountable regarding strategic direction, risk profiles, assessment of management and compensation but not public sector banks. Unlike private and foreign banks, public sector banks do not require a licence from the RBI to operate. This means that the RBI lacks the power to cease the operations of the latter, should such a need arise.

Second, as a corollary of the previous point, public sector banks are subject to dual regulation by the finance ministry and the RBI. The finance ministry issues numerous circulars to give formal directives to the banks. When the government launches special programmes such as the campaign to open bank accounts for all under the Jan Dhan Yojana, it issues special directives to public sector banks that do not apply to private banks. The government also gives verbal, undocumented direction to these banks. At the same time, in matters such as CRR, SLR, capital adequacy ratio, classification of assets into standard and non-standard assets, and numerous reporting requirements, the banks are subject to regulations issued by the RBI.

Under the dual regulation, the government appoints all directors of public sector banks other than those elected by the shareholders. These directors cannot be considered as independent. This means that when it comes to listing public sector banks on the stock market, they are in violation of the guidelines of the Securities and Exchange Board of India. Unlike private banks, the boards of public sector banks do not have power to bring directors with special skills. The tenures of chairmen and executive directors of boards of public sector banks are short, which greatly undermines their ability and motivation to exercise control over management.

Third, with government ownership come government rules applicable to employees that differ from those that apply to employees of private sector banks. Over time, this has led to a significant widening of differences in salaries and compensation between public and private banks. In turn, this has also led to differences in skills, which has contributed to differences in performance of the two sets of banks.

Equally important, should they err in discharging their duties as per rules, public sector bank employees are subject to vigilance enforcement of the Central Vigilance Commission (CVC) and Central Bureau of Investigation (CBI). While even systematic good performance of loans advanced by an employee promises to bring few rewards, failures of even a small number of loans can trigger action by the CVC and CBI. This situation greatly impacts the risk-taking behaviour of bank employees when taking decisions on loans. At the same time, the short tenures of the top management and board members complemented by the absence of commercial pressures similar to those faced by private sector banks provide fertile ground for fraudulent transactions for private gain by corrupt but enterprising regular employees. The episode of a major fraud at the Punjab National Bank in 2019 highlights this problem.

Fourth, ownership by the government leads to political interference in ways that has worked to greatly weaken public sector banks and, given their disproportionate share in total banking assets, the entire banking sector. This interference has typically taken two forms. One, politically powerful private entrepreneurs are able to manipulate the system to obtain loans even when they have no intention of paying them back in full. Two, the government directs public sector banks to advance loans to entities, both private and public, operating in infrastructure, transportation and energy sectors, even when the projects are not commercially viable. Often, the lack of commercial viability itself is the result of difficulties in land acquisition and slow clearances by various government ministries, most notably the environment ministry. Both types of interferences have resulted in the accumulation of large volumes of non-performing assets in recent years.

Finally, the ownership of banks creates serious conflicts across various roles that the government must play. First and foremost, the government is the policymaker for the banking sector. But as the owner of public sector banks, it also becomes a service provider. In addition, through various channels, it also acts as a regulator of banks. Therefore, we have a situation of the policymaker making policy for itself and the regulator regulating itself. While few analysts would question the right of the government to give direction to the regulator in a crisis situation, the exercise of such right on a day-to-day basis leads to conflict-of-interest situations and undesirable interference in the functioning of the sector.

Will There Be Takers for Public Sector Banks?

Sceptics sometimes argue that the government may not find any takers when it tries to sell public sector banks. This fear is based on the assumption that the government will be selling its entire equity in each bank at one go within a short period. But the assumption is unfounded.

All public sector banks are currently listed on the stock market. What the government will need to do is begin the process by selling just enough shares in a bank to bring its equity below 50 per cent. At that stage, after the appropriate change in law, management of the bank can be passed on to a private board. The government can then reduce its stake gradually over time and take advantage of increases in share prices that would follow. A simple path to privatization can thus be chalked out.

The assumption that the government must privatize all banks at once or within a short period also lacks basis. It can have a plan extending to three or four years during which its share in equity in each bank will be reduced below 50 per cent. The State Bank of India can be placed at the end of the queue. As it dilutes its equity in more and more banks and passes on control of management to private boards, it will have the opportunity to assess whether this is unduly undermining its ability to achieve social objectives. If the answer turns out to be in the affirmative, it can choose not to privatize the State Bank of India.

An Alternative to Privatization and Towards Bank Consolidation

It is sometimes argued that many of the objectives of privatization of banks can be achieved without the government having to give up the ownership of public sector banks. The Nayak Committee report, submitted in 2014, has outlined one such plan. Under it, the government would form a Bank Investment Company (BIC) under the Companies Act, which would have the character of a passive sovereign wealth fund for the government's banks. Legislation nationalizing banks would be repealed and ownership rights transferred to the BIC, which would also become the holder of the government's equity in the banks. In the final stage of reform, the BIC would transfer all ownership functions to the bank boards and would be left to exercise investor functions only. Public sector banks would be governed the same way as private banks with the positions of the chairman of the board and CEO held by different individuals. The RBI would adopt a uniform licensing regime across all board-based banks serving similar functions and ensure that publicly owned and private banks were subject to the same set of regulations. The government would withdraw from regulating banks and pursue all social objectives through the RBI regulation that would apply uniformly to the two types of banks.

Theoretically, these reforms can achieve approximately the same outcome as privatization. But I am sceptical whether within the complex system of governance that India has, these reforms will reach their logical conclusion. The intent may well be to achieve the outcome as per the report but as the reform works its way through the labyrinth of India's political-bureaucratic process, it will morph into something quite different or get stalled altogether. It is best to repeal the legislation nationalizing the banks, dilute the government equity below 50 per cent in a short period of time and offload the rest of it over a five-year period in a time-bound manner. The RBI should license the banks as private banks so that any distinction between them and existing private banks from the viewpoint of regulation would be eliminated.

Among other reforms, India also needs to consolidate its banks. Banking is subject to substantial economies of scale and scope, which means that the existence of too many small banks undermines efficiency. In this respect, the decision in 2019 to merge several public sector banks into a smaller number of larger banks is a very welcome development. These decisions in the past have brought down the number of public sector banks from twenty-seven before 2017 to twelve. The government should work towards bringing this number further down to half a dozen, since creating even larger banks will make the banks more efficient and competitive. Moreover, privatization will be easier to accomplish when the number of banks is smaller.

Government Policies and Private Investment

Before concluding this chapter, three aspects of government policy bearing on the availability of financial resources to private investors through financial markets should be noted. First, taking the GDP and private consumption as given, the higher the level of government expenditure, the lower is the level of resources available to private investors. The government finances its expenditure principally by tax revenue or borrowing from financial markets. When the government raises tax revenue by taxing household income, corporate profits or consumption of goods and services, it lowers savings available to private investors. Reduced savings in turn result in reduced private investment. If the government finances expenditure by borrowing from the market, it crowds out private investors, once again reducing private investment. No matter how the government finances expenditures, it has an effect on private investment. This fact must be given due consideration when considering increases in government expenditure.

Second, India has had a longstanding policy of requiring banks to offer a specified percentage of their credit to a set of listed sectors or entities including agriculture, renewable energy, education, micro and small enterprises, low-cost housing and small businesses and service enterprises. This policy of priority sector lending has an adverse effect on the allocation of available investment funds across sectors. To the extent that a floor on lending to priority sectors results in the diversion of investment funds from higher return projects in 'non-priority' sectors, there is a loss of efficiency in the use of the funds. In the 1990s, the first Narasimham Committee on banking reforms had recommended phasing out priority sector lending, but the government did not accept it. It is time to return to a discussion of this reform.

Finally, despite considerable liberalization, the interest rates on many small savings schemes including the Public Provident Fund, Senior Citizen Savings Scheme, and Sukanya Samriddhi Scheme (Girl Child Prosperity Scheme) continue to be administered by the government. Interest rates paid on savings deposits under these schemes are held well above market rates. To attract deposits, banks in turn have to compete against these schemes with the result that the connection of lending rates to the policy interest rate of the RBI is weakened. The pass through of reductions in the latter rates to lending rates is at best partial. In order that the monetary policy work smoothly, the government needs to free up all interest rates and use alternative instruments to protect the interests of the groups being helped through above market interest rates currently.

Concluding Remarks

Channelling finance to projects with high returns is a highly critical function in any economy. In a developing economy where available funds are limited and high-return projects are spread in isolated pockets not easily identified, this function assumes even greater importance. Only a well-functioning banking system, manned by staff with the skills to identify high-return projects, can satisfactorily solve this problem.

India has a substantial banking sector today. But it is underperforming by a wide margin and has been afflicted by repeated bouts of accumulation of non-performing assets. A key factor in the underperformance of the sector is public ownership of banks accounting for two-thirds of banking assets. This ownership has been justified on the ground that banks must perform a set of social goals. But the argument is flawed. All banks must contribute equally to the pursuit of social goals, as is currently the case with priority sector lending. Requiring one set of banks to perform functions that another set of banks need not perform creates not just an uneven playing field but also leads to gross inefficiency. The RBI must use one set of regulatory rules for publicly owned banks and another set of rules for private banks. In turn, public sector banks must answer to two masters, the RBI and the government. Public ownership also means that the banks are not subject to the usual commercial pressures. All these features of the current Indian banking system point to the urgent need for their privatization. If the government must retain ownership, it should limit it to one bank, the State Bank of India. If this is done, the government must place the State Bank of India at arm's length with a special purpose vehicle so that the regulatory anomalies discussed in this chapter are minimized.

A healthy financial sector is critical to the accumulation of physical capital in high-productivity activities. Equally important, however, is human capital formation. Indeed, it may be argued that with technology taking centre stage in all aspects of human life, human capital formation has become even more important than physical capital formation. A critical element in human capital formation is the availability of first-rate higher education. This sector has been much neglected in India, necessitating a detailed treatment in the next chapter.

HISTORY OF BANKING PRIOR TO 1991 REFORMS

THE HISTORY OF BANKING in India, prior to the launch of economic reforms in 1991, can be divided into three periods: the pre-Independence era (1720–1947), the early post-Independence years (1947–67), and the nationalization phase (1967–1991). These three periods are discussed below in greater detail.

Pre-Independence Era (1720–1947)

The first Western-style joint-stock variety bank in India was the Bank of Bombay, established in 1720 in Bombay. But it lasted for only sixty years.[65] More substantial activity started later and was located on the eastern side of the country, where the British East India Company was successful in establishing its control during its early years. The Bank of Hindustan was established in 1773 and General Bank of Bengal and Bihar in 1773. Three Presidency banks with government participation followed: Bank of Bengal in Calcutta in 1806, Bank of Bombay in 1840 in Bombay and Bank of Madras in Madras in 1843. Royal Charters governed the Presidency banks. The banks also issued currency notes until the enactment of the Paper Currency Act, 1861, which transferred the right to issue currency to the government.

65 Amladi, 2014

Until 1860, banks and insurance companies were subject to unlimited liability. Beginning in 1860, Indian law permitted limited liability, which led to an increase in banking activity. Allahabad Bank, the first Indian-owned bank, came into existence in 1865. The Punjab National Bank was established in Lahore in 1895 and the Bank of India in Bombay in 1906. The Swadeshi movement of 1906 accelerated the process of establishing joint-stock banks of Indian ownership. It led to the founding of the Central Bank of India, Bank of Baroda, Canara Bank, Indian Bank and Bank of Mysore between 1906 and 1913. By December 1913, India had fifty-six reporting commercial banks.

During the First World War, many banks with low capital base and limited liquid assets failed. The failed banks included some large ones such as the British-owned Indian Special Bank. In large part, the failures were due to imprudent management, involving large unsecured advances to directors and their companies. Such lending was possible due to the absence of adequate regulatory safeguards.

In 1921, the three Presidency banks were merged to form the Imperial Bank of India. Later, several banks belonging to princely states such as Jaipur, Mysore, Patiala and Jodhpur were merged into the Imperial Bank of India. In addition to functioning as a commercial bank, Imperial Bank also discharged the functions of a central bank until the establishment of the RBI in 1935 via the Reserve Bank of India Act, 1934. The RBI was assigned four functions: act as a banker to the government; issue notes; act as a banker to other banks; and maintain the exchange rate. In its role as banker to other banks, the RBI also became the lender of the last resort.

In its early years, the RBI lacked adequate powers of control and regulation. The Companies Act, 1913, which governed ordinary non-banking companies, also governed banks. New banks could be set up under this law without the permission of the RBI. In this environment of virtual free entry and exit of banks and no real regulation, small banks mushroomed. At the same time, banks also remained subject to a high rate of bankruptcy. The Companies (Amendment) Act, 1936, introduced a separate chapter on banking companies and specified norms with respect to minimum capital and cash reserve requirement but the provisions fell far short of creating an adequate regulatory regime. It was not until the Banking Companies Act, 1949, which was renamed the Banking Regulation Act in March 1966, that the RBI acquired comprehensive powers of supervision and control of the banking system.

Wartime expenditure on defence and supplies led to rapid expansion of currency. This correspondingly increased incomes of some sections of the population. With supplies of consumption goods including through imports restricted, however, unspent margins expanded and created a large pool of bank deposits. In turn, this led to a rapid expansion of bank branches of scheduled commercial banks between 1940 and 1945. Several banks spread out thin and the risk of failure increased. Luckily, with the sector highly fragmented and interbank linkages missing, failures remained localized with no contagion effect.

Early Post-Independence Phase: 1947–1967

At the time of Independence, Indian banks were entirely in the private sector. Even the RBI was not fully state-owned until its nationalization via the Reserve Bank of India (Transfer to Public Ownership) Act, 1948. The Imperial Bank of India was the largest commercial bank. There were five other large banks with deposits of one billion rupees each: Central Bank of India, Punjab National Bank, Bank of India, Bank of Baroda and United Commercial Bank.

Scheduled commercial banks, numbering ninety-seven, dominated the baking system at the end of December 1947. Non-scheduled banks and cooperative banks, though large in number at 557 and 395, respectively, jointly accounted for only 13.6 per cent of the total deposits.[66] Scheduled banks had a regional focus, with West Bengal

66 Reserve Bank of India, 2008, Table 3.10, p.85. An urban cooperative credit movement had begun in the State of Baroda in the late 19th century.

having the largest concentration of them, followed by Madras and Bombay. Regarding the concentration of non-scheduled banks, Madras led by a wide margin with West Bengal and Bombay claiming distant second and third positions, respectively.[67]

The era immediately after Independence saw an acceleration in bankruptcies of banks. This was in part due to disruptions resulting from the Partition. The western and eastern parts of the country, which had been impacted heavily by Partition, also witnessed a larger incidence of bankruptcies. To address the problem and protect the interests of depositors, the government passed the Banking Companies Act, 1949—renamed the Banking Regulation Act in March 1966—giving the RBI wide powers to regulate banks. This helped slow down bank failures but did not eliminate them. Therefore, efforts were made to force mergers or liquidation of weaker banks. A total of eighty-three banks were merged with other banks between 1954 and 1960. This process accelerated after the enactment of the Banking Companies (Amendment) Act, 1961, which gave clarity to and supplemented the provisions of compulsory merger of banks in the original legislation. Between 1960 and 1966, 217 banks were merged with other banks. The total number of non-scheduled banks fell from 474 in 1951 to 210 in 1961 and just twenty in 1967.

While consolidating banks, India also made it a high priority to use the sector as an instrument of mobilizing savings for economic development. On the one hand, this required the expansion of bank branches, including in rural areas and smaller towns, and on the other, improving the flow of credit to agriculture, which employed 70 per cent of India's workforce. According to the All India Rural

---

Recognition of the need for the provision of rural credit led to the spread of the movement in rural India as well. As a result, by Independence, a large number of cooperative banks had come to exist in India.

67 Source: https://www.rbi.org.in/scripts/publicationsview.aspx?id=10487 (last accessed on 15 January 2020)

Credit Survey (AIRCS) Committee, which submitted its report in 1954, commercial banks provided only 0.9 per cent of the total credit of ₹7.5 billion to farmers in 1951–52. Therefore, the committee recommended proactive measures to increase the flow of bank credit to agriculture.

A key specific recommendation of the AIRCS Committee was the nationalization of the Imperial Bank of India and merger of the former state-owned and state-associated banks with it. Accordingly, an act was passed in May 1955, which led to the constitution of the State Bank of India in July 1955. More than a quarter of the resources of the banking system came into the public sector as a result. In 1959, another act led to the takeover of eight former state-associated banks as subsidiaries of the SBI. This brought nearly one-third of the banking resources into the public sector. To maintain an arm's length relationship between the government and the SBI, the ownership of the latter was given to the RBI. This step was also seen as helpful in preserving the original corporate character of the Imperial Bank of India under its new name.

At the direction of the RBI, the SBI speeded up branch expansion in general and in rural areas in particular. Other commercial banks also expanded their network, though their focus remained largely on urban India. Between 1952 and 1967, rural branches expanded from 540 to 1,247, semi-urban branches from 1,942 to 3,022 and urban branches from 1,451 to 2,716. Advances to agriculture rose from ₹120 million in 1951 to ₹570 million in 1967, but this amounted to only a marginal increase in its share in the total bank credit from 2.1 to 2.2 per cent over the period. In 1967, industry had the largest share in total advances at 64.3 per cent, followed by commerce at 19.4 per cent.

By 1967, two key concerns with the banking sector occupied the attention of policymakers. First, through ownership of banks, a handful of business families managed to concentrate bank deposits in their hands. These families loaned the funds to their own or each other's industrial arms. Second, as far as bank credit was concerned, agriculture remained neglected. Its share in total bank credit remained minuscule.

In the early years, this situation may well have resulted from the priority that Prime Minister Jawaharlal Nehru gave to industry, especially heavy industry. But after Nehru died in 1964 and his successor, Prime Minister Lal Bahadur Shastri, shifted the focus of policy to agriculture, the concern with the low share of agriculture in bank credit became more acute. Under Prime Minister Indira Gandhi, Indian socialism turned far more aggressive and populist, with industrialists becoming its direct target. The concern that the nexus between banks and industrial houses had led the latter to hog the bulk of the credit with agriculture and small enterprises left bereft of financial resources assumed centre stage.

Social Control and Nationalization: 1967–1991

From 1967–69, the government tried to address these concerns through social control of banks. The government amended the Banking Companies Act, 1949, which had been renamed as the Banking Regulation Act in 1966, to require commercial banks to induct members in their boards with special knowledge of accountancy, agriculture and rural economy, banking cooperation, economics and small-scale industry. The amendment also required the banks to appoint a whole-time chairman who was a professional banker and not an industrialist. Furthermore, it gave the RBI the power to appoint and remove the chairman, any director, chief executive officer or any other officer or employee of the bank. It was understood that in exercising these powers, the RBI would keep in view not just the interests of the banks and depositors but also the larger public interest. A key component of public interest in this context was to make banks a more effective instrument of development via faster expansion of bank branches in unbanked areas and channelling of credit to priority sectors such as agriculture and small-scale industries.

Before social control had the opportunity to prove its worth, however, political considerations led Indira Gandhi to nationalize all fourteen banks that had deposits worth ₹500 million or more in July 1969.[68] With the SBI already nationalized, this action gave the government the ownership and control of more than 90 per cent of banking assets and deposits. In due course, deposits of another six private banks grew to ₹500 million or more. On the recommendation of the RBI governor, Gandhi nationalized them as well in 1980. Therefore, beginning in 1969 until 1991, when the Licence-Permit Raj finally gave way to more liberal policies, the government remained in firm control of the banking sector.

This control in turn allowed the government to freely employ the country's banking resources to promote the twin goals of expanding the banking network to rural and semi-rural areas and diverting credit flow to priority sectors, which were considered underfinanced. In the early years following nationalization, the government used the Lead Bank Scheme (LBS) to expand the branch network. Under it, a 'lead bank' was designated for each district and given responsibility to provide leadership for the expansion of banking infrastructure in that district. The programme was effective in expanding the branch network by 129 per cent between 1969 and 1975. Half of the new branches opened during this period were in rural areas. As a result, the share of rural branches in the total number of branches increased from 17.6 per cent in 1969 to 36.3 per cent in 1975.

In 1977, the government introduced a branch licence policy under which banks were allowed to open one branch each in metropolitan and urban areas for every four branches opened in rural areas. To ensure that branch expansion also resulted in the expansion of credit, rural and semi-urban branches were directed to maintain a 60 per cent credit-deposit ratio at the minimum. Bank branch expansion as

---

68 I have discussed the political circumstances leading to nationalization in greater detail in my book, *India: The Emerging Giant* (2008), Chapter 3.

well as correction to the urban bias continued during the 1980s. By 1990, rural branches came to account for 58.2 per cent of the total bank branches. Semi-urban branches accounted for an additional 19 per cent of all branches. But this indiscriminate expansion of branches proved costly. Many of them could not be sustained on a commercial basis. In 1990, the government decided to discontinue its bank branch expansion programme.

The second major initiative of the government was to reorient credit in favour of what it considered to be priority sectors. The government had been making efforts to raise the share of agriculture in credit through the instrumentality of the State Bank of India and its subsidiaries. The nationalization of another fourteen of the largest banks imparted the government the ability to intensify those efforts. In 1972, it went on to adopt a formal definition of the priority sector and, in November 1974, directed all public sector banks to raise the proportion of priority sector credit in total outstanding credit to one-third by March 1979. In November 1978, it also directed private sector banks to reach the same target by March 1980. Both sets of banks achieved the target by the assigned dates. Subsequently, the target was raised to 40 per cent of outstanding credit, which too was achieved.

These efforts led to a decline in the share of formal industry in total credit from 67.5 per cent at the end of 1967–68 to 38.9 per cent at the end of 1979–80 and 37.5 per cent at the end of 1988–89. The share of agriculture rose from 2.2 per cent at the end of 1967–68 to 15.8 per cent at the end of 1988–89. Exports and small-scale industry came to account for 22.6 per cent of the credit by the end of 1988–89.

From the mid-1960s onward, India practised extensive credit controls. Interest rates were controlled and varied by sector as well as the size of the borrower. Credit was rationed so that not everyone wishing to borrow could do so, or borrow in the quantity she wanted to. At a broad level, priority sector lending was at subsidized rates, which resulted in an effective tax on the rates charged to non-priority sector lending. Within each of priority and non-priority sectors, multiple rates prevailed. Under the Credit Allocation Scheme, approval of loans of value exceeding a relatively low threshold by the RBI was mandatory. The government offered low interest rates on its debt. These low rates were sustained by a high SLR that banks were required to maintain. Empirical estimates suggest that the low rates on government debt resulted in very substantial financial repression.[69]

Finally, nationalization of banks gave depositors a certain degree of confidence in the security of bank deposits. This fact helped shift household savings from the physical to the financial sector. As incomes rose, overall household savings comprising physical and financial savings rose as well. The result was a rise in financially intermediated household savings as a proportion of the GDP. They rose from 3 per cent in 1970–71 to 5.9 per cent in 1980–81 and to 8.7 per cent in 1990–91.

69 Kletzer, 2005

10

TRANSFORMING HIGHER EDUCATION

A SOUND HIGHER EDUCATION system, capable of providing not just up-to-date education in all fields but also producing scholars who compete internationally with the best in their domains, is essential for any country aspiring to become a leading economic power. Good educational and health outcomes depend on the availability of good teachers and doctors, respectively. Delivery of justice, likewise, depends on the availability of good lawyers and judges. Industrial and technological development requires the availability of first-rate engineers, managers and technology experts. In sum, to build a nation, one must create excellent institutions of higher education.

Apart from meeting the challenge of creating a human capital base essential to sustaining rapid growth, the higher education system in a country must grapple with a variety of issues including access, equity, efficiency, quality, financing and public-versus-private provision. In this chapter, I do not propose to offer an exhaustive treatment of all these issues. Instead, my main focus is on how best to replace the current archaic regulatory regime introduced more than sixty years ago via the University Grants Commission (UGC) Act, 1956, with a more modern one that is consistent with a market economy and suits contemporary India. In addition, I offer a roadmap for how best to speed up the quality of higher education and research.

I begin by giving some historical background on higher education in India along the quantity and quality dimensions. While doing so, I assess the progress made by the country against that made by China, a country that is marginally larger in terms of population and that started out equally poor in the 1950s. The Chinese experience is helpful in understanding what is feasible for India in the forthcoming decades.

The Quantity Dimension: Healthy Expansion

India has made accelerated progress in expanding higher education in the post-reforms era, especially during the current century. Accelerated growth has yielded larger public revenues as well as rising private incomes and investment resources. The former have allowed the government to invest larger volumes of resources in higher education while the latter have brought private players into the sector. Private higher education institutions (HEIs), especially colleges, and student enrolments in them have been the fastest-growing segment of higher education.

Table 10.1 shows the total number of universities, colleges and students for a few selected years. During the first fifty years between 1950/51 and 2000/01, India added 227 universities, 9,574 colleges and 8.2 million students. The corresponding additions during just sixteen years of the current century have been 610 universities, 29,874 colleges and 27.1 million students. In absolute terms, the accomplishment during the first sixteen years of the 21st century has been three times that during the preceding fifty years.

Table 10.1: Number of Recognized Educational Institutions and Enrolment in Them

Year	Universities (Number of)	Colleges (Number of)	Students (Million)
1950/51	27	578	0.4
1980/81	110	6963	4.8
2000/01	254	10,152	8.6
2016/17	864	40,026	35.7

Source: Ministry of Human Resource Development, 2016 and 2017

The progress India has made in expanding the absolute number of enrolments in higher education since 2000/01 broadly matches that of China. The latter saw its enrolments rise from 5.9 million in 2000 to 37 million in 2016. Indeed, when we consider that this growth in enrolments in China took place at substantially higher income levels, India's performance looks even more impressive.

The increase in enrolments in India has taken place against a demographic transition of the college-age population that is very different from the one in China. As a result, the Gross Enrolment Ratio (GER), which measures the gross enrolment in higher education as a percentage of the total college-age population, defined as the age group spanning eighteen to twenty-three years, has evolved very differently during the relevant period in the two countries. In India, the GER rose from 8.1 per cent in 2000/01 to 25.2 per cent in 2016/17. For approximately similar absolute enrolments in China, it rose from 12.5 per cent in 2000 to 42.7 per cent in 2016. Because of the smaller and rapidly decreasing population in the age group eighteen to twenty-three years, the GER in China has been higher and risen faster.[70]

Table 10.2: Public and Private Institutions and Enrolments in Them

Institution Type	**2000/01**	**2016/17**
Universities (Number)		
Public	245	522
Private	31	330
Colleges (Number)		
Public	4097	8177
Private	8199	28675
Enrolment: University plus college (Million)		
Public	3.44	14.2
Private	4.95	19.3

Source: Agarwal, 2006, Table A3 for 2000/01 and Ministry of Human Resource Development, 2017, for 2016/17.[71]

Note: Private institutions include government-aided but privately managed colleges and universities

70 Enrolments and GER data in China other than those for the year 2016 are from Li and Yang, 2014, Figure 1.2. The data for 2016 is from a newspaper report http://en.people.cn/n3/2017/0711/c90000-9240278.html, which in turn attributes it to a communiqué by the Ministry of Education, China.

71 For 2016/17, estimates come from different tables in Ministry of Human Resource Development 2017. Specifically, the figures for universities is from the table on p. 39; for colleges from Table 5 on p. T-5; for college enrolments from Table 5(a) on p. T-5; and for university enrolments from Table 27 on p. T-27.

The private sector has been crucial to the expansion of higher education in India. Table 10.2 provides the division between public and private sectors in terms of universities, colleges and enrolments. Perhaps the most dramatic figure in this table is the large number of private (including government-aided but privately managed) colleges in 2016/17. These colleges have expanded more than threefold since 2000/01 and now stand at more than three times the number of public colleges. This means that undergraduate education has progressively moved to the private sector in India. This movement has been especially pronounced in technical fields such as engineering and medicine.[72] At the university level, the public sector continues to dominate, despite a substantial growth in the number of private universities. More disaggregated enrolment data (not shown in Table 10.2) reveals that during 2016/17, enrolment in public universities stood at 5.6 million as opposed to only 1.5 million in private universities. Therefore, university education remains concentrated in the public sector.

The Quality Dimension: Some Progress but a Long Way to Go

Even as India is winning the battle of bringing higher education to the doorstep of a large and increasing proportion of its youth, it is failing along the quality dimension. Colleges and universities are falling well short of providing up-to-date and quality education to students. Relative to comparable countries, scholars from India are performing poorly on the research and innovation fronts.

It may be stated at the outset that the decline in quality is to be interpreted in the relative sense. India has not been able to move as fast as other countries in producing quality education and research. As

72 See Kapur and Mehta, 2008

far as the absolute output, either in terms of the number of graduates or the number of research papers and patents of a given quality is concerned, the country has been making steady progress.

Rapid growth during the current century has led to a rapid rise in the demand for qualified engineers and managers. Had the economy failed to generate their supply in adequate numbers, the potential for high growth could not have translated into actual growth. In a similar vein, the momentum in the start-up space in India and the continued growth in information technology offer evidence that the supply of skilled personnel has largely kept up with demand and that the current talent pool is substantially larger in absolute terms than its size even ten years ago.

The number of articles published in leading science and engineering journals provide objective evidence of the progress India has made in absolute terms. The National Science Foundation (NSF) has compiled country-by-country data on the number of journal articles published in the fields of physics, biology, chemistry, mathematics, clinical medicine, biomedical research, engineering and technology, and earth and space sciences beginning with the year 2003. Currently, this series is available till 2016. In 2003, India ranked eleventh. Remarkably, by 2016, India had climbed up to outrank eight out of the ten countries it trailed in 2003. As Figure 10.1 shows, in terms of the absolute number of scientific and engineering articles published in leading journals, India now stands ahead of such countries as Japan, Germany and the United Kingdom. Only the United States and China remain ahead of India.

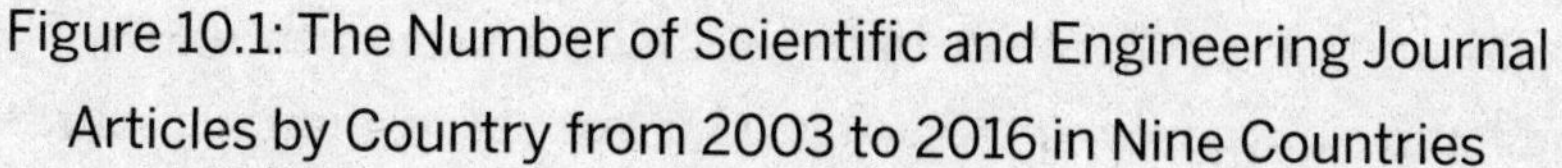

Figure 10.1: The Number of Scientific and Engineering Journal Articles by Country from 2003 to 2016 in Nine Countries

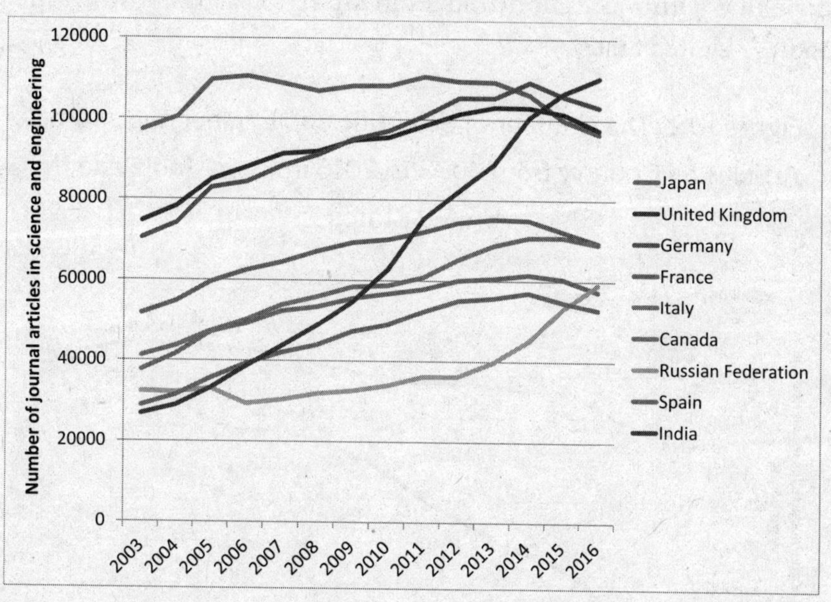

Source: WDI online series 'Scientific and Technical Journal Articles', attributed to the National Science Foundation (last accessed on 3 June 2018).

Figure 10.1 shows the clear progress that India has made in catching up with some of the comparable countries. Yet, its achievements remain well below what its size would demand. India is sixteen times the size of Germany in terms of population, the country right below it in 2016. Even Russia, the largest among the comparator countries shown in Figure 10.1, is one-ninth the size of India. The point is brought home by Figure 10.2, which shows the United States, China and India on a common graph. In 2003, papers published by authors in China stood at 27 per cent of those by authors in the United States. By 2016, China had outdone the United States. India too has made progress relative to the United States. Papers by it as a proportion of those by the United States rose from 8.3 per cent in 2003 to 27 per cent in 2016. But this progress fades in comparison to China. The proportionate gap between India and China bottomed out in 2009 and has been recovering thereafter. This last observation is a source of hope that with more effort, India can aspire to catch up with China and the United States.

Figure 10.2: The Number of Scientific and Engineering Journal Articles by Country from 2003 to 2016 in China, India and the United States

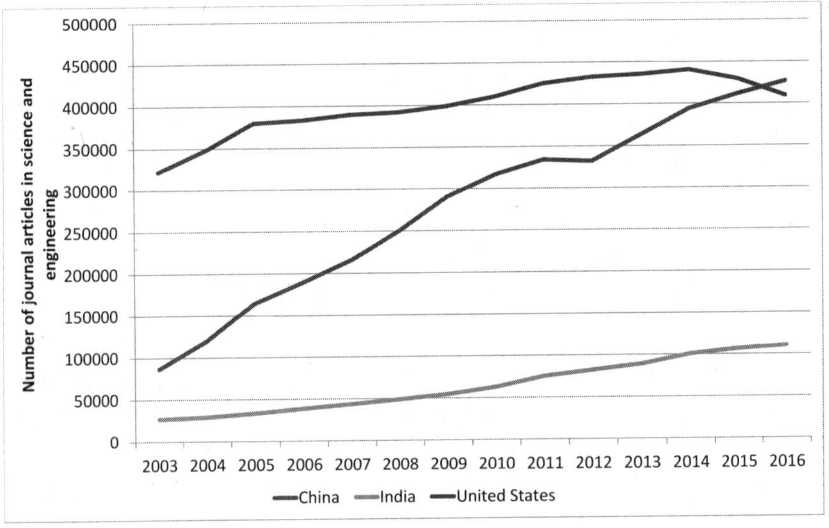

Source: WDI online series 'Scientific and Technical Journal Articles' (attributed to the National Science Foundation; last accessed on 3 June 2018).

With 21,950 peer-reviewed journals as of August 2017, the Scopus database provides the most comprehensive view of the world's research output in the fields of science, technology, medicine, social science and arts and humanities. The starting date of the database is 1996 and it is updated annually. Among other things, it allows us to rank countries by not just the number of journal articles but also by citations, with and without self-citations. Citations, especially those excluding self-citations, are an important measure of the visibility of an author's research papers.

Table 10.3 provides the rankings of India and China in 1996 and 2017 by the total number of articles in journals in the Scopus database, the total citations and citations excluding self-citations. The picture that emerges is further discouraging. Although India has gone from the thirteenth to the fifth position between 1996 and 2017 when ranked by the total number of papers, improvement is only from sixteenth to eleventh, based on total citations, and from nineteenth to fourteenth, based on citations excluding self-citations. In 1996, India had ranked higher than China based on the total citations and citations excluding self-citations. But by 2017, China had not only surpassed India but also achieved the second and third ranks, based on the two criteria respectively.

Table 10.3: Rankings Based on the Scopus Database According to Articles in All Subject Areas

Criterion	India		China	
	1996	**2017**	**1996**	**2017**
All Subject Areas				
Total Papers Published	13	5	9	2
Total Citations	16	11	19	2
Total Citations Excluding Self-citations	19	14	21	3

Source: Author's compilation based on Scopus database at https://www.scimagojr.com/countryrank.php?order=it&ord=desc (last accessed on 7 June 2018)

The Scopus database also allows us to rank countries by subject areas. Such rankings help us identify areas of strength and weakness. Accordingly, Table 10.4 shows the rankings of India and China in the years 1996 and 2017 according to total citations in some key subject areas. India does reasonably well in physics, chemistry, mathematics, engineering and business, and management and accounting. But it does poorly in agricultural and biological sciences; arts and humanities; biochemistry, genetics and molecular biology; medicine; and social sciences. In the majority of these areas, the progress between 1996 and 2017 has also been minimal.

Table 10.4: Rankings Based on the Total Number of Citations in Different Subject Areas

	India		**China**	
Subject Area	**1996**	**2017**	**1996**	**2017**
All Subject Areas	16	11	19	2
Agriculture and Biological Sciences	17	14	22	2
Arts and Humanities	28	25	15	6
Biochemistry, Genetics and Molecular Biology	17	14	20	2
Business, Management and Accounting	22	10	27	3
Chemistry	11	5	13	1
Engineering	14	4	10	1
Mathematics	20	7	11	1
Medicine	19	17	23	3
Physics and Astronomy	17	8	13	2
Social Sciences	21	14	24	5

Source: Author's compilation based on the Scopus database at https://www.scimagojr.com/countryrank.php?order=it&ord=desc (last accessed on 7 June 2018)

In contrast to India, China has made impressive progress across all subject areas. Even in arts and humanities, where it ranked a low twenty-eight in 1996, it has moved up to the sixth rank in 2017, a solid nineteen ranks ahead of India. In social sciences, it rose from the twenty-fourth position in 1996 to the fifth position in 2017. In chemistry, engineering and mathematics, it now ranks first in terms of the total number of citations.

The superior progress achieved by China is reflected in the international rankings of HEIs. This is shown in Table 10.5, which reports the latest available HEI rankings from three commonly used sources: QS, Times Higher Education (THE) and Shanghai. China has seven institutions in the top 200 according to QS rankings, four according to THE rankings and ten according to Shanghai rankings. India has only three institutions in the top 200 according to QS rankings and none according to the remaining two rankings. None of the Indian institutions in the top 200 in QS rankings makes it to the top 100.

Table 10.5: Number of Universities from India and China in International Rankings

Country	**Top 100**	**101–200**	**201–600**	**601–1000**	**Total**
QS 2018					
China	4	3	24	9	40
India	0	3	6	11	20
THE 2018					
China	2	2	19	31	54
India	0	0	6	24	30
Shanghai 2017					
China	2	8	49	33	92
India	0	0	1	6	7

Source: Author's construction from the rankings available online

Taken as a whole, this evidence carries both good and bad news for India. The bad news is that while India has made substantial progress in expanding enrolments in higher education, it has achieved minimal progress along the quality dimension. The good news is twofold. One, even without focused effort, rising enrolments have led to progress along the quality dimension, especially in the areas of science and engineering. And two, the experience of China shows that with focused effort, India can achieve substantial improvements along the quality dimension in the next two decades.

There are two key areas on which India needs to focus. First, the existing regulatory regime under the auspices of the UGC Act, 1956, though suitable for the India of the 1950s, has been stifling competition among institutions at all levels today. India must learn from the experience of the successful countries and replace the current UGC regime with a more pro-competitive regulatory regime. Second, India must enhance and redirect its investments in research to improve quality while also promoting greater cooperation among the HEI, industry and the government.

International Experience

By all measures, during the last several decades, the United States and the United Kingdom have had the best universities. The United States has been the home to the largest number of top-ranking universities in the world. In terms of historical ties and governance, the Indian higher education system has the greatest affinity to the system in the United Kingdom. Finally, China is a developing country with a large population that has made the greatest progress in higher education during the past two decades. Keeping these factors in view, the regulatory experiences of the three countries can offer useful lessons for India. Accordingly, in the following sections, I review their experiences in higher education with special reference to governance.

The United States

In the United States, degree-giving institutions are classified into three categories by control: public, private non-profit and private for profit. In the academic year 2013–14, the country had 3,039 four-year-degree granting institutions.[73] In the fall of 2015, of the 13.5 million students enrolled in four-year-degree institutions, 62 per cent were in public institutions, 30 per cent in private non-profit and 8 per cent in private for-profit institutions.[74]

The sources of revenue

The sources of revenue of the three types of institutions vary considerably. As Figure 10.3 shows, tuition fees are the single largest source of revenue for private institutions, both non-profit and for-profit. For the latter, tuition fees contribute as much as 90 per cent of their total revenue. Private non-profit institutions raise a large part of their revenue from gifts and private grants and contracts, which are included in 'all other revenue'. Public institutions depend most heavily on federal, state and local government grants, though even they raise one-fifth of their total revenue from tuition. Tuition fees are generally significantly lower in public than in private institutions. Private non-profit institutions charge the highest tuition fees, on an average.[75]

---

73 See https://nces.ed.gov/fastfacts/display.asp?id=84 (last accessed on 8 June 2018). In addition to four-year-degree institutions, the United States had 1,685 two-year colleges in the academic year 2013–14.

74 See https://nces.ed.gov/programs/digest/d16/tables/dt16_301.10.asp (last accessed on 8 June 2018).

75 See Figure 2 in https://nces.ed.gov/programs/coe/indicator_cud.asp (accessed on 8 June 2018).

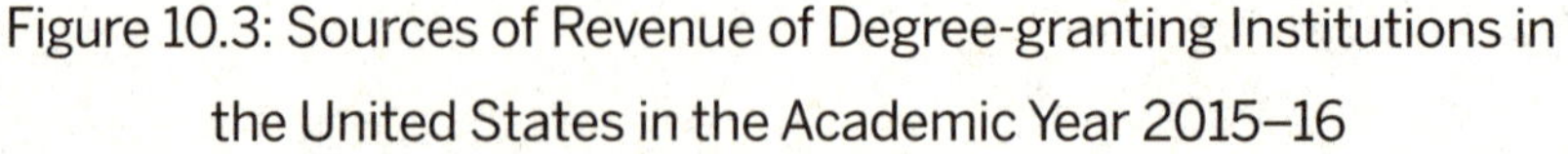

Figure 10.3: Sources of Revenue of Degree-granting Institutions in the United States in the Academic Year 2015–16

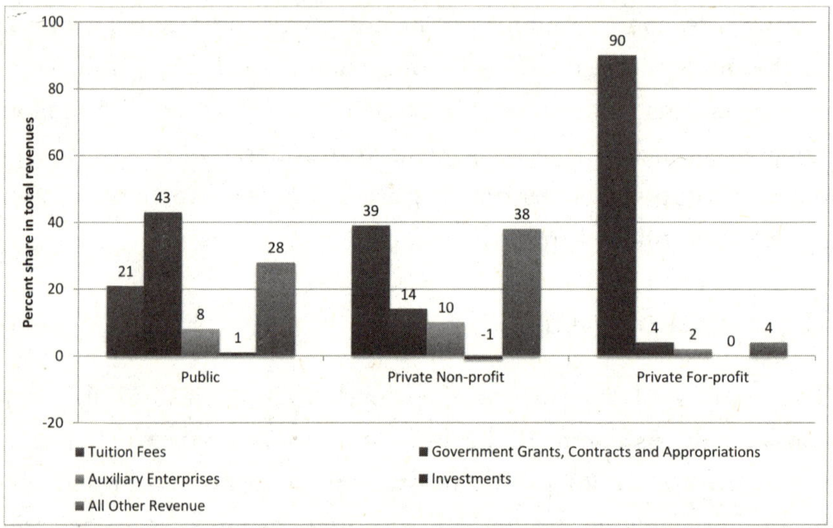

Note: 'All other revenue' includes gifts, capital or private grants and contracts, hospital revenue, sales and services of educational activities, and other revenue. Auxiliary enterprises include campus housing, dining services, on-campus bookstores and vending machines, parking and transportation services and on-campus hotels.

Source: https://nces.ed.gov/programs/coe/indicator_cud.asp (last accessed on 8 June 2018).

Governance

The United States higher education system is highly decentralized. A university or college, once established, is independent of federal- or state-government regulation. To start an HEI, all that is required is a degree-granting licence from the state in which the HEI is to be located. The level of difficulty of obtaining the licence varies by state. The most liberal states such as Virginia, Colorado and Wyoming do not require even a site visit. At the other extreme, in states such as Maine, inspectors visit the campus, other university presidents must be informed and a state legislator must introduce a bill for grant of the licence.

Public as well as private institutions are typically chartered as corporations in the United States. They are governed by boards of trustees, appointed by a state governor or state legislature in the case of public institutions and elected by the board itself in the case of private institutions. The institutions can have single or multiple campuses. In some cases, they can also be systems comprising several independent institutions, as is the case with the University of California system. All institutions are autonomous with respect to administrative and academic decision-making.

Universities are also decentralized in terms of course offerings. Each department decides its course offerings and teaching assignments to the teaching staff. As long as the academic department can muster resources, it can start new courses, with the design of the course normally left to the assigned faculty member. Indeed, with individual faculty members giving their own separate examinations for the purpose of grading their students, even the contents of the same course taught in two or more sections by different faculty members during the same semester may differ.

A key instrument for promoting excellence in teaching is the evaluation of the instructor by students. At the end of each course, students at most institutions routinely fill an evaluation form answering questions relating to the design of the course, assigned readings, classroom lectures and overall performance of the professor. Students may also offer additional written comments on the course.

Secret of success

The success of HEIs in the United States should be attributed to two key factors: availability of sufficient research and development

(R&D) funds and competition. Historically, the federal government has played a key role in funding university-based R&D. In the late 1960s, its share in the total R&D expenditures of HEIs had reached 73 per cent.[76] The share has subsequently declined, dropping to 54 per cent in 2016. Alongside, industry and especially university shares have risen. In 2016, industry and university shares in the R&D expenditure of HEIs stood at 5.9 per cent and 25 per cent, respectively. The total R&D expenditure has seen steady increases with the amount in constant 2017 dollars rising from $27.8 billion in 1990 to $73.3 billion in 2016. Figure 10.4 depicts the evolution of R&D expenditures of HEIs from 1990 to 2016.

Figure 10.4: University Science and Engineering R&D Funding in the United States by Source, 1990–2016

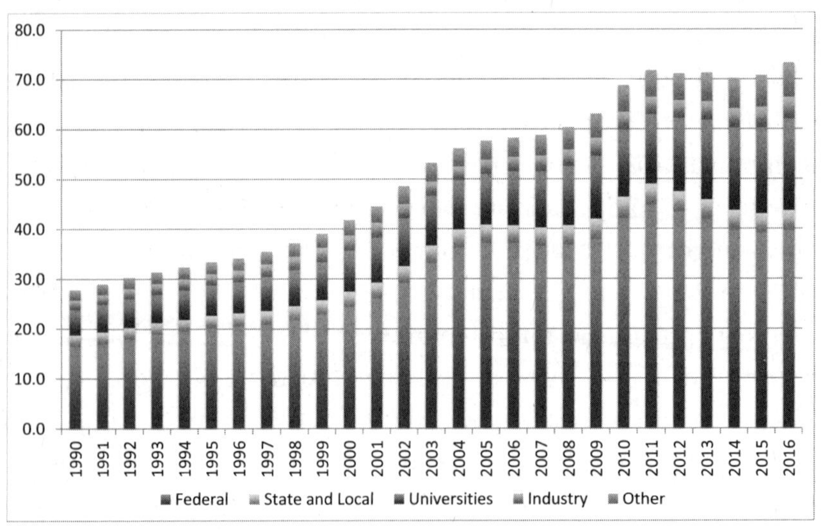

Source: National Science Foundation, Higher Education R&D survey data series, available at http://www.nsf.gov/statistics/herd/

76 See https://www.aaas.org/page/rd-colleges-and-universities (last accessed on 9 June 2018).

The second important factor behind the success of HEIs in the United States has been competition for excellence across all dimensions. Universities compete for the best students, best faculty and research funds. Faculty salaries are set competitively, with individual faculty rewarded for their higher productivity. Faculty salaries differ not just across different academic departments but also within the same department, depending on productivity and what the market forces dictate. Universities try to build up their faculty by hiring the best faculty from other institutions, so that each institution has to respond to the bids for their best faculty by offering matching emoluments. In this system, individual faculty members earn their respect through publications in prestigious journals and their visibility is reflected in the offers they receive from peer institutions. Even within the same academic department of a university, salaries reflect their relative standing. In a similar fashion, universities also compete for the best students. In addition to offering fellowships to the best students, members of the faculty personally reach out to them to woo them to their universities.

China

Western-style HEIs in China, which began in the late 19th century, first followed the Japanese and then the American model. Beginning in 1949, the higher education system switched to the Soviet model. The system did well for sixteen years but then came the Cultural Revolution, which turned HEIs into battlegrounds and administered a near-fatal blow to them. It was only after Mao Zedong died and Deng Xiaoping came to the helm that higher education had a revival.

Empowering of HEIs: The Higher Education Law, 1998

The Higher Education Law, 1998, governs the current Chinese higher education system.[77] While this is a central law and vests the authority to permit the opening of new universities and provide overall guidance to HEIs in the central government, it is operationally very liberal. It decentralizes the higher education system in a manner similar to that in the United States.

The State Council formulates the specific standards for the establishment of new institutions. Applications may be made to the Department of Education Administration under the States' Council with a report on the proposed institution, feasibility report, articles of association and other prescribed material. The Department of Education Administration then examines the application and takes a decision.

Article 32 of the 1998 law calls upon the HEIs to 'work out schemes for admission and independently regulate the percentage of admission for departments and disciplines'. Article 33 gives them independence to 'set up and adjust disciplines and specialties'. Articles 34 empowers them to 'work out teaching plans, select and compile textbooks and organize activities of imparting teaching in accordance with the requirements of teaching'. Article 36 authorizes the institutions to 'independently carry out scientific, technological and cultural exchanges and cooperation with foreign institutions of higher learning in accordance with the relevant provisions of the state'. Article 37 imparts administrative freedom to the institutions, stating that they 'independently decide on the setting up and personnel employment of such internal organizational structures as teaching, scientific research and administrative functional departments in the light of actual requirements'. Finally, Article 41 fixes the responsibility of outcomes on the president of the institution, while also conferring on him wide-ranging powers:

---

77 The text of the law can be found at http://www.asianlii.org/cn/legis/cen/laws/helotproc422/ (last accessed on 24 January 2020)

The president of an institution of higher learning shall be fully responsible for the teaching, scientific research and other administrative work of the respective institution and exercise the following duties and powers:

(1) to draft development planning, formulate specific rules and regulations and annual work plan and organize their implementation

(2) to organize teaching activities, scientific research and ideological and moral education

(3) to draft schemes for the setting up of internal organizations, recommend candidates for vice presidency, appoint and relieve persons in charge of internal organizations

(4) to employ and dismiss teachers and other internal workers, administer students' school roll and give rewards or impose penalties

(5) to draft and implement annual fund budget proposal, protect and manage school properties and safeguard the legitimate rights and interests of the school and

(6) other duties and powers provided for in the articles of association.

Tuition fee a major source of revenue

Article 54 of the Higher Education Law explicitly recognizes the right of the HEI to charge tuition fees. It states, 'Students of institutions of higher learning should pay a tuition fee in accordance with state provisions.' Students whose families face financial hardship 'may apply for subsidy or reduction and exemption of the tuition fee'. Giving the institutions considerable freedom to charge tuition fees has been an important step towards placing them on a firm footing as far as finances are concerned. A modest fee of RMB 100 for accommodation and RMB 20 for tuition was first introduced in 1989. Subsequently, the tuition fees at public institutions rose rapidly to RMB 600 in 1992, RMB 4,000 in 1999, RMB 5,000 in 2001 and RMB 6,000 in 2005. By the mid-2000s, some private universities came to charge fees as high RMB 10,000. In 2003, higher education fees amounted to

RMB 40 billion, in comparison to the national expenditure on higher education of RMB 70 billion.[78]

Promoting excellence: Projects 211 and 985

Although the higher education law in China leaves academic and administrative decisions to the HEIs, the Chinese government has actively intervened with substantial financial resources to foster quality improvements. This has been done through two major programmes called Project 211 and Project 985.[79] The former was intended to help the top universities improve teaching, research and infrastructure and the latter to turn some top universities into world-class institutions.

Initiated in 1995, Project 211 derived its name from the slogan, 'For the 21st century, to manage one hundred universities successfully.' The project allocated RMB 36.8 billion ($4.6 billion) across 107 universities between 1995 and 2005. Of this amount, RMB 16.5 billion was spent on developing some key disciplines, RMB 7.1 billion on the establishment of a system of public service, RMB 2.4 billion on strengthening teaching staff and RMB 10.8 billion on infrastructure.[80] Engineering and new technology, social sciences and humanities, medical and health, environmental sciences and agriculture and basic research were the key disciplines the project supported.[81]

Project 985 was so called because it was launched in May 1998. Its objective was to create a number of world-class universities and all universities under this programme were drawn from Project 211. The project provided for (i) reforming and improving administrative and operational mechanisms in universities; (ii) recruiting leading scholars inside or outside China to establish strong research teams;

---

78 Li and Yang, 2014, pp. 13-14

79 Two additional, less prominent interventions are the 863 Project and 973 Project.

80 Zhang, Patton and Kenney, 2013, p. 767, footnote 8

81 Li, 2010

(iii) establishing a Science and Technology Innovation Platform and a Social Sciences Research Base in the selected universities; and (iv) improving university infrastructure and supporting international collaborations.

Different universities entered Project 985 on different dates and received different levels of funding.[82] The top two universities, Peking and Tsinghua, were the first to enter the programme and received a whopping RMB 1.8 billion ($240 million) each during the first three years. Seven other universities, with much reduced funding, were added to the list in 1999. By 2003, the number of covered institutions had risen to thirty-four.[83] During Phase I, spanning 1999 to 2003, special funding by the central government to these thirty-four universities amounted to RMB 14 billion. During Phase II, spanning 2004–2007, funding was RMB 18.9 billion and covered thirty-nine universities.[84] Provincial governments provided additional funds. In 2011, the entry of new universities into both Projects 211 and 985 was closed.

The United Kingdom

In the academic year 2016/17, the United Kingdom had 162 HEIs, which received public funding via one of the UK funding councils and returned data to the Higher Education Statistical Agency. In addition, there were nine privately owned institutions, which did not receive funding for teaching and research from the government. In 2016/17, a total of 2.32 million students were studying at UK higher education institutions. The GER in UK in higher education in 2015 stood at 57 per cent. The Higher Education and Research Act 2017 has brought about important changes in the governance of the higher education

82 Li, 2010, pp. 278–79

83 See Li and Yang, 2014, p. 17, footnote 2

84 See Zhang, Patton and Kenney, 2013

system. In the following, I first describe the system as it has functioned until 2016/17 and then describe the latest reform.

Governance of institutions and degree-granting power

The HEI in the United Kingdom are independent and autonomous legal entities with councils or governing bodies managing them. Individual institutions are fully free to appoint their own academic and administrative staff. They also determine their own entry requirements and admission procedures.

The power to award degrees in the UK is regulated by law and is granted by a royal charter (mostly before 1993) or by an Act of Parliament. The Higher Education Act, 1992, empowered the Privy Council to grant HEIs powers to award their own degrees.

Funding for education

The UK government funds the institutions but it neither owns nor governs them. Government funding has been managed at arm's length through independent funding councils.[85] Funding councils attach conditions to the grants, requiring the institutions to use the funds as per the law, undertake quality assessments of education and research and meet the specified governance standard.

During the decades immediately following the Second World War, undergraduate education for UK students was free. But rapid expansion of education during the 1980s and 1990s resulted in declining expenditure per student, with universities finding it difficult to maintain the quality of teaching. This situation led the government to introduce tuition fees for undergraduate students beginning in 1997. The initial fee cap was set at £1,000, which was revised to £3,000 in 2006 and to £9,000 in 2010.

---

85 There are four funding councils for each of the four regions of the United Kingdom: England, Scotland, Wales and Northern Ireland.

Students are able to finance their tuition by taking loans from the government, offered through the Student Loans Company. After the student begins earning and her annual earnings cross the threshold of £21,000, she must begin repaying the loan. If, during the period, the earnings fall below the threshold, repayments are suspended. After thirty years, the debt is written off.

Funding for research

Until recently, institutionalized research funding by the government has been channelled through two sources. First, the funding councils gave an annual block grant to each institution for research infrastructure and for promoting research according to the latter's mission and priorities. These funds could also be used for research on pedagogy. Second, seven research councils, organized by fields of research, provided grants for specific research projects, contracts and post-graduate programmes. In addition to these institutionalized sources, HEIs also received funds from charities, industry, the European Union and individual UK government departments. In the last few years, some changes to funding infrastructure have been made. These changes are discussed below.

Overall HEI resources

Table 10.6 provides the total incomes of the HEI and their sources in the years 2014/15, 2015/16 and 2016/17. The total revenue of the HEI has risen from £33.5 billion to £35.7 billion during the three years. Tuition and education contracts constitute the largest source of revenue and rose to almost half of the latter by 2016/17. This large share is truly astounding when we consider the fact that tuition fees for UK undergraduates were non-existent until the late 1990s. Funding body grants and research grants and contracts are the other two major sources of revenue for the UK HEIs.

Table 10.6: Income of the HEI in the UK: 2014/15–2016/17

Source of income	£Billion			Percentage of total		
	2014/15	2015/16	2016/17	2014/15	2015/16	2016/17
Tuition Fees and Education Contracts	15.5	16.8	17.7	46.4	48.4	49.7
Funding Body Grants	5.3	5.2	5.1	15.9	14.9	14.3
Research Grants and Contracts	6.0	5.9	5.9	17.8	16.9	16.6
Other Income	5.9	6.0	6.1	17.6	17.4	17.0
Investment Income	0.2	0.3	0.3	0.7	0.8	0.7
Donations and Endowments	0.5	0.6	0.6	1.6	1.7	1.6
Total Revenue	33.5	34.7	35.7	100	100	100

Source: https://www.hesa.ac.uk/data-and-analysis/providers/finances (last accessed on 11 June 2018)

A new architecture for higher education and research

The UK legislature has enacted the Higher Education and Research Act, 2017. This act replaces the earlier governance through the funding councils and research councils with a new set of institutions. It has created two corporate bodies, the Office for Students (OfS) with jurisdiction over all higher-education-related issues and the UK Research and Innovation (UKRI) with jurisdiction over research.

The OfS establishes and maintains the Register of Higher Education Providers. It formulates the regulations (including fee caps) that a proposed new institution must satisfy to be entered into the register, as well as regulations that the existing HEIs must satisfy to maintain entry in the register. It also lays down conditions under which an institution may be deregistered. It has the power to impose penalties in case of violations.

Under the new law, OfS grants HEIs the power to grant degrees. It can also empower HEIs to authorize other institutions to grant degrees on their behalf. It further grants authority to HEIs to use 'university' in their titles.

Assessing and rating the quality of and standards applied to higher education by HEIs is another important function of the OfS. A Quality Assessment Committee helps the latter in discharging this function. The OfS also designates other bodies to perform the assessment function on its behalf. Designated bodies are permitted to charge HEIs fees to provide assessment. The law lays down rules for the oversight of the designated bodies. The fee cap applicable to an institution can be related to its quality rating, with a higher cap permitted for an institution with a higher quality rating.

The OfS is empowered to give grants and loans to the governing body of an HEI for the provision of education and facilities or activities that the governing body considers desirable for education. Given this provision, no need is left for the Higher Education Funding Council of England. Therefore, the new law has abolished it.

The UKRI, a separate body corporate created under the new law, has jurisdiction over research. It has the following committees that are referred to as 'councils':

(a) The Arts and Humanities Research Council,
(b) The Biotechnology and Biological Sciences Research Council,
(c) The Economic and Social Research Council,
(d) The Engineering and Physical Sciences Research Council,
(e) The Medical Research Council,
(f) The Natural Environment Research Council,
(g) The Science and Technology Facilities Council,
(h) Innovate UK, and
(i) Research England.

UKRI is empowered to carry out as well as encourage and support research in science, technology, humanities and new ideas. It is also charged with facilitating and supporting knowledge exchange in these areas. The UKRI may delegate these functions wholly or partially to councils (a) to (g) in their respective areas. The Innovation Council is supposed to carry out activities that will help promote economic growth. Research England aims to give financial support to governing bodies of HEIs for research and knowledge exchange and for facilities required for research and knowledge exchange in science, technology, humanities or new ideas.

The UKRI also develops an overall research and innovation strategy to be approved by the government. Within this overall strategy, each council must prepare a strategic delivery plan for the period specified in the UKRI strategy paper. The delivery plan requires approval by the corporate body.

A Possible Roadmap for India

Evidence shows that India has done well in increasing enrolments in higher education and made some progress in increasing research output but has lagged in terms of quality of education and research during the past two decades. Research quality, as measured by citations, is of particular concern. In 1996, India ranked ahead of China along this dimension but by 2016, it had fallen very far behind it. The good news, however, is that China's experience shows that rapid progress is feasible with concerted effort.

Creating Autonomous and Independent HEIs

One feature common to the United States, the United Kingdom and China is that their HEIs are autonomous corporate entities. In the United States, many universities receive funding from state governments but enjoy full autonomy in running their academic and administrative affairs. In the UK, all but a few HEIs receive federal funding and students are funded by generous government loans. But they remain independent in making their own decisions in academic and administrative matters. Even in China, where much of the funding of a large number of institutions comes from the central or provincial governments, HEIs have a high degree of autonomy.

India too has begun to grant its top universities and colleges autonomy, getting excellent results even within a short period of time.[86] The experience of other countries suggests that this process must be accelerated. The degree of autonomy must be increased and it should be extended to many more institutions. The system should now evolve into one in which HEIs are given autonomy, unless there is positive evidence to indicate that this will be harmful to the quality of education and research they deliver.

One possible option could be to adopt the British system, under which HEIs are independent and autonomous legal entities with their own governing boards. Under such a system, the government funding beyond a minimum level would be subject to quality standards. HEIs that perform well would be entitled to a larger volume of funds than those that perform poorly. And if the performance falls below a threshold, the institution would face the prospect of losing funding.

A Higher Education Promotion Commission

Building on the autonomy first extended to the Indian Institutes of Management and then to top-ranking universities and colleges, the key reform India needs is to replace the UGC Act with a new law whose aim would be to promote rather than control higher education.[87] To convey that this is the intent of the new law, it could be called the

---

86 Panagariya and Kumar, 2019

87 Panagariya and Kumar, 2018a, discuss some recent reforms, while Panagariya and Kumar, 2018b and 2018c, offer suggestions on reforming the current governance system of higher education.

Higher Education Promotion Commission Act. In the 21st century, India can ill afford to work with an institution conceived in the 1950s. No matter how suitable at the time of inception, today, the UGC Act is an obstacle to the growth of quality education.

The HEPC should be designed such that it is unable to resurrect the Inspector Raj that has become the hallmark of the UGC regime. Illustratively, we can imagine it having nine members, all eminent persons of unimpeachable integrity with a passion for the promotion of excellence in higher education. Under this conception, in the initial round, three members would be appointed for six years, three for four and three for two. Subsequently, every two years, the commission would replace three outgoing members by three new members that it would select and appoint for six-year terms. A high-level committee would choose the initial nine members, after which the commission members would select all the new members.

The commission would be assisted in its work by three bodies: (i) Advisory Council; (ii) Office of Registration of HEIs; and (iii) Committee for Quality Assessment.[88] The Advisory Council would consist of representatives of the states and eminent scholars from different fields. It would meet at least once a year, more frequently if the commission so desires. Its role would be advisory but important, since it would link the commission to active academics and sensitize it to the ongoing issues that it must address.

The Office of Registration would maintain the Register of HEIs. It would develop a classification of HEIs (for example: fully autonomous, partially autonomous, degree-granting, private, public, foreign-owned, college, university and HEIs of national importance) and list

88 This design is heavily influenced by the design of the Office for Students in the United Kingdom, with the key difference that it does not vest the power to disburse government funds in the commission. Government funds should be disbursed by another arm's length agency of the government, with some consideration given to institution quality as assessed by the Committee for Quality Assessment.

each HEI using this classification in the register. The commission can formulate transparent criteria for entry of an entity, including those of foreign origin, into the register under one or more categories. It would take decisions on the entry of an HEI applicant, whether domestic or foreign, in a time-bound manner. It would also formulate transparent criteria for the existing HEIs to maintain entry into the register. Failure to satisfy these criteria would attract punitive action including, in extreme cases, removal of the institution from the register.

Access and quality of education should be the only criteria for gaining entry into the register and maintaining that entry. Any input-based criterion should be included only if there is a clear and direct link between it and the quality of education. Enforcement should be entirely through a clear statement by the HEI on its website that it is in compliance with all the stipulated conditions. Any false claims should attract severe penalties.

Degree-granting power should be vested in the commission and implemented through the Office of Registration. The commission should translate this power into action by developing transparent criteria, under which an HEI can be empowered to grant degrees. Degree-granting power should be available to both universities and colleges, as is the case in the United States. This will allow the first-rate colleges to develop their brand names without having to convert into full-fledged universities. The commission must also specify transparent criteria under which an HEI will be granted power to authorize other HEIs to confer degrees on its behalf. This power should be available to both public and private universities as long as they satisfy the stipulated criteria.

The commission should also develop transparent criteria under which an HEI can use 'university' in its title. These criteria should offer paths to directly set up an institution as university as well as to convert an existing HEI into a university. No central or state government legislation should be required to set up a university. The commission should make decisions in a time-bound manner.

The Committee for Quality Assessment will help the commission in developing criteria for the entry of a new HEI applicant into the register. It will also help it develop criteria for continuation of existing institutions under various classifications to maintain their entries. Most importantly, it will help develop criteria for rating different categories of institutions. With its help, the commission will also identify and designate outside agencies to rate HEIs in different categories.

The commission will refrain from developing curriculums. Instead, universities and colleges with autonomy will be entirely free to develop their own curriculums. They will also be free to choose their own textbooks and other reading material for students. Universities and colleges without autonomy would follow the curriculums and textbooks of these universities and colleges identifying on their websites clearly for each course the university or college whose curriculum they are following. In rare cases, when a university or college without autonomy wishes to start a course that is not given by any university or college with autonomy, the commission should appoint a committee of two or three experts who would provide such curriculum in a time-bound fashion.

Allocation of Government Funds for Education and Facilities

The function of allocating government funds for education and facilities (but not research) should be assigned to a separate committee that is at arm's length from the government. In drawing up the criteria for such disbursements, this committee must give considerable weight to the quality of institutions as assessed by the Committee for Quality Assessment of the commission. The Rashtriya Uchchatar Shiksha Abhiyan (RUSA) has made an important beginning in this direction by channelling a part of the central funds on merit-based criteria. But a large chunk of the central funds does not flow through RUSA. Instead, it goes directly to the states and contributes to the salaries paid at state institutions. This automaticity needs to be replaced by merit with public and private institutions competing for the funds on equal footing. As long as recipient institutions accept quality-related conditions, they should be eligible to compete regardless of their public or private character. Once the commission is operational, all central government funding including that under RUSA may be unified and channelled through this committee.

Tuition Fees

Various state committees currently fix tuition fee caps. This practice may be continued, though there is a need to connect the caps to the quality of education. Institutions that provide quality education should be subject to more generous caps. States may be encouraged to accomplish this by connecting the caps to quality assessments by the Committee for Quality Assessment. States should be required to inform the fees to the commission.

There also needs to be transparency in the collection of fees. Therefore, institutions should have the obligation to provide a clear statement on their websites regarding all fees that students are required to pay. Outside of the listed fees, no other fees should be permitted and any violations must attract punitive action by the commission.

There is a serious need for promoting a culture of tuition fees. The United States, China and the United Kingdom charge hefty tuition fees for higher education, including undergraduate education. In contrast, India has ended up with a system in which students enrolled in private colleges and universities pay high fees while those lucky enough to get into publicly owned colleges and universities pay almost nothing. With the central and state governments both financially strapped, this has created a huge resource crunch for publicly owned colleges and universities. This needs to change.

One possible course is to adopt the British system whereby generous loans are provided to cover tuition fees but once the beneficiary begins working and her income reaches a certain threshold, repayment begins. After thirty years, any unpaid debt may be written off. Such a system will provide institutions additional resources to improve the quality of education. It will also create a greater equality between public and private institutions and encourage students to choose institutions based on quality instead of always preferring public institutions because they charge almost no fees.

A National Research and Innovation Foundation

Under the existing system, research in India has been relegated to independent councils such as the Council for Scientific and Industrial Research, Indian Council of Social Science Research and Indian Council of Agricultural Research, with the HEIs largely turning into teaching-only institutions. This separation of education and research has been highly detrimental to productivity in both areas, since they go hand in hand, and the vast faculty resources at HEIs go unused as far as research is concerned. To be sure, some research does take place at HEIs but only at a tiny fraction of them, and it is often driven by individual faculty member interest with no institutional reinforcement.

This state of affairs needs to change. The role of research at HEIs needs formal recognition, as in countries such as the United States, United Kingdom and China. India must incentivize research by faculty at a significantly larger fraction of HEIs than is the case currently, with due credit given for research via both funding and reduced teaching responsibilities. To make a significant impact, much larger budgetary resources will need to be devoted to be mobilized for the purpose.

The only relevant R&D expenditure data available for India are those allocated to research councils (CSIR, ICAR and the Indian Council of Medical Research), the Defence Research and Development Organization (DRDO), Department of Atomic Energy, Department of Biotechnology (DBT), Department of Science and Technology (DST) and Department of Space. In 2014–15, the total expenditure by all these units was ₹350 billion (approximately $5.4 billion). If DRDO is excluded, the expenditure was ₹218 billion ($3.4 billion) and if only the research councils, DBT and DST are included, the expenditure was a tiny ₹119 billion ($1.8 billion).

The upshot is that the total academic R&D expenditure in India is small and the proportion that reaches the HEIs is negligible. If India is to realize its potential, there is a need to beef up the funds available for R&D to HEIs. This would require both a rapid increase in R&D funds and some diversion from the councils. Indeed, an effort must be made to incentivize the best researchers and their labs at the councils to move to universities. If students do not get to interact directly with the top researchers, they are not going to get the necessary inspiration for research. The movement of some researchers and labs to universities will also help improve the HEI–industry research collaboration.

Institutionally, there is a need for the creation of a National Research and Innovation Foundation empowered to promote research and innovation at HEIs by offering project-based research grants to the latter via a peer review process. At present, only small grants are channelled to researchers at HEIs in the fields of science, technology and biotechnology through DST and DBT (totalling just ₹37.22 billion or approximately $570 million in 2014–15). Funds going into social sciences and arts and humanities research at HEIs are close to nil.

World-class Universities

Apart from improving quality in general, India must also create a few world-class HEIs that can serve as models and inspiration for other institutions. Prime Minister Narendra Modi has already announced the project to turn ten public and ten private universities into world-class institutions. My personal view is that this project needs to be fundamentally rethought along three dimensions.

First, the total number of institutions at twenty is excessively large for two reasons. One, at present, India does not have twenty universities that could rise to rank among even the top 200 universities at the global level in one to two decades. And two, given the tight fiscal constraints it faces, India lacks funds to genuinely aspire to bring as many as twenty universities to the global level in one to two decades. Therefore, betting on as many as twenty universities at once with the tight fiscal constraint would spread resources too thinly. The experience of China reinforces this point. Even though, with its larger resource base, it has tried to invest in nearly three dozen universities under Project 985, it devoted a significantly larger volume of resource to its two best universities: Peking and Tsinghua.

Second, while cutting down the number of universities to be promoted, it is also important not to divide the total number equally between public and private institutions. Good economics says that it will be best to pick the top half a dozen universities, regardless of ownership type. The reputation of the country will gain equally, whether the universities that acquire high rankings are public or private.

Finally, it is important to include two or three entirely new, greenfield universities in the group. A big advantage of new universities is that the rules under which they operate can be written from scratch. One of the challenges an established university will face is the existing entrenched culture, which often emphasizes equity over excellence. A new university can stipulate from the beginning that excellence will not be sacrificed in the name of equity. If a superstar scholar can only be attracted at twice the average of the salaries of existing faculty, a new institution can write rules such that it is acceptable. The faculty to be hired by a new institution is also entirely new, so that it is in a better position to go after a block of the world-class faculty with common research interests than an established university, which can hire only a small number of additional faculty members at a time. Scholars have a strong preference to be where they have other scholars with similar interests. Therefore, the ability to hire a large number of faculty members in one go has a big advantage in attracting top scholars.

Concluding Remarks

Beginning in 2000, India has made impressive progress in raising its Gross Enrolment Ratio in higher education. It has also made progress in research output, but not at the speed necessary to place the country among the leading institutions of the world. Going by citations, in 1996, China was behind India. But today, China is not only ahead of India, its research productivity in terms of papers published and citations places it at the top, second or third place in most fields.

Indeed, the progress China has made during the last two decades is a source of great hope for India in the next two decades. India has two important advantages. First, with English as the medium of instruction as well as research, it can readily anchor itself in English-language journals and other publications. Unlike countries such as China, Japan and Russia, its researchers are not handicapped in terms of accessing scholarly outlets both as readers and as contributors. Second, India also has a large number of scholars in the United States, Australia and Canada among the diaspora who can be attracted back home to rapidly build up faculty in the targeted institutions.

Working in the opposite direction is the fact that several countries including Russia, Japan and China are ahead of India and are investing a significantly larger volume of resources to improve their rankings. Therefore, as a latecomer, India will need to make a truly big push to hit what is a moving target. Nevertheless, through focused efforts, India can turn its higher education system around to rapidly advance its quality and improve its standing in the world university rankings. Reforms and mobilization of substantial financial resources will be the key to this turnaround.

As a final point, it may be noted that India also needs to reform higher education in areas covered by laws other than the UGC Act.

The National Medical Commission Act, which has replaced the Indian Medical Council Act, has been a breakthrough legislation from this viewpoint. Similar change needs to be brought about in areas such as the Indian systems of medicine, homeopathy, dentistry, nursing, pharmacy, veterinary and rehabilitation. Although the UGC Act covers legal education, that area also needs special attention.

11

GOVERNANCE

CHOOSING THE RIGHT POLICIES, programmes and projects is only half of the story. The precise translation of broad policies into concrete laws, rules and regulations, and the effective delivery of programmes and projects depends on the implementation process. This is where governance is critically important. In the absence of effective governance, even the best of policies, programmes and projects can fail due to poor translation into action. This is why almost all successful cases of sustained rapid growth and poverty eradication can be traced to able leadership capable of making right policy choices as well as implementing them. It is inconceivable that Singapore and South Korea could have achieved the success they did during the 1960s and 1970s without Lee Kuan Yew and Park Chung-hee, respectively, at the helm.

Implementation is integral to nearly everything that the government does. Good policies can be subverted if they are not translated into appropriate laws, rules and regulations. Delivery of every service by central and state governments, whether it is related to health, education, infrastructure, international trade, tax collection, defence, rule of law or dispensation of justice, depends on the process of implementation and quality of personnel along the chain of delivery. Given this all-encompassing importance of governance, it should be evident that a single chapter in a book can hardly do justice to the subject. What I offer instead are a few ideas to improve the delivery of outcomes in a selected set of areas in which suggested changes offer high returns.

I discuss improvements in governance in three areas: consolidation of ministries, reform of bureaucracy and economic administration. Reform of bureaucracy includes matters such as the selection and promotion processes of civil servants, training of officers, file management within ministries, work culture and the role of vigilance agencies. Economic administration has numerous aspects, of which I discuss a few such as implementation of reforms in mission mode, transparency in fiscal accounting, sunset clause on centrally sponsored schemes, tax administration, monitoring export growth and trade negotiation administration. With some tweaking, some of these ideas can also be applied to governance in Indian states.

Consolidation of Ministries

The central government in India has far too many ministries. Based on data gathered by my student Vishnu Narasimhan in early 2018, India had a total of fifty-three ministries. Out of nineteen major countries around the world, only Sri Lanka, with fifty-one ministries, came close to India. For the next position, Canada and South Africa were tied with thirty-four ministries each. As Table 11.1 shows, twelve out of the nineteen countries on which Narasimhan collected data had twenty-five or fewer ministries. At thirteen, Germany had the smallest number of ministries followed by France, which had sixteen.

The large number of ministries is detrimental to governance for at least three reasons. First, ministries judge their importance by how much they get to spend. Therefore, they compete within the government for as large a share in the total expenditure as possible, regardless of the social good they might do with those resources. This competition often leads to inefficient allocation of resources, with some high-return areas underfunded and low-return areas overfunded. When the number of ministries is large, many ministries on the margin do not have credible social or public purposes. As a result, the damage on account of allocation of expenditure to these ministries can be disproportionately wasteful.

Table 11.1: Number of Ministries in Selected Countries, 2018

Country	Total Number of Ministries
India	53
Sri Lanka	51
Canada	34
South Africa	34
Pakistan	32
Indonesia	30
Brazil	28
China	25
Nigeria	25
Malaysia	24
Chile	23
UK	23
United States	22
Kenya	20
Mexico	19
Thailand	19
South Korea	18
France	16
Germany	13

Source: Collated by the author's student Vishnu Narasimhan

The second reason why a large number of ministries is detrimental to governance is that it slows down the decision-making process in the government. This happens because too many ministries end up having jurisdiction over any given decision that the government must take. Because senior bureaucrats often pursue the narrowly defined interest of their ministries—sometimes even their own interests, such as maximizing power and influence within the government or improving prospects for the next promotion—which often do not coincide with the national interest, decisions reached through negotiation and bargaining among multiple ministries fail to maximize the national interest. Divergence between what serves the national interest and what actually transpires rises with the number of ministries.

The third and final reason why a large number of ministries is detrimental to governance is that it aids mission creep in administration. The government gets centrally involved in sectors that should be off limits to it. The existence of a large number of sectoral ministries in areas that should be the exclusive preserve of the private sector illustrates this point. Unlike most countries, India has ministries for steel, textiles, electronics, information technology, food processing, heavy industries, mines, chemicals and fertilizers. These ministries perpetuate and expand the scope of public sector enterprises in these sectors. They also become focal points for lobbying by narrowly defined special interests.

The existence of ministries that buy from or sell to other ministries sometimes gives rise to gross inefficiencies. For example, the railway ministry is a buyer of steel and the steel ministry is a seller. Because both activities are a part of the government, it is expected that the railway ministry would buy steel from the steel ministry, even if it is a costly supplier. There have been feuds between the two ministries, with the steel ministry crying foul at the insistence of the railway ministry to buy steel from private sector suppliers. When public sector steel companies perform poorly, the ministry also manages to convince the government to impose all kinds of duties on imported steel. That makes steel costlier still for the railway ministry and dents progress in the expansion of railway lines.

Sectoral ministries have also been principal barriers to the closure of many loss-making and sick enterprises. For instance, textile firms acquired by the government during the 1980s continue to impose a cost on the taxpayer, even though they have not been engaged in any manufacturing for years. At the same time, valuable land owned by these firms remains unused, despite scarcity of land for new private sector enterprises.

There is a need to phase out many of the ministries and amalgamate others to create more encompassing ones. For instance, replacing the numerous sectoral ministries by a ministry of industry and a ministry of services would make it more difficult for narrow special interests to successfully lobby them. Such ministries would not be able to do favours to individual sectors such as steel, textiles or information technology. Instead, they would have to address broader interests of industry and services as a whole.

Similar amalgamation could also be done to bring several other ministries together to create larger, more encompassing ministries. A single transport ministry could replace the ministries of roads, shipping, civil aviation and railways. An energy ministry could be created by merging coal, power, petroleum and gas, and new and renewable energy. Numerous social-welfare-related ministries such as minority affairs, tribal affairs, women and child development, and social justice and empowerment could also be consolidated into a single ministry. Likewise, the skill ministry could be merged with the human resource development ministry.

Reform of Bureaucracy

A merit-based civil service system may be either a career-based closed system or a position-based open system. In the former, civil servants are selected using a set of merit criteria that may include a competitive examination at an early age. Appointments to different positions are then made through promotions within this pool of civil servants. In a position-based system, emphasis is placed on selecting the best-suited candidate for a given position, with the choice made through open competition among internal candidates and lateral entrants from outside.

Till date, India has relied nearly exclusively on the former system. Various top Indian civil services, which are classified into All India Services and Central Civil Services (Group A and B), recruit their employees at a young age through competitive examinations offered to candidates satisfying eligibility criteria. Positions are then filled from within the pool by successful candidates who choose to join the services.[89]

Bringing Competition to the Top Civil Service

Of greatest importance among the myriad government services requiring reform is the Indian Administrative Service (IAS). Sardar Vallabhbhai Patel, the first deputy prime minister and first home minister of India, had conceived this service as the 'steel frame' of the country. In his address to the first batch of IAS officers at Metcalfe House in Delhi on 21 April 1947, he had exhorted the new recruits to be impartial, honest and incorruptible, serve without expectation of reward and behave as servants of the public rather than rulers.

More than seventy years later, members of the service have all but abandoned these ideals. They predominantly see themselves as rulers rather than servants of the public. Bribe-taking is far from uncommon. And a majority among them is guided by narrowly defined personal

---

89 There are three All India Services, namely, the Indian Administrative Service, Indian Police Service and Indian Forest Service. Central Civil Services are far more numerous and include, but are not limited to, the Indian Foreign Service, Indian Economic Service, Income Tax Service, Indian Engineering Service, Indian Railway Service and many others.

interest and expectation of private rewards rather than a desire to serve the public.[90]

Some of these changes were inevitable once the fervour to serve the nation, which characterized the generation that fought against the British to win national freedom, had dissipated. In the ultimate, public servants are not an exception to the human race and they were bound to eventually turn to pursuing the same dreams of personal progress and prosperity that other fellow citizens do. It should have come as no surprise that the enormous power that the near-complete monopoly over the top-level civil administration of the nation, which Patel conferred upon them, would corrupt most of them in the broader sense and some of them in narrower sense as well.[91] The decision in favour of a socialistic development model in the 1950s, with its attendant command and control features, contributed to speeding up that process.

To be sure, as one would expect from the highly selective recruitment process and the prospect of influencing the lives of more than a billion people it offers, the service continues to produce some highly dedicated, honest and brilliant officers. These officers also do their best to keep up with developments in economic thinking, technology and other relevant areas. But there are two reasons why the downside is no longer something that can be overlooked.

---

90 This was forcefully driven home to me when, as the vice chairman of NITI Aayog, a think tank of the government on which the prime minister serves as the chair, I offered to deliver a few lectures on the Indian economy to freshly recruited IAS officers. Much to my disappointment, my staff told me that most of the young officers would not attend the lecture unless they were served dinner with a non-vegetarian dish after the lecture. That led me to withdraw my offer after the first lecture.

91 Corruption in a broader sense is to be interpreted as the replacement of the high ideals espoused by Patel by the pursuit of power and a good life for oneself. Corruption in a narrower sense is meant to refer to an exchange of private favours, financial or otherwise, for services provided legally or illegally in an official capacity.

First, from the steel frame of India, the service has become an armour that protects its own. Taken as a whole, it functions like a monopoly and works towards safeguarding its own power, interests and privileges. Because the service has successfully reserved for its members nearly all the top-level positions at the centre and in states, even the most poorly performing officers can count on becoming secretaries in states before retirement. And mediocre performance is generally sufficient to reach the position of secretary in the central government. The absence of any threat of competition from outside, almost no punishment for poor performance and nearly guaranteed promotions based on the length of service have led to stagnation among officers, while also making many of them arrogant to the point of believing that they know what is there to know as far as administration and policymaking are concerned. The result is resistance to change and an unwillingness to constructively engage with experts.

Second and more importantly, the old bias in favour of general rather than specialized skills in the service has continued. This bias made sense immediately after Independence since the primary duties of officers were limited to general administration, most prominently, maintenance of law and order and provision of standard public goods such as education and health. Even when it came to policymaking, the economy still being in a primitive state at the time, common sense could go a long way.[92] But today, the economy is large and complex, requiring specialized knowledge.

---

92 I hasten to add that even during the early years there were occasions when expert advice could have helped avert some highly damaging decisions. One such moment was when a lone bureaucrat in the Ministry of Finance decided to introduce a strict foreign exchange control in response to a balance-of-payments crisis in 1957/58, without considering the possibility of devaluation of the rupee (see Panagariya, 2008, pp. 26–29). Had India chosen to devalue the rupee at the time, it could have maintained a far more open import regime than the one that followed the imposition of exchange control. In the early 1960s, faced with a similar situation, South

For example, the finance ministry must deal with whole host macroeconomic policy issues ranging from inflation, fiscal deficit and debt to banking, capital markets, tariff policy, taxation, investment treaties and privatization. Each of these subjects is highly specialized and forms a separate area of research in economics. It is preposterous to think that an officer can acquire expertise in these areas within a few months, as many officers of the service like to claim and believe.

The same can be said of the tasks performed by the Ministry of Commerce. Officials of this ministry must represent India in negotiations for multilateral agreements at the World Trade Organization as well as those for bilateral and multilateral free trade agreements with trading partners. They must also negotiate on bilateral trade issues and dispute with large countries such as the United States. The economics of these negotiations and agreements is a subject of much research and debate among trade economists. Once again, it is difficult to appreciate that officers who entered the service some twenty or twenty-five years earlier and have not studied the subject in any depth would be in a position to adequately represent the country's interest in the negotiations.

The impact of this lack of specialized knowledge and intellectual stagnation has manifested itself in two forms: slow pace of reforms and avoidable mistakes. With no scope for injecting fresh blood into it at top levels, the bureaucracy remains entrenched in its conventional ways and, with rare exceptions, resistant to change. With its strong bias in favour of the status quo, it has also designed rules and regulations that make any change difficult. Often, multiple layers of regulations must be removed before a change can become effective. The result is that even when the political leadership wants reform, change is excruciatingly slow.

Korea had chosen multiple devaluations, which allowed it to pursue more outward-oriented policies subsequently.

A good example is the decision by the Cabinet to privatize a number of public sector enterprises in 2016 and 2017. Despite such a decision, the Department of Investment and Public Asset Management (DIPAM) had not privatized a single private sector enterprise until as late as August 2019. This is particularly damning because some of the units identified for privatization are listed on the stock market and the government stake in them is 60 per cent or less. Therefore, DIPAM needed to sell no more than 10 percentage points of its shares in those units to pass their control to independent boards. The decision by the Cabinet to privatize Air India also remains unimplemented.

With India in the midst of reforms aimed at replacing the old order, partially inherited from the British but mainly created during the first four decades of Independence and during the second term of the UPA government, the need for bureaucrats who understand the basic principles of economics is especially acute. This point is reinforced by the fact that within the Indian system, ministers are elected members of Parliament and usually not professionals with specialized knowledge. Membership in the Rajya Sabha offers a chance to bring professionals into the Cabinet but political parties have exploited this route sparingly. Therefore, the government must rely heavily on permanent bureaucracy for designing and implementing new laws and accompanying rules and regulations to bring about necessary change.

To be sure, an officer can compensate for the lack of specialized knowledge by reaching out to outside experts. But this avenue has two limitations. First, to seek such knowledge, officers have to know what they do not know. Unfortunately, with intellectual stagnation and arrogance simultaneously characterizing many of them, this is not always the case. Second, the ability to identify the right expert, absorb her advice and correctly translate it into action may require a certain minimum level of expertise on the part of the officers, which may be lacking.

A good recent example illustrating these problems is the slow pace at which the Department of Financial Services (DFS) in the Ministry of Finance responded to the problem of NPAs of public sector banks. To experts in the field, the problem had been apparent as early as 2013. By 2015, it had also been a subject of at least informal discussions within the government. Yet, with the leadership in DFS unable to grasp the implications of the problem, it neither initiated corrective action in a timely fashion on its own nor made an effort to sensitize the higher levels of the government to the urgency of tackling it. It was only after growth in bank credit came to a standstill in early 2017 and the top leadership recognized the need for action that the DFS bureaucracy swung into action.

Another example relates to the reform of labour laws. Economists have spilled much ink pointing to these laws as a key to the poor performance of labour-intensive sectors in India as well as to the predominantly small size of Indian firms. Therefore, they have pitched for making labour laws employment-friendly. In response, the government recently decided to replace the existing forty-odd central labour laws by four labour codes. The Code of Wages, which Parliament has already passed as a law, speaks to the poor understanding of the labour ministry bureaucrats as to how labour markets work. The code retains the provisions in existing labour laws for rising minimum wages with rising levels of skills. This is a bizarre provision and one that exists in hardly any other important country. The ethical argument for a minimum wage is that the wage received by an individual should be enough to attain a minimum living standard as per prevailing social norms. This minimum living standard cannot by higher for more skilled individuals than for less skilled ones.

For nearly two decades, I have been suggesting lateral entry as a possible solution.[93] Appreciating fully well that such entry strikes at the heart of the monopoly power they enjoy, IAS officers as a group remain opposed to it. With proponents of lateral entry gaining traction in recent years, officers from the service have responded by interpreting

93 Panagariya, 2000 and 2005

the reform as opening the system to the entry of specialized staff as consultants. This, however, is a tactical response to give the appearance of receptivity to the reform while fully protecting the monopoly of the service over positions with real decision-making power. Genuine lateral entry requires opening positions with decision-making power such as those of directors, joint secretaries, additional secretaries and secretaries to lateral entrants.

Lateral entry will bring two major advantages. First, it will subject regular IAS bureaucracy to competition. The resulting pressure would force the members of the service to continuously improve themselves through acquisition of skills and augmentation of knowledge base rather than stagnate under the protection of guaranteed and automatic promotions. Even if new entrants end up filling only 10 to 15 per cent of the positions with members of the IAS taking the remaining ones, the accompanying competition will impact the entire service. It is contestability of the position rather than the final outcome that is the key to change. Second, lateral entry will offer the opportunity to bring specialized skills and knowledge centrally into the corridors of power. Once inside the system and bestowed with decision-making authority, the entrants would be in a position to influence the thinking of the permanent bureaucracy on a daily basis.

The government has made two radical shifts in policy with regard to appointments of senior officials. First, it has opened joint secretary positions to officers of services other than the IAS in a big way. As part of this shift, in July 2019, out of a total of thirty-three new joint secretaries, it chose only seven from IAS. The remaining twenty-six officers came from services such as the Indian Railway Service of Mechanical Engineers, Indian Post and Telecommunication, Indian Defence Accounts Service, Indian Audit and Accounts Service, Indian Railway Accounts Service, Indian Railway Service of Signal Engineers and Indian Statistical Service.

Second, the government has opened the door to lateral entrants for senior positions. In April 2019, it announced the appointment of nine outsiders with specialized knowledge as joint secretaries. According to media reports, the government plans to bring more outsiders with special skills and knowledge at lower-ranked positions such as directors and deputy secretaries into the government.

Five observations relating to these unprecedented shifts in policy towards senior appointments in the central government are in order. First, appointment of officers from non-IAS services as joint secretaries is administratively much easier and faster than through lateral entry. As such, these appointments constitute a very effective instrument of rapidly weakening the IAS monopoly on senior jobs and of establishing the principle of opening up of senior levels of bureaucracy to individuals other than IAS officers. Keeping this in mind, some further movement in this direction is desirable. But it is equally important to recognize a key limitation of this avenue to enhanced competition for senior positions. Whereas IAS officers have the occasion to think about policy making at various stages in their careers, the duties of officers in non-IAS services are predominantly of administrative nature. Insofar as a key function of joint secretaries is making policy, this limitation calls for caution in relying too heavily on appointments of officers of non-IAS services to increase competition for senior positions in the central government. Once the stranglehold of the IAS is weakened and the principle of openness in the appointment of senior officers is firmly established, most appointments should be thrown open to all applicants, whether insiders or outsiders. There is no reason why one monopoly should be replaced by another consisting of all services, even if it happens to be more encompassing. Talent must be tapped from wherever it exists.

Second, it is extremely important that the number of non-IAS hires is rapidly expanded. Past experience suggests that IAS officers may try to discredit non-IAS entrants, whether from other services or from outside, to reassert their control. If the number of non-IAS appointees is small in relation to the existing stock of senior IAS officers, the latter will be in a good position to ensure the failure of the former.

Third, the dominant view among IAS officers is that non-IAS appointees must be subject to higher age and experience requirements than their IAS counterparts. This is wholly inappropriate. It is time to recognize that talent is not a prisoner of age or experience. Truly talented individuals advance rapidly in their fields and they would not want to join the government if made to wait because their talent is not backed by their age or years of experience. The goal of policy should be to simply eliminate the age and experience requirement for all and appoint officers according to qualifications of the candidates. If younger existing IAS and non-IAS officers within the government wish to compete for positions open to lateral hires, they should be permitted to do so as well.

Fourth, it is also important that outside candidates are brought in on a fixed term. Once the term is over, they must return to a non-government job. This will help ensure that only those confident enough of finding a good outside job after completing their stint in the government will take up these roles. Any promise of a permanent job in the government is likely to attract candidates with limited talent, looking for a comfortable job in which they can eventually retire.

Finally, the government must exhibit utmost transparency in and protect the integrity of the process of hiring an outside candidate. Vested interests have every incentive to discredit the entry of non-IAS appointees by alleging favouritism and political interference. The present government is particularly vulnerable to allegations that it is appointing party cadres to the coveted positions. Selection through the Union Public Service Commission, which is known for its independence, and making the qualifications of non-IAS hires available for public scrutiny can go a long way towards blunting such criticisms.

In concluding the discussion on lateral entry, it is useful to touch upon a tension of sorts between general and specialized skills in the running of the government. There is need for greater acceptance of the view that certain tasks and positions within the government require specialized skills and knowledge. Because IAS officers tend to be generalists, they promoted the fiction that they can learn to perform any specialized task within a matter of months and that those among them who go for higher studies in areas such as economics and return with specialized knowledge can do nothing that they cannot do. In its extreme form, this view translates into hostility towards those with specialized knowledge. It then results in deliberate placement of younger IAS officers with specialized skills and knowledge in positions that are entirely unrelated to their expertise. In turn, this discourages other younger officers from seeking specialized knowledge. This is counterproductive and there is need for accommodation of younger officers with specialized knowledge on the part of senior IAS officers.

At the same time, this pitch for a greater role for and acceptance of specialized skills is not to be interpreted as a rejection of generalized skills that characterize the IAS officers. Generalists will always remain pivotal to any well-functioning government. Indeed, to be successful in a bureaucratic setup, any outside entrant will have to acquire some generalized skills as well. In the ultimate, a balance between generalized and specialized skills through greater acceptance of the latter is what is needed.

Temporary Exit to Non-Government Sectors

While bringing in outsiders on fixed terms, the government must also encourage the temporary exit of at least a small fraction of its permanent staff to non-government sectors including the private corporate sector. Such exits can serve three purposes. First, they would allow officers to see the world from the other side. They will get to see and experience first-hand how those they serve feel about their services. This may help sensitize them to serving better when they return to the government. Second, outside employment will help them acquire skills that may make them more effective employees in the government in the future.

Finally, some officers may discover that their comparative advantage lies outside the government and may choose to permanently leave the government. This too will represent better allocation of the nation's human resources.

A common fear expressed with respect to government employees working outside the government is that this would lead to a conflict of interest during employment outside or after they return to the government. But these fears are highly exaggerated and should not deter experimenting with temporary exits for three reasons. First, ultimately, it is the individual character of the officer that determines her behaviour. Officers with integrity would refrain from profiting personally at the expense of the public even if they serve in the private sector for short periods, while those without scruples are likely to sacrifice public interest for personal gain even if forced to stay all their lives in the government. Second, should an officer indulge in wrongdoing on account of contacts developed while working outside government, vigilance agencies can bring them to justice just as they do in the case of wrongdoing by officers who never leave the government. Finally, even if there is risk of conflict of interest in allowing officers to take temporary outside employment, we must measure this cost against the potential benefit of such movement. The movement of individuals into and outside the government is a common feature in many countries, including the United States.

File Management, Lower Levels of Bureaucracy and Young Professionals

Under the current system, the lowest-level official (in most cases, clerical staff) in a ministry initiates a file or writes the first set of comments on a file that comes for scrutiny from another ministry. Once this official has done so and the file travels up, the tendency of successively higher-level officers is to echo the view of the official below. The lowest-level official goes by history, sticking to the line the ministry took in the past on any given issue. This gives him a good defence in case bosses above him raise any questions. As the file travels up, higher-level officers also feel secure in endorsing what comes from below, since they can blame the latter in case questions are raised about the stance of the ministry. The lack of specialized knowledge reinforces this view: if you do not know the subject well, best to endorse what officers below you noted on the file. Indeed, this is a perfectly safe system for senior officers who claim that they can become specialists in any area within a matter of months but actually don't.

This process leaves little room for innovative thinking within the ministry, so that any major change has to invariably come from the top. To promote innovative thinking at the middle and lower levels, the government should shift to a system under which the first noting comes from an officer of the rank of director or higher. The officer may take inputs from those below her but the initiation of a file or first comment on a file from another ministry must be hers. This would even encourage the officer to discuss the matter upfront with those senior to her and force greater interaction and thinking.

A related reform would be to overhaul the staff below deputy secretary. Rather than rely on a large body of permanent staff at these levels, it may make more sense to bring bright and tech-savvy young professionals in their early to late twenties on three- to five-year contracts. These youngsters can bring energy and innovative thinking to the ministry while also gaining exposure to and experience of working in the government. Once past files and records are digitized in the form of searchable documents, the young professionals can help the senior staff readily track down history of how the ministry handled any specific subject in the past. Digital archives would eliminate the need for permanent staff as keepers of institutional memory. The government's think tank NITI Aayog has made effective use of young professionals since its inception and other ministries may learn from its experience.

Reining in Vigilance Agencies

India has far too many vigilance agencies and there are widespread complaints that they launch investigations of officers on flimsy grounds. Such investigations demoralize officers and discourage them from taking innovative actions and decisions. Fearful that any deviation from the past may open the door to questioning by the agencies, officers take the safe course of continuing with past practices, thereby perpetuating the status quo. This fear is often also behind officers endorsing what their juniors write on official files, since in case of an investigation the blame can be shifted to the lower-ranked officer. The fact that all those whose signatures appear on a particular file take the same view of the matter further serves as a protective shield. There is a need to curb frivolous investigations that do not lead to convictions and instead create an atmosphere of fear among officers. India needs to create an ecosystem in which officers can freely take decisions in the national interest.

Reforming Training Institutions for Officers

The government must also take a fresh look at its various training institutes and programmes. Under the current system, there is a strong internal bias in training, in the sense that trainers are predominantly from within the government. Some outsiders are invited to speak but officers' exposure to them is limited. The process should not be one in which, serving as trainers, senior officers effectively try to turn junior officers into their clones. A rethink of how training institutes are administered and training conducted is required.

Correcting Colonial and Princely-Era Practices in the Daily Lives of Officers

A sensitive yet important issue concerns the discontinuation of certain practices in the daily lives of officers inherited from colonial and princely eras that should have no place in a modern society. These practices manifest themselves in many aspects of the officers' lives such as multitasking staff (MTS) carrying their bags, opening the doors of their offices and cars, delivering files from one office to another and serving them tea and coffee. Officers often insist on two cars and multiple drivers with one car exclusively for family use. When it comes to very senior officials, almost an army of MTS and contract workers can be found hanging around their residences and offices. Few modern countries indulge in these practices. In today's time, officers must learn to carry their own bags, open doors of their offices and cars and get their own coffee and tea. As regards amenities, the government should consider moving to a system of cash allowances rather than the current opaque system of in-kind benefits such as cars, drivers, workers to assist at home and large bungalows in the most expensive part of New Delhi.

Economic Administration

There are numerous areas of reform that can be loosely classified under the rubric of 'economic administration'. The potential list of these areas would be quite long. Therefore, what I discuss in the following paragraphs is illustrative rather than exhaustive.

Reforms in Mission Mode

During his first term, Prime Minister Narendra Modi successfully deployed a governance model that relied on bureaucratic initiatives under his guidance. A key element of this governance model was the appointment of a number of groups of secretaries with each group assigned the task of preparing presentations on projects, programmes and policies to be implemented the following year in key sectors of the economy. The prime minister, his entire Cabinet and top bureaucrats then discussed the presentations over long sessions. Once finalized, these presentations became the roadmaps for the following year for the major sectors.

An advantage of this approach was that bureaucrats jointly owned the proposals and therefore diligently implemented them. But when it comes to radical reforms, this approach has a downside. By nature, bureaucrats are cautious and lean heavily in favour of projects and programmes. Even when they propose policy changes, these are piecemeal and rarely go beyond tinkering.

To pave the way for radical reforms, the government must adopt a different approach. At the outset, it must identify half a dozen key areas of reform. These could potentially include labour laws, land acquisition laws, higher education, international trade, privatization of public sector enterprises and banking reforms. In each area, a time-bound mission must be launched, headed by a senior bureaucrat with domain knowledge. Within two months, the mission head must provide a precise roadmap for radical reforms with a time-bound action plan.

Each mission head must have a professional with deep knowledge of the area of reform as adviser. A team of bright and energetic young professionals should in turn assist the mission head and adviser. The experience of NITI Aayog shows that young professionals, unencumbered by the compulsions of regular bureaucracy, can play a critical role in helping speed up the work of ministries and missions. Designing, piloting and implementing the reforms should be the sole responsibility of the mission.

Each mission should have its own budget, with the mission head having full authority to decide how the funds are used. Rather than seeking prior approval for each expenditure item, it should suffice for the mission to send a statement of its expenditures each quarter to the financial adviser representing the department of expenditure. It is important for India to move away from a system that relies on multi-layered bureaucratic rules to one that places trust in at least its senior officers. The mission should have similar autonomy in other areas to add to the speed of its work.

Finally, the prime minister must oversee the implementation of each of these missions and take periodic reports from the mission head. In turn, each mission head should have direct access to him for one-on-one meetings so as to be able to freely seek his help in removing obstacles to the mission's work posed by any functionaries, departments or ministries.

This mission-mode implementation of reforms assumes special importance during the second term of Prime Minister Modi. His government has a two-thirds majority in the Lower House of Parliament. Though it does not have a majority in the Upper House on its own, it is able to muster enough votes from other parties and independents to pass even contentious legislations. Such a favourable situation for bringing about major changes in the economy is unlikely to be realized in the future.

Implementation of an Export Strategy

A central theme of this book has been that rapid growth of the kind that the East Asian tiger economies achieved from the 1960s to the 1980s and China during the last three decades cannot be attained without major success in export markets. India must increase its share in export markets to reach a significantly larger scale of operation in its manufacturing enterprises. For this, in addition to various policy changes, it also needs to signal to enterprises its commitment to remove barriers that hinder its cross-border trade in general and exports in particular.

Here India can learn from the experience of South Korea. In the 1960s, as South Korea embarked on its export-oriented strategy, it not only adopted policies that helped make its goods competitive in the world markets but also sent clear signals to enterprises that it wanted them to expand their engagement in the world economy.

Beginning in December 1962, President Park Chung-hee initiated a process of regular, institutionalized consultations with stakeholders including relevant ministries, industry groups, policy analysts and exporters to effectively communicate the policy and identify and remove bottlenecks facing exports. He enacted the Export Committee Regulation within which he created an Export Promotion Committee to discuss important policies and plans for export expansion. Initially, the Ministry of Commerce and Industry was given the charge of coordinating across different departments and the prime minister chaired the committee.

Because the process did not work satisfactorily in the early years, in February 1965, Park himself assumed chairmanship of the committee, which began meeting once a month. The committee discussed and devised policies to expand exports and address the bottlenecks facing exporters. As Korea began achieving success in expanding exports, the scope of the committee widened. Beginning in 1969, its participants came to include government ministries, the Korea Chamber of Commerce and Industry, the Korea International Trade Association, representatives of export industries, professors and even political and legal figures.

The fact that Park himself presided over the committee sent a strong message to all relevant actors that the government was serious about its objective of expanding exports. The meetings also offered the government departments an opportunity to communicate, discuss and modify policies while giving a chance to industry representatives to bring to the notice of the government the bottlenecks they faced. Reviews of progress at the meetings in Park's presence also placed the burden of explanation of any failures on relevant actors. This kept all involved on their toes.

The Korean approach to international trade stands in sharp contrast to that of India. India's trade concerns have been predominantly focused on imports. According to media reports, in June 2019, the government announced its intention to monitor the top fifty tariff lines accounting for 60 per cent of India's imports to find ways to 'reduce import dependence'[94]. Once again, in September 2019, the commerce minister stated that the government was monitoring import trends of important goods and would take corrective steps to control sudden surges that harm the Indian industry.[95]

Going by the experience of every single successful country, India would do well to build exports, which would effectively eliminate the need to cut imports to promote industry. By adopting an institutional approach involving regular reviews of trade policies and export performance under the chairmanship of the prime minister, as done by President Park in the 1960s and 1970s, it can make a success of 'Make in India' through industries in which it enjoys a comparative advantage. As in Korea, regular reviews by the prime minister will go a long way towards signalling to industrialists the government's commitment to building export industries. They will also put India's policymaking bodies on notice that they must work to remove the barriers exporters face. Such a process may also lead to a sincere exploration of the prospects for FTAs that may help open markets for Indian exports in return for imports.

A New Entity for Trade Negotiations

The Ministry of Commerce has had a longstanding protectionist history in India. It has supported tariff hikes on numerous products to promote import substitution. It has also taken a rather negative approach to negotiations at the World Trade Organization as well as those for free trade agreements with the European Union and Asian countries under the auspices of the Regional Comprehensive Economic Partnership (RCEP). At the WTO, India has refused to join negotiations on

---

94 Chakraborty, 2019

95 The report appeared on the front page of the *Economic Times* on 4 September 2019: https://www.pressreader.com/india/the-economic-times/20190904/281569472407866/textview

e-commerce that seventy-plus countries, including China, have initiated. In negotiations for a free trade agreement with EU, the ministry makes impossible demands such as opening up of the labour market for skilled workers from India and upon being rebuffed, reports back that the latter are not interested in negotiating with India. It is critical to break these logjams to maximize the opportunities trade offers India.

A possible solution to the problem is to create a new entity similar to the United States Trade Representative (USTR) and place it in charge of all negotiation. Ideally, this entity should report directly to the prime minister. If this is administratively awkward, it may be placed in the Ministry of External Affairs (MEA). In contrast to the inward-looking attitude of the commerce ministry, the MEA appreciates better the value of external engagement and is also better able to carry out negotiations with trading partners.

Tax Administration

The central government collects taxes on personal income, corporate profits, purchase and sales of goods and services, and international trade. The administration of each of these four components of taxes has governance problems specific to it. As such, the subject of tax administration is vast and can hardly be covered satisfactorily in a short section of a chapter. Accordingly, I have confined myself to some basic issues at a conceptual level.

Currently, at 18 per cent of the GDP, the combined tax revenue of central and state governments in India is well below those in comparator countries. This creates a serious revenue problem for a government that is committed to significant social expenditures, building infrastructure and raising defence expenditure on the one hand and maintaining fiscal discipline on the other. As a result, the pressure on tax authorities to raise more revenues is immense.

Tax authorities can raise a larger volume of revenue by expanding the tax base, collecting more revenue from the existing base or both.

Unfortunately, they have found it more convenient to increase revenue from those already bearing a large part of the burden of taxes. This approach has translated into higher tax rates on individuals in the upper tax brackets, cesses on products subject to higher GST and challenges by tax collectors to exemptions claimed by richer taxpayers including corporates. Additionally, recognition of the fact that the government desperately needs a larger volume of tax revenue has heightened the sense of impunity on the part of tax collectors keen on extracting more bribes from taxpayers. The end result has been greater harassment of taxpayers, including demands of bribes at higher rates and damage to investor sentiment.

It is high tax rates and a complex web of exemptions that is at the heart of this unhappy situation. Despite the embrace of reforms for three decades, policymakers in India have been unable to rid themselves of a socialist mindset. They continue to find popular appeal in taxing the rich and corporates at ultra-high rates while simultaneously loading up the system with all kinds of exemptions conveniently labelled as incentives. Such a system encourages rent-seeking behaviour and impedes wealth creation. What India needs instead are moderate tax rates with fewer or no exemptions. Such a system will automatically minimize the scope for tax officials to extract bribes by challenging exemptions sought by taxpayers. It will also have a favourable impact on investment and growth and undercut rent-seeking behaviour.

A related problem India faces is that of a very large number of tax disputes. A complex tax system with ambiguously defined exemptions, scope for extracting bribes and the fear on the part of tax officials that vigilance agencies might investigate them if they settle tax disputes rather than appeal all the way up to the final judicial authority have resulted in the accumulation of a large number of tax disputes at different levels of the judicial system. According to available data, there were more than 137,000 such cases related to indirect taxes and 145,000 cases related to indirect taxes at the appellate tribunal, High

Court and Supreme Court levels.[96] Though the government loses more than two-thirds of the cases at all levels, officials continue to pursue them either because they want to extract bribes or they want to avoid being accused of taking bribes to close the case by vigilance agencies. The slow pace of the Indian judicial system only makes matters worse.

To clear the backlog of disputes, judicial reforms aimed at speeding up resolution are needed. But there is also a need for tax simplification and administrative reforms that would help minimize the scope for bribe extraction and discourage officers from pursuing frivolous cases against taxpayers. Greater reliance on modern technology to conduct audits can help reduce human involvement in selecting returns that are subject to scrutiny. It will shrink the space for bribe extraction while also reducing the scope for vigilance agencies to investigate officers. The decision in mid-2018 to increase monetary thresholds of additional tax claim below which the income tax department cannot file an appeal to the next judicial level is an important step towards reducing backlog of cases. The government should regularly revise these thresholds for appeals at various judicial levels upward.

Sunset Clause on Centrally Sponsored Schemes

The government devotes a substantial proportion of its expenditure to Centrally Sponsored Schemes (CSS). For the vast majority of these schemes, we lack any assessment of their impact. It is time that the government carries out a serious audit of the schemes and those failing to meaningfully serve a social purpose should be closed down. In the future, when a new scheme is begun, the ministry proposing it should be required to provide a clear statement of objectives and a timetable for their delivery. In this manner, a sunset clause will accompany each CSS. Continuation beyond the sunset clause should be seriously evaluated by the Prime Minister's Office in the light of outcomes

96 Ministry of Finance 2018, p. 137

delivered by it. With rare exceptions, the government should require pilot projects prior to full launch of a scheme. Finally, states should be given full flexibility in the choice of different CSS. Based on the choices made by the states, central allocations should be continuously rejigged across schemes. This will also help separate schemes that are aligned to states' interests from those that are not.

Transparency in Fiscal Accounting

The main documents providing public sector revenues and expenditures in India are the annual budgets of central and state governments. These documents give a somewhat partial picture of public sector revenues and expenditures. In particular, public sector entities such as the Food Corporation of India, National Housing Bank, Rural Electrification Corporation, Power Finance Corporation, Higher Education Finance Agency and the National Agricultural and Rural Development Bank borrow funds from the market that finance expenditures on social schemes and infrastructure. These funds, called 'extra-budgetary resources' (EBRs), remain on the balance sheets of the entities borrowing them and are not included in the borrowing reported on the government budget. At the same time, the government covers the interest and losses of these entities that they are unable to cover from their income streams.

There are two separate issues related to this borrowing. First, an exhaustive account of EBRs and payments made by the government to cover the interest or other expenses of borrowing entities remains unavailable. Transparency requires that all sources of funding for government expenditure, whether on or off budget, be listed. Likewise, public resources spent on servicing loans of off-budget entities should be transparently listed.

The second issue concerns the calculation of fiscal deficit. Conceptually speaking, to the extent that EBRs finance expenditures on government projects, they should be incorporated in the calculation of fiscal deficit. If the sums involved were small, this would not be a major issue. But according to some calculations, the fiscal deficit of the central government in 2017/18 becomes 5.85 per cent of the GDP if EBRs are included, whereas the officially reported fiscal deficit is only 3.5 per cent of GDP.[97] Even if the exclusion of EBRs from official fiscal deficit is as per international practice, it is important to report the figure inclusive of it. When assessing the impact of public sector borrowing on private investment, it is the larger figure that is relevant.

The final point worthy of note is that while off-budget borrowing may help the government to hold the official fiscal deficit figure low, it is a costly form of borrowing. Interest rate paid by public sector entities is generally 2 to 3 per cent points higher than what the government pays on sovereign borrowing. Therefore, the eventual cost to the taxpayer would be significantly lower if the government shifted off-budget borrowing to the budget.

Concluding Remarks

The choice of policy and identification of projects and programmes are critical to development and growth. But they can yield desired outcomes only if implemented effectively. This is where governance comes into play.

The subject of governance is wide ranging, with the result that even an entire volume exclusively devoted to it would be insufficient to do justice to it. As such, this chapter does no more than scratch the surface. I have taken a handful of important selected topics and briefly touched upon them. My focus has been on subjects relating to

97 A media story attributes the calculation to a presentation made by the Comptroller and Auditor General of India to the Fifteenth Finance Commission. The story can be found at https://economictimes.indiatimes.com/news/economy/indicators/cag-demonstrates-how-govt-relies-on-off-budget-resources-to-fund-deficit/articleshow/70360281.cms (last accessed on 13 August 2019).

governance at the level of the central government. The topics covered have included consolidation of ministries, reform of the bureaucracy and several selected aspects of economic administration of the central government.

I have deliberately chosen not to discuss two of the most important areas of governance: police and judiciary. While insufficient expertise has been a contributing factor, my primary reason for this choice is that justice cannot be done to these subjects without devoting at least full chapters to each of them. Nevertheless, in concluding this chapter, it is important to explicitly acknowledge the critical importance of reforms in these areas. The police and judiciary are central to achieving peace, security and order and enforcing contracts. When peace, security and order are missing, no amount of good policy can lead to development and growth. For instance, as long as Bihar remained unsafe, it was unable to make much economic progress. When Chief Minister Nitish Kumar came to the helm in 2005, the first thing he did was to establish some order and security of life in the state. Only then was he able to reap the benefits of good policy. In a similar vein, repeated bouts of terrorist attacks and the resulting insecurity have been a major obstacle to the development of the state of Jammu and Kashmir.

A poorly functioning judiciary not only undermines the objectives of peace, security and order, it additionally exerts negative effect on growth by failing to enforce contracts in a timely fashion. Indian courts at all levels—district and subordinate courts, High Courts and the Supreme Court—have been notoriously slow in dispensing justice. More than 10 per cent of the civil cases in district and subordinate courts take five years or longer to resolve.[98] In the Delhi and Bombay High Courts, the average life of unresolved cases is approximately six years.[99] India thus needs major reforms in the areas of police and the judiciary.

---

98 Ministry of Finance, 2019, Figure 4, p. 100.

99 Ministry of Finance, 2018, Table 1, p. 134.

12

NUGGETS: A MISCELLANY OF REFORMS

I HAVE ALREADY SYSTEMATICALLY analysed the key areas requiring deep reforms to accelerate growth to double-digit levels. The account will remain incomplete, however, without a brief reference to a number of additional reform measures. Arguably, some of these measures deserve detailed consideration and separate chapters of their own. But doing so would make the volume unduly long, something I wish to avoid. Hence I choose to follow the middle path.

Macroeconomic Reforms

During the last two years of the UPA government, 2012/13 and 2013/14, inflation, fiscal deficit and current account deficit had been high. During its first term, its successor, the NDA government, managed to stabilize the economy, bringing all three indicators down. Early on in its term, the NDA government adopted inflation targeting with the RBI required to keep inflation at 4 per cent and deviations from this rate not allowed to exceed 2 percentage points in either direction. The RBI has been successful in achieving this target. It has also been able to hold the current account deficit below

2 per cent of GDP. For the first time in history, the government has kept fiscal deficit as a proportion of GDP from rising for seven consecutive years.

Given this macroeconomic stability, there would seem to be little reason to change course. Yet, not all has been well. Although GDP growth has averaged a respectable 7.5 per cent during the five years spanning 2014/15 to 2018/19, it has not accelerated in a robust manner towards a double-digit rate. Bringing prosperity to nearly all Indians within one to two decades requires growth at rates 8 per cent or higher, year after year. That India remains some distance away from that goal is testified by the fact that the growth rate declined to 5.8 per cent in the last quarter of 2018/19 and to 5 per cent in the quarter that followed. During the full year from 1 July 2018 to 30 June 2019, growth averaged only 6.1 per cent. No doubt, in large part, this fragility reflects the restructuring that is under way due to the implementation of GST, clean-up of non-performing assets of commercial banks and anti-corruption drive of the prime minister. But macroeconomic policies have something to do with it as well.

In particular, it is my view that the inflation rate in India has been kept excessively low in recent years. Although the assigned inflation target is 4 per cent with a 2 per cent-point deviation permitted in either direction, going by its behaviour, the RBI has treated this mandate as that of holding inflation rate at or below 4 per cent. Any time inflation appears to rise above this level, it rushes to raise its policy interest rate (the rate at which commercial banks can borrow funds from the RBI overnight) called repo rate. But it is less inclined to cut policy rate when the inflation rate falls below the 4 per cent threshold. The result has been a large increase in the real lending interest rate of banks over the past five or six years. This trend can be seen in the data presented in Table 12.1.

According to Table 12.1, the inflation rate has steadily fallen from 10.1 per cent in 2012/13 to 3.4 per cent in 2018/19. Alongside this 6.7 percentage points decline in inflation, the RBI policy rate has fallen just 1.25 percentage points. The small decline in the policy rate has in turn been reflected in the small movement in the average lending rate of banks to businesses, which has fallen by barely 2 percentage points. The result has been a large increase in the real interest rate paid by borrowers. Admittedly, in 2012/13, the real lending interest rate was negative, which was unsustainable. But the average real lending rate of 4.5 to 4.65 per cent in 2018/19 was also on the high side, by any standard. For borrowers without access to one of the major banks, interest rates are higher, and for those having to borrow from non-bank sources, it is significantly higher.

Table 12.1: Inflation Rates, RBI Policy Interest Rates and Bank Lending Rates, 2012/13–2018/19

Year	Consumer Price Index	Repo Rate (End of Fiscal Year)	Lending Rate (Range)*
2012/13	10.1	7.5	9.7–10.25
2013/14	9.3	8	10–10.25
2014/15	5.8	7.5	10–10.25
2015/16	4.9	6.75	9.3–9.7
2016/17	4.5	6.25	7.75–8.2
2017/18	3.6	6	7.8–7.95
2018/19	3.4	6.25	7.9–8.05

*Based on rates charged by five major banks

Source: Author's construction using data in real time, RBI *Handbook of Statistics on Indian Economy* (last accessed on 6 September 2019)

In addition to pushing the real interest rate facing borrowers to unduly high levels, low inflation poses another risk. A fast-growing, developing country needs to restructure its economy on a continuous basis, with resources moving out of declining sectors to rising sectors. For this restructuring, adjustments in the relative prices of different products and activities must serve as signals. But if inflation is held to excessively low levels, space for relative prices to adjust shrinks. Potentially, this absence of price signals can impede the reallocation of resources from less to more efficient activities.

The possibility of money illusion on the part of businesses provides another reason why excessively low inflation, which translates into low growth in nominal profits, can undermine business sentiment and animal spirits. Symmetrically, if household decisions on financial savings suffer from money illusion, excessively low inflation, which partially translates into low nominal interest rates, can impact financial savings. These considerations add to the reasons why the government should consider revisiting its current inflation target with a view to revising it upwards to 5 or 6 per cent. If the original intent of the 4 per cent target with a 2 percentage point deviation in either direction was that a rise in inflation rate above 4 per cent should not invite the ire of RBI, it has not been fulfilled.

One further subject in the macroeconomic area worthy of further thought is government expenditure. Prime Minister Modi has set many very ambitious targets in his quest to build a New India by 2024. Achieving many of these targets requires rapid expansion of expenditures. Push for this rapid expansion of expenditures in turn has generated pressures at two different levels.

First, tax collection agencies are having to scramble for revenue collection as never before. In turn, this has led to increased harassment of honest and law-abiding taxpayers in high-tax brackets, since they present an easier target for collecting yet more revenue. Such harassment ends up vitiating the atmosphere for economic activity in general and investment in particular. For instance, it is increasingly in the news these days that entrepreneurs prefer to register their companies abroad and then operate in India through wholly owned subsidiaries.

The second impact of the ambitious targets has been that ministries responsible for delivering those targets are increasingly resorting to off-budget borrowing. According to one reliable estimate, this borrowing may be adding another 2.4 per cent of GDP to overall public sector borrowing.[100] With household financial savings already low, such large public sector borrowing can starve the private sector of investment resources. To the extent that economic growth crucially depends on the growth of the private sector, there is need to allow some more time for the achievement of targets that are dependent on large expenditures.

Closure and Sale of Public Sector Enterprises, Monetization of Assets

Most economists adhere to the principle that the government should not enter an activity unless it serves a public purpose. Activities such as defence, education and health fulfil this condition. But in India, the government has also entered into many activities that serve no real public purpose, in the sense that moving them to the private sector would result in no sacrifice of any public good. Indeed, in many cases, after an activity is brought into the public sector, over the years the ministry serving as host to it attaches a public good purpose to it. If nothing else works, it labels the activity as having 'strategic' importance or serving a 'development' objective or simply a 'priority' for the government.

In large part, the reason for the government to have taken over many activities with no substantive public purpose is historical. As

---

100 See: https://economictimes.indiatimes.com/news/economy/indicators/cag-demonstrates-how-govt-relies-on-off-budget-resources-to-fund-deficit/articleshow/70360281.cms

India launched its development programme, the government took the view that it was necessary for the country to build its own heavy industries such as steel, aluminium and defence, which required large investments. It further felt that the private sector did not have the necessary financial resources to undertake these large investments. Therefore, the government had to step into these activities in public interest. Complementing this reason was the government's objective of building a socialistic pattern of society in which it would have a progressively larger share of new investments. Later, under Prime Minister Indira Gandhi, this objective acquired greater vigour. She went on to increase the government's share in production activity and ownership of resources not just through increased share of public sector in new investments but also outright nationalization.

With the private sector having access to investment resources aplenty and the economy having been opened to foreign investors, the first of these rationales for the entry of the government into many activities no longer applies. Moreover, with India having chosen the market economy model over the socialistic one since 1991, the second rationale has also lost its force. Therefore, there is now a strong case for the government to exit activities it currently undertakes that do not have a public purpose. And it should make no new investments in such activities.

Privatization of Public Sector Enterprises

Unfortunately, as the saying goes, old habits die hard. Not only has the government shown no propensity to exit activities without public purpose into which it had entered in the past, it has continued to enter into more such activities. If India is to attain and sustain near-double-digit growth for one to two decades, it must do course correction in a major way.

Today, the scale of the government's involvement in areas in which it has legitimate reason to be present has greatly expanded:

administration, education, health, defence and numerous anti-poverty programmes. Increasingly, it finds itself seriously short of fiscal resources to fulfil its obligations in these areas. One of the unintended consequences of this resource scarcity has been the deterioration of governance in tax collection, with increased harassment of taxpayers being the result.

In such a situation, it makes no sense for the government to continue owning and managing loss-making large public sector enterprises such as Air India and BSNL. Even if the debt of these is currently outside the government budget, the taxpayer will eventually have to repay it in some form. There is no credible argument against privatization of these and other perpetually loss-making enterprises. Ministries that do not want to part with their enterprises often use the argument that the government should revive them before privatization to maximize sales value. But the harsh reality is that this is merely a ploy to delay, possibly even thwart, privatization. Past experience shows that attempts to revive sick public sector enterprises have usually amounted to good money being thrown after bad.

The government, of course, needs to go much farther than selling just the loss-making enterprises and extending privatization to the ones that may be in profit, as long as such action has no adverse impact on public welfare. On the one hand, it needs additional revenues to stay the course on fiscal consolidation and on the other, ministries need to focus on their core functions such as policymaking and implementing schemes directly related to public welfare. In cases in which looking after public sector enterprises is virtually the only activity of a ministry, after privatization of the enterprises under its jurisdiction, it needs to be closed down. Looking after enterprises that the private sector can profitably run is an unnecessary burden on public sector human resources.

Sometimes, the ownership of public sector enterprises by ministries creates a conflict of interest. Responding to the poor performance of their units, ministries seek protective tariffs and other restrictions against imports. Such actions end up positively hurting rather than promoting the public interest. This has been the case, for example, with fertilizer imports. There have even been instances when a ministry producing an input tries to forbid another ministry using that input from buying it from private suppliers even though the latter may sell it at a lower price. This has been an issue, as mentioned earlier, between the steel and railway ministries.

A final point in favour of privatization of public sector enterprises is that private entrepreneurs are in a much better position to take risks associated with commercial activity. The government appoints chief executive officers of public sector enterprises from amongst bureaucrats, often after their retirement. Not being professional entrepreneurs, they lack the skills necessary to undertake commercial activity efficiently. Their tendency is to minimize taking risk, including personal risk arising out of possible investigation by vigilance agencies. The impact of this factor can be seen in the generally poor performance of public sector enterprises relative to their private sector counterparts.

A study of the experience with privatization during the administration of Prime Minister Atal Bihari Vajpayee showed that the gains are vastly more when the government sells majority stakes with management transferred into private hands than when it sells a minority stake and retains management control. Specifically, it found out that on an average, the gains from majority privatizations exceeded those from minority privatizations by 23 per cent in terms of sales, 21 per cent in terms of profits and 28 per cent in terms of employment.[101] Figure 12.1 offers further evidence. Net profits as well as earnings before tax (EBT) as proportions of revenue of listed private enterprises turn out to be uniformly several times those of central public sector enterprises in manufacturing as well as services.[102]

101 Gupta, 2013, pp. 141–167

102 Gupta and Panagariya, 2019

Figure 12.1: Earnings Before Tax (EBT) and Net Profits as Proportions of Revenue in Central PSEs and Listed Private Enterprises

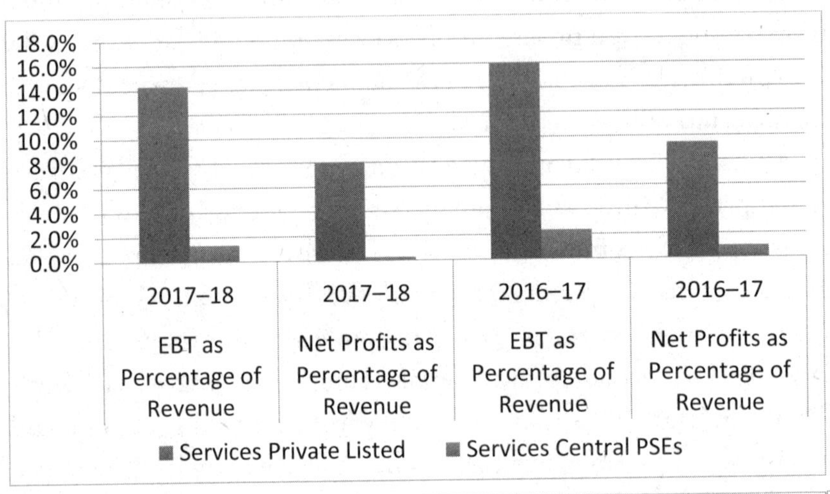

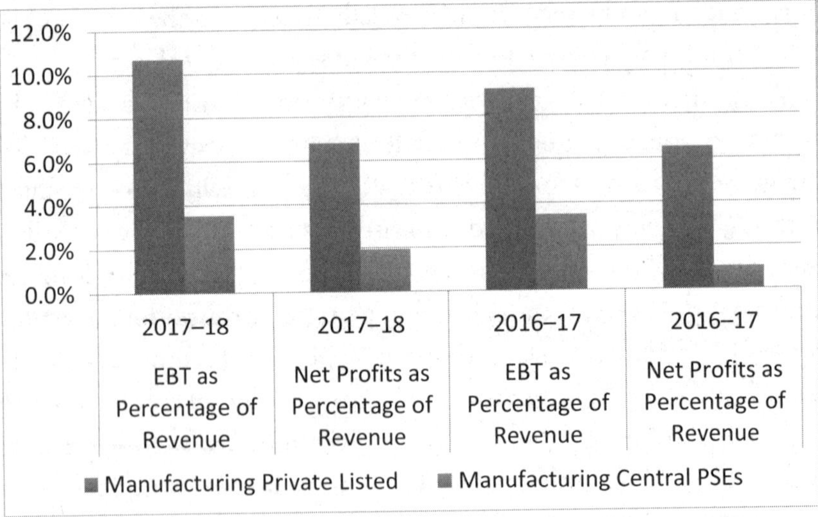

Source: Gupta and Panagariya 2019

A common bureaucratic tactic to delay privatization is to argue that it is necessary to wait so as to maximize the value of the enterprise to be privatized. Clearly, such an argument has no validity in perpetuity.

Even in the short run, the argument is a red herring when the public sector enterprise is listed on the stock market and the government has no more than 60 per cent share in it. In such cases, all the government needs to do is to sell 10 percentage point shares, which is sufficient to pass control to a private board. The government can then wait on selling its remaining shares in the enterprise till such time as it feels confident that the share value has peaked. Today, a number of public sector enterprises exist in which the government has less than 60 per cent stake and they have had Cabinet approval for privatization for nearly three years. Yet, the bureaucracy continues to drag its feet.

Restructuring and Closure of Loss-making Public Sector Enterprises

At the end of 2017/18, there were 339 central government public sector enterprises. Of these, seventy-one showed losses during the year with their combined losses summing to ₹312.6 billion. Many of them have been running in perpetual loss with no prospects that they will turn into profit-making enterprises thereby costing the taxpayer large sums of money every year. These enterprises perpetuate themselves by implementing repeated restructuring plans. In some cases, such as Air India and BSNL, the cost of restructuring falls directly on the taxpayer. In other cases, ministries carry out restructuring plans by using money obtained from selling a small part of the land available to the public sector enterprise. In this case, it is public resource that pays for restructuring.

The government should put an end to this charade of restructuring. The ones that serve no public interest must be allowed to restructure only if their restructuring plans meet the market test. The rule should be that any public sector enterprise that serves no public interest must seek funding from a bank for its restructuring plan at commercial terms. If the plan is commercially viable, the bank will provide financing for it. If not, restructuring should not be permitted. At that point, the enterprise should be sold to the highest bidder if a buyer can be found; if not, it should be closed down.

The government has a number of public sector enterprises, which have been dormant for many years with no production activity whatsoever. These enterprises are a net drain on public resources since workers must be paid their salaries and factory premises maintained. In most cases, the only asset with financial value that these enterprises have is land. The government must close them down and either retire workers with appropriate severance packages or re-employ them elsewhere in the government. As regards land owned by the enterprises, it should be deposited in a land bank or auctioned off. The NITI Aayog has made such recommendations in a number of cases over the past three or four years, with the Cabinet accepting them. But ministries have not implemented the Cabinet decision.

Monetization of Public Assets

In addition to entering manufacturing activity, over the years, the government has also invested heavily in many public projects such as roads, bridges, railways, airports and ports. Each of these projects is a public good, in the sense that at least to a limited degree, its use by one customer does not reduce its availability to another. More importantly, investment in it is characterized by lumpiness such that though its combined benefits across all customers exceeds the cost, the benefit to any single customer or subset of customers falls short of the latter. As a result, without some government intervention, the project may not be undertaken.

Conventionally, these public projects have been undertaken and maintained by the government. Consequently, the government owns and maintains many of them today. At the same time, the private sector has become financially far more capable than in the past and has acquired considerable expertise in the building and maintenance of these projects. This has led to the two sectors coming together to form public–private partnerships with private entrepreneurs investing in building many public projects. Unfortunately, however, many of these projects have got stuck on account of delays in land acquisition and environmental and other clearances with their costs rising unduly.

As a result, private entrepreneurs have lost appetite for greenfield public projects. They are nevertheless willing and able to invest in brownfield projects that are fully de-risked and have established revenue streams in the form of tolls and other user charges. There are many highways, bridges, railway stations, ports and airports that the government owns and manages currently. It can raise substantial revenues in exchange for long-term leases on them to private operators. This will be a win-win since it will bring revenues to the government, good returns on investment for private operators and better service for customers of the projects.

One another extremely important asset that the government can monetize in win-win transactions is land. Public sector units often own substantially more land than they need. Similarly, loss-making public sector units that are closed down have substantial volumes of land. Finally, many ministries such as railways and defence own large amounts of land. All these tracts of land are principally located in urban areas and are effectively unproductive. Auctioning them would not only bring the government revenue but, more importantly, turn valuable unproductive assets productive. It is a major national loss when so much urban land is left unused in the face of huge scarcity.

Consolidation of Subsidies, Scaling Down of Food Corporation of India

In December 2018, the government introduced a cash transfer scheme for farmers called PM-KISAN. Under the scheme, each farmer household receives a cash transfer of ₹6,000 per year. Though the sum of the transfer is modest, this scheme established the principle of direct cash transfers to farmers. The government can take advantage of this new instrument to eliminate inefficiencies associated with several other transfer schemes.

The first such subsidy is that on fertilizers. The purpose of this subsidy is to keep the price of fertilizers paid by farmers below the level that would prevail in the absence of government intervention. As such, farmers are its ultimate intended beneficiaries. It follows that the government can transfer this subsidy directly to farmers in proportion to their land holdings along with PM-KISAN transfers. Once this is done, fertilizer price may be allowed to find its equilibrium level in the market and restrictions on imports eliminated. To provide modest protection to domestic producers, the government may impose a 10 per cent customs duty on imports. On the supply side, this will allow efficient fertilizer producers to expand operations and force inefficient ones to contract them. On the demand side, it will help eliminate wasteful use of fertilizers.

Another subsidy that can be replaced by cash transfer is that provided through minimum support price (MSP). Because procurement at MSP is confined principally to wheat and rice, this subsidy is concentrated in relatively rich states such as Punjab and Haryana and goes mainly to large farmers who often have a lock on official procurement. This makes the subsidy regressive as far as income distribution is concerned. The government can make the system more efficient and less regressive by distributing the subsidy among all farmers based on the size of the holding. This will eliminate the need for procurement of grain to provide price subsidy to farmers. It will also eliminate the artificial incentive to wheat and rice that currently exists due to above-market MSP for these crops. Once the subsidy is given according to the size of land holding, on the margin, farmers will have the incentive to diversify into other crops.

One other important closely related subsidy worth converting into cash transfer is food subsidy. This subsidy is not targeted specifically at farmers, though the vast majority of them do receive it on account of poverty. Since the beneficiaries of this subsidy are already identified in each state and they have Aadhaar cards, the subsidy implicit in below-market grain prices under the public distribution system can be transferred in cash to each beneficiary household. Initially, the government can even begin by offering an option between cash and in-kind transfer and let the conversion to cash take place gradually as more and more households opt for cash. It is a reasonable conjecture that the vast majority of the beneficiaries will shift to cash within three years, since it gives them greater control over what they wish to buy and from whom. Once 80 per cent of the beneficiaries have switched, the government can extend the cash mode of transfer of subsidy to all.

If MSP and food subsidies are both replaced by cash transfers, the government can achieve a major efficiency-enhancing reform of the Food Corporation of India (FCI). With the provision of subsidy to farmers and consumers through this institution eliminated, its operations can be dramatically scaled down. Its mandate can be limited to maintaining a small emergency stock and public distribution system in areas where the private sector has poor reach. Procurement for both purposes should be done at market prices. If the FCI wishes to maintain public distribution in areas served by the private sector, it must do so on a commercial basis, with no public funds provided to support such operations.

The FCI has a huge workforce. The proposed reform would release most of these employees from their current employment. They may be shifted to other parts of the government that currently face personnel shortages. In some cases, this may require retraining the workers.

Electricity Distribution Companies

The power sector in India has faced repeated crises. The sector is too complex to be considered in detail here. Instead, I will briefly discuss one component of it, distribution. In India, it is this component that is at the heart of the key problems facing the sector. Distribution companies (discoms) buy power from generation companies and supply it to users. If they are insolvent, generation companies are not willing to contract to sell power to them. The result is that even if users are willing to pay, they are deprived of power.

In India, discoms in most states have remained in poor financial condition. Among the reasons are large transmission and distribution losses, power theft, poor metering, non-payment of bills and uncovered subsidies to users. Businesses pay ultra-high rates to cross-subsidize home users and many state governments provide additional subsidies. But these payments remain grossly insufficient to cover the losses on low-price electricity to homes and free electricity to farmers. The result is accumulation of losses and debt by distribution companies. The poor financial condition of distribution companies means that they are not credible buyers of electricity from generation companies.

At the heart of the problem is the absence of genuine commercial pressure on distribution companies. With rare exceptions, they are state-level public sector companies, run by state government employees whose jobs do not depend on the health of the companies they serve. The situation is made worse by State Electricity Regulatory Commissions (SERC), which do not function as independently as their central counterpart, the Central Electricity Regulatory Commission, does. State governments interfere with tariff setting to keep them low. They also forbid distribution companies from charging tariff to favoured sections, especially farmers, without compensating them through budgetary resources.

The government has made repeated attempts to solve the problem but without success. The latest was the Ujjwal Discom Assurance Yojana (UDAY), translated as Bright Discom Assurance Scheme, under which state governments undertook to shift 75 per cent of discom debt to their budgets and improve efficiency along a set of specified parameters in return for certain subsidies from the central government. Although the scheme temporarily relieved the financial burden of discoms, it has not been successful in restoring their long-term health. Aggregate Transmission and Commercial (AT&C) losses, which represent power for which the discom did not receive any payment as a proportion of the total electricity it procured, fell from 20.8 per cent in 2015/16 to 18.8 per cent in 2017/18. But as of September 2019, they rose back to 21.4 per cent. Likewise, as of July 2019, the gap between the average cost of supply (ACS) and average revenue realized (ARR), which UDAY had sought to eliminate, remained 0.25 rupees per unit of electricity.[103]

Ultimately, the problem cannot be solved without reforms that will put commercial pressure on distribution companies. And this requires subjecting the electricity supply to competition. The government had placed the Electricity (Amendment) Bill, 2014, before the Lower House of the previous Parliament to achieve this goal but the latter failed to pass it. The reform proposed in this bill is a sound one and the government needs to implement it at the earliest.

The key proposal in the bill was to separate distribution into network and supply business. This would allow multiple supply licencees in any area of supply, thereby bringing competition into the distribution of electricity. The network would still be owned by a public entity, which would be regulated to ensure that it gives equal access to potential suppliers of electricity. The bill also provided that any subsidies to users will be provided by the central or state governments in the form of direct benefit transfer with suppliers setting their own prices to recover their costs. In this manner, price discrimination among users will be eliminated with DBT subsidies protecting disadvantaged users of electricity.

One further reform concerns the independence of SERCs. An independent, competent and honest SERC has the potential to bring about significant improvement even under the current system. An effective SERC can ensure that state governments wishing to subsidize

103 Mishra, 2019

certain groups of customers pick the full cost of it with the discom receiving the subsidy amount in full. In addition, discoms may be encouraged to contract out collection of electricity bills to private agencies, with rewards and punishments built into contracts for extra collections and shortfalls, respectively, relative to initially specified collection amounts.

The opponents of discom reform sometimes appeal to the good performance of public sector distribution companies in certain states to bolster their case. To be sure, cases of excellent management and sound financial condition of distribution companies in the public sector exist. The problem, however, is that such performance sustains only as long as the top leadership in the state is sound and it appoints competent staff to manage discoms in the state. Once the leadership changes, the management and financial condition of the companies deteriorates as well. For instance, discoms performed very well during the rule of Chief Minister Narendra Modi in Gujarat until 2014. But it did not take long for the performance to deteriorate after he became the prime minister and a new chief minister succeeded him in Gujarat.

The Right to Education Act

The Right to Education (RTE) Act, whose principal objective was to give every child from the age of six to fourteen years access to school, was passed in 2010. By that year, only 4 per cent of children in this age group were out of school. Therefore, broadly speaking, the act's mission had already been accomplished when it was passed. It was trying to solve what was yesterday's problem.

From widely available data, even at the time the law was passed, tomorrow's problem in school education was its quality. Data, painstakingly collected by non-governmental organization Pratham and published in its Annual Status of Education Report (ASER) since 2005, was repeatedly showing low student achievements in reading, writing and mathematics. The reports also showed at best limited improvement over time.

Unfortunately, the RTE Act was not just neglectful of the education quality problem, which stared India in the face. Under the pretence of doing good, the act even incorporated provisions that made the problem worse. Just as the Industrial Disputes Act had deprived Indian workers of decent jobs, the RTE Act carried provisions that promised to deprive children of decent education. Only recently has the trend of declining levels of achievement in reading, writing and mathematics begun to exhibit signs of reversal.

If India is to seriously address the issue of quality of education, it must overhaul the RTE Act. Provisions that inhibit improvements in learning outcomes need to be replaced by those that will facilitate them. Here I discuss two specific provisions that are clear candidates for amendment.

First, the minimum norms and standards for schools to retain recognition by the government in the act are laid down entirely in terms of inputs and none in terms of learning outcomes. They include a student–teacher ratio of thirty for primary and thirty-five for middle-level education; a well-equipped library; an all-weather building with one classroom per teacher; a kitchen for midday meals; a playground; sports equipment; and more. The act says that the government may force schools that fail to achieve these norms by 31 March 2013 to close down. Several schools have met this fate under the act.

Studies show little correlation between norms and standards in the act and education outcomes. There are numerous low-budget schools that do not satisfy these norms and standards, cater to low-income families and deliver better educational outcomes than their publicly run counterparts that satisfy these conditions. Indeed, in rural India, parents are progressively moving their children into low-budget private schools precisely because public schools fail to provide meaningful education. It is this gap in outcomes that has been behind the large-scale hollowing of public schools. For example, during the four years following the implementation of the RTE Act from 2010 to 2014, the number of schools with fifty or fewer students rose sharply to 370,000 in 2014/15. The figure represented a gigantic 36 per cent of all public elementary schools in existence at the time. Per pupil cost in teacher salary alone in these schools amounted to ₹40,800.[104]

Closing private schools on the grounds that they do not meet the norms and standards in the RTE Act is nothing short of criminal. By doing so, the government deprives children of better quality education than what public schools in their areas offer them. The government must amend this provision by basing school recognition norms primarily on learning achievement outcomes and diluting greatly or even removing input norms.

In this context, the provision in the RTE Act that state governments must set salary norms for all teachers, including those in private schools, should also be removed. Numerous low-budget schools run on teacher salaries that are a fraction of their public school counterparts. Raising salaries to the levels of the latter would lead to a closure of all but a tiny number of elite private schools. This too would be tragic since studies show no correlation between teacher salaries and learning outcomes. A careful study of schools in Andhra Pradesh has shown that private schools are able to deliver at least as good learning outcomes as their public sector counterparts at less than one-third the cost.[105]

The second major provision in the RTE Act which needs amending to improve learning outcomes relates to the promotion of every child to the next grade each year regardless of whether or not she has achieved some minimum threshold level learning prescribed for the grade level from which she is promoted. This provision has two detrimental effects on learning. One, for many children, automaticity

104 Kingdon, 2017

105 Muralidharan and Sundaraman, 2015

of promotion means that they need not bother learning the material, since they would be promoted to the next level anyway. And two, difficulty of learning higher-level material rises exponentially as the child moves to higher and higher grades. By not having learned the material prescribed for earlier grades, the child is unprepared to learn more demanding material.

The common argument made to defend automatic promotion is that holding children back leads them to drop out of school. But it must be asked if staying in school has any value if the child is not learning anything there. Indeed, such forced stay in school may even deprive the child from picking up skills working at home in the family trade. If there is going to be any real value-add of school attendance, the school must motivate the child rather than rely on automatic promotion to the next class.

Concluding Remarks

For a country that has spent many decades pursuing counter-productive economic policies, there is no escaping a long list of reforms. During the first four decades following Independence, India adopted numerous growth-retarding policies. In 1991, it began to dismantle those policies. But along the way, it also added new anti-growth policies, especially during the second term of the United Progressive Alliance government between 2009 and 2014. Future reforms must address these policies as well.

In an economy with a policy regime as distorted as that in India, reforms pose an uphill battle, both because the list of reforms is long and significant beneficial impact comes with long lag. Though the 1991 reforms had resulted in quick macroeconomic stabilization and some early payoff in terms of growth, it was not until 2003/04 that the economy shifted to an 8 per cent plus growth trajectory. And even then, failure to maintain the pace of reforms and return to some dirigiste policies resulted in a loss of momentum. Under Prime

Minister Modi, the economy has returned to reforms but there is considerable distance to cover. Despite setback to growth during three quarters beginning on 1 October 2018, the current policy regime can be counted on yielding 7 per cent growth in the medium run. But acceleration beyond this level will require sustained reforms.

CONCLUSION
REVISITING THE PAST, LOOKING TO THE FUTURE

THE CIRCUMSTANCES FOR INDIA to become the third largest economy in the world in less than a decade and to bring genuine prosperity to the bulk of its citizenry could not be better. In May 2019, the people of India gave Prime Minister Narendra Modi the strongest possible mandate. The NDA, which he leads, returned to power with two-thirds majority in the Lower House of Parliament. Not since Prime Minister Jawaharlal Nehru, who contested his elections in the immediate post-Independence era when the opposition parties were still emerging, have the people of India given a leader such a strong mandate twice in a row. The NDA has also come to enjoy enough support from other parties and independent members in the Upper House of Parliament to be able to pass its legislations in that house. Modi now has an unprecedented opportunity to transform the nation. Given the unflinching faith that people have placed in him, this is also his obligation.

Many commentators argue that India cannot repeat China's performance because the global economy will not be as hospitable in the next twenty years as it was during the last twenty. But these commentators forget that the global economy was rocked by a major financial crisis triggered in 2008. Indeed, China also had to contend with the Asian financial crisis a decade earlier in 1997. But even setting these crises aside, the global economy was much smaller and export opportunities far less generous during the years that China transformed than they are today.

For instance, in 2000, world merchandise and commercial services exports respectively amounted to just \$6.1 trillion and \$1.5 trillion in current dollars. In 2017, these figures had grown to \$17.2 trillion and \$5 trillion, respectively. Though growth in trade has slowed down in recent years, it remains positive despite the United States–China trade war. No one predicts that global exports would fall in the forthcoming decades but even if that were to happen, combined goods and services exports would continue to be \$20 trillion.

Therefore, if economic policies within India are designed to promote efficiency so that the country can become progressively more competitive in the global economy, it has ample scope for expanding its exports. In 2017, India's share was just 1.7 per cent in global merchandise exports and 3.5 per cent in global commercial services exports. If it raises these shares to even 4 and 5 per cent, respectively, in a decade and maintains them at these levels in the following decade, global exports cannot be a constraint on its growth.

To put these shares in perspective, China accounted for 12.8 per cent of the global merchandise exports and 4.3 per cent of the global commercial services exports in 2017. For India, the real constraint in the next twenty years will not be the size of the global export pie; instead, it will be the size of the slice it is able to carve for itself from this pie. As such, rather than freeze into inaction on account of the fear that the global economic environment would be unfavourable over the next decade, it needs to aggressively implement reforms that make its goods and services competitive in the global economy.

Productivity growth in rich countries is constrained by the rate of technological change. But this is not the case for poorer countries such as India. Low per capita income in India compared to its richer counterparts implies that its level of productivity is far below that of the latter. My discussion of massive underemployment in all three broad sectors of the economy corroborates this observation. It follows that India has a large scope for productivity growth through playing catch-up with these richer economies. What is needed once again is a set of policy reforms that would enable its enterprises to imbibe more and more of the superior technologies that are already available. This is precisely what the East Asian economies did from the 1960s to the 1980s and China during the last two to three decades.

Therefore, it stands to reason that the problem of economic growth and transformation for India is wholly one of getting its own internal policies right. If India progressively adopts policies that would improve its efficiency as measured by its ability to capture a larger and larger share of the world export markets in both goods and services, it will accomplish in the next twenty years what China did in the last twenty. While I have discussed the detailed roadmap of these policies in the preceding pages, in this chapter, I will discuss the political economy challenges that Modi faces as he implements radical reforms.

Reduced but Continuing Influence of Socialism

The dominance of socialist ideas in the thinking of policymakers, whether we consider politicians or bureaucrats, has been the bane of the development effort in India. It is ironic that when it comes to the economy, communist countries such as China and Vietnam have shown a greater propensity to embrace pro-market reforms than India. In India, even many entrepreneurs remain infected by the old socialistic ideas and readily approve of the government taking on tasks that are best performed by the private sector. The result has been an acceptance of the heavy hand of the government and consensus around policies that undermine individual initiative and wealth creation.

In the immediate post-Independence era, building a 'socialistic pattern of society' was a formal objective of the government. Under Nehru, the pursuit of this objective translated into a progressive expansion of the public sector, including into production activities that served no direct public purpose. This era saw the government determining even the allocation of private investment through the instrumentality of investment licencing. It subjected all private investments above a relatively low threshold to a licence that only it could issue. The licence specified the product to be produced, its volume and the firm's location. On top of that, import licencing often denied the entrepreneur access to the latest technologies as well as high-quality machinery and inputs. The result was high production cost and abysmal quality of Indian products.

After Nehru, the stranglehold of socialism became tighter still. Prime Minister Indira Gandhi, who ruled from 1966 to 1984 with a small break in between, went on to expand the scope of the government through nationalization of enterprises. She began with banks that had assets above a modest threshold and then proceeded to take over the entire insurance sector. This was followed by nationalization of coalmines and all major oil companies. She went on to amend labour laws such that they deprived manufacturing firms with 100 or more workers of the right to terminate a worker under any circumstances. She also introduced an Urban Land Ceiling and Regulation Act, which gave the government the right to acquire an empty urban lot exceeding a low threshold for a throwaway price.

After the launch of the liberalizing reforms in 1991, the hold of socialism, no doubt, progressively weakened. Yet, politicians and bureaucrats have been unable to fully free themselves of their socialist mindset. For politicians in the major national parties—the Congress and the BJP—the problem remains that their founding leaders, who serve as inspiration for the current leaders, have all been socialist. In the Congress, Prime Ministers Nehru and Gandhi were committed socialists. Both Sonia Gandhi and Rahul Gandhi, who currently lead the party, fully subscribe to the ideology of these earlier leaders. The Congress party has also entirely disowned Prime Minister P.V. Narasimha Rao, who had initiated pro-market reforms in 1991. In the BJP, while Prime Minister Modi himself is reform-minded and appreciates the role of markets, many in his party draw inspiration from Pandit Deendayal Upadhyaya, who was a socialist. Therefore, reform initiatives under the present government have predominantly come from Modi himself.

As regards the bureaucracy, its adherence to socialism remains deeply rooted in the education its members received in Indian universities, where faculty members are wedded to anti-business and anti-market ideology. Given the dream of an ideal world that the socialist ideology offers, the young are naturally drawn to it. This attraction is reinforced by anti-market ideas that their teachers in colleges impart them. Civil services in India pick up many among these youngsters at an early age. Once inside the government, they find themselves safely in the company of others like them for the remainder of their professional lives.[106]

The impact of this continued even if the somewhat weakened grip of socialist ideas is visible in many policy choices made even in the post-reform era. For all intents and purposes, pro-market reforms came to a standstill under the Congress-led UPA government between 2004 and 2014. During the second term of this government, legislations dominated by socialism proliferated. They included the Land Acquisition Act, Right to Education Act and the Food Security Act. Though apparently intended for the poor and the weak, each of these legislations did the exact opposite by undermining growth. Under the Modi government, import substitution, which is also associated with socialist policies, has seen a revival. Similarly, preoccupation with micro and small enterprises, which cannot become engines of growth without flourishing medium and large enterprises, has its roots in a socialistic mindset.

---

106 As an example, on a visit to St Stephen's College during my years at the NITI Aayog, I was surprised by the deep scepticism towards pro-market reforms among students there. The college has been a steady contributor of IAS officers for decades.

The impact of bureaucracy has taken two forms. First, the institution has taken few initiatives of its own towards building a pro-market economy. A few senior officials can be heard echoing pro-reform sentiments when expressed by the country's top leadership of the day but bureaucracy as a whole has done little to move the reform agenda forward. Prime Minister Modi even offered them an explicit opportunity to put radical reform ideas on the table through groups of secretaries he constituted to prepare annual roadmaps of actions in different areas of the economy. But projects and programmes, rather than radical policy reforms, dominated the proposals these groups put forth in their presentations.

Second, in many instances, the bureaucracy has served to slow down, even block, reforms that the top leadership has sought to implement. For instance, cumulatively, the Modi government has taken the decision to privatize a large number of public sector enterprises. In 2016, the Prime Minister's Office directed NITI Aayog to carry out an analysis of public sector enterprises and identify enterprises that would be good candidates for privatization. After NITI Aayog undertook the exercise and sent lists of such enterprises, the prime minister saw to it that the Cabinet gave its approval for privatization of those enterprises. But once the matter went to the Department of Investment and Public Asset Management, it remained stuck there. At the time of writing (September 2019), not a single public sector enterprise had been privatized.

Labour law reform offers another example. In this case, the top leadership decided to simplify and consolidate forty central government laws into four codes and asked the Ministry of Labour to perform the task. This was an excellent opportunity for bureaucrats in the Ministry of Labour to propose reforms of various anti-growth and anti-employment laws while simplifying and consolidating the existing laws. But so far it has failed to rise to the occasion. The Code on Wages, which has now been enacted into a law by Parliament, did little to make minimum wage laws employment friendly. Even more important, according to media reports, the Code on Industrial Relations it has proposed fails to incorporate even the reforms many states have already implemented with the consent of the central government.

A final example relates to civil service reform. Prime Minister Modi has pushed for lateral entry at the top levels of bureaucracy for several years. But going by publicly available information, it is a reasonable conclusion that the bureaucracy slowed down the process to such a degree that it was only at the very end of his term that nine officers could be inducted from outside. According to media reports, there had been plans to induct many more officers from outside but this had not happened.

It may be asked how the bureaucracy can block actions desired by the prime minister and his Cabinet. Why can the prime minister not replace obstructionist bureaucrats by those that would carry out his mandate? There are two answers to this important question. First, a seasoned bureaucrat never says no to those above him. Instead, while stalling progress, he conveys to his superiors that he is in the process of taking necessary actions. When questions get asked from above about the lack of progress, he takes one of many steps in the process and conveys that progress is under way. Given the multi-layered processes in India to bring a project to its conclusion, this tactic can be deployed for long enough that either the bureaucrat responsible for the delay retires or the government changes.

The second problem concerns the shortage of officers who are both competent and are devoted to the agenda of the top leadership. Often these officers are already placed in departments where they are needed the most. Therefore, the prime minister does not have the luxury of moving around non-performing officers. He only risks replacing one non-performing officer by another while additionally creating disruption.

Remarkably, in India, even business leaders have played an insignificant role in pushing for market-friendly reforms. In most countries, businesses try to use an economic crisis as an opportunity to seek removal of regulations that impede their progress. But in India, they see a crisis as the opportunity to seek subsidies and protection from imports. They want the government to intervene more, not less, to save their specific sector or industry.[107] With rare exceptions, even business organizations and associations, which are expected to represent the collective interest of business, have not bothered to push for pro-growth reforms.

What Makes Reforms Possible

This discussion points to rather bleak prospects for reforms. Indeed, it begs the question how reforms till date have been possible in the first place. My broad answer to this question is that it is principally the top political leadership that must be credited with reforms that have taken place so far. Prime ministers who have been determined to see India progress faster and have been perceptive enough to appreciate that the dirigiste policies of the first four post-Independence decades cannot deliver prosperity to Indians have successfully navigated reforms despite India's difficult polity and bureaucratic machinery.

A complementary factor aiding progress in reforms is the positive role that specific individuals within the system have played. Though the central tendency of each set of players in the system—politicians, bureaucrats and business leaders—has been to lean against reforms, each group has also produced some exceptional individuals who joined hands with the enlightened leadership at the top to push reforms. This has been particularly true of a handful of bureaucrats who knew how to navigate the system and became partners of the top leadership in the reform project.

107 The case of the auto industry during the slowdown in 2019 is a case in point. See Panagariya, 2019c, in this context.

From a longer-term perspective, the writings of a handful of economists, which have gradually helped change the minds of all Indians, have strengthened the hand of pro-reform actors in the system. Like the movement in the hour hand of a clock, gradual evolution in public opinion is not noticeable. But the change becomes visible when we consider the central tendency of the opinion at two distant points in time. For example, in the mid-1980s, the Licence Permit Raj had near-universal approval in India. But today, it is subject to near-universal opprobrium. In 1970, when Jagdish Bhagwati and Padma Desai published the first full-scale case for a more liberal policy regime in India, they found no takers.[108] Today, those ideas have wide acceptance while the opposite ones, espoused most prominently by Amartya Sen, are in retreat. The result is that even though a diluted form of socialism continues to have appeal in certain powerful circles, advocates of reforms have come to command a great deal of respect, especially among the young who want change and want it sooner rather than later.

In the early phase of reforms, three events helped these ideas gain greater acceptance. First, the poor performance of the Indian economy had gradually led at least a few Indians in positions of power to conclude that the command-and-control system had failed the country and that there were no prospects that it would deliver even modest growth. Second, the collapse of the Soviet Union, on which Nehru had modelled India's development strategy, brought out into the open the fact that the emperor had no clothes. Finally, for a long time, Indian policymakers had disdainfully rejected the extraordinary performance of East Asian economies, arguing that they were too small to carry any lessons for India. But when China, a country more populous than India and a communist one at that, shed its command-and-control-cum-autarkic model and produced double-digit growth for a full decade, their defence of the old system fell flat.

108 Bhagwati and Desai, 1970

These developments paved the way for Prime Minister P.V. Narasimha Rao—a politician from the south with no past baggage—to use the occasion of a balance of payments crisis to give a dramatic turn to economic policy.[109] A pragmatic politician, who had survived multiple splits in the Congress party, Rao dismantled the Licence Permit Raj in one stroke and began opening the economy to foreign trade and investment in his very first year. In the years that followed, he kept opening the door to trade and foreign investment wider while also implementing reforms in the financial sector, telecommunications and civil aviation.

Some observers argue that Rao embraced reforms under pressure from the international Monetary Fund (IMF) and World Bank. But this is a mistaken view. At most, one can make the case that these institutions had a significant role to play in the first bout of reforms, though even this is arguable.[110] After the initial loan from these institutions, the Indian economy had recovered quickly with macroeconomic stability restored. As such, it no longer needed additional loans from the IMF and World Bank and could have eschewed further reforms. But the impetus for reforms had come from within and Rao was determined to take the process forward.

The role of the top leadership in determining the course of reforms remained crucial in subsequent years. In the midst of corruption charges, Rao lost the 1996 election and a series of unstable coalition governments followed. They ruled the country for approximately two years. Setting aside a few isolated actions, reforms witnessed a pause during this period. But in 1998, a BJP-led coalition government, with Atal Bihari Vajpayee as prime minister, came to the helm. Like

---

109 In the 1991 parliamentary elections, former Prime Minister Rajiv Gandhi led the Congress. But he was assassinated during the election campaign, leading his widow, Sonia Gandhi, to ask Rao to take the helm. Consequently, Rao, who had been all set to retire with his bags packed to ship to Hyderabad, became the prime minister.

110 Panagariya 2008, Chapter 5, especially footnote 1.

Rao, Vajpayee was reform-minded and decisive. He sought double-digit growth to eradicate abject poverty. Helped by able bureaucrats, he implemented wide-ranging reforms touching almost all areas of the economy. By the last year of his rule, 2003/04, India had finally entered an 8 per cent-plus growth trajectory.

It was this 8 per cent-plus growth for almost a decade that strengthened the hand of reform advocates and helped shift politics in favour of liberalization. For the first time, people saw their fortunes perceptibly improve within a decade. That fact greatly sensitized them to the power of growth.

In earlier decades, improvement in the living standards at snail's pace had left people resigned to their fate, as captured in the classic Hindi phrase '*Aise hee chalata hai*'. Translated into English, the phrase means, 'It goes like this only'. This fatalism led people to repeatedly return the same government to power. But once they found that better policies and governance could deliver dramatically superior outcomes, their voting behaviour changed. Henceforth, governments that delivered significantly better economic outcomes would be returned to office while those failing to do so would bite the dust.[111] During the past decade, people have returned to office state and central governments that have delivered superior economic outcomes and bundled out those failing to do so.[112]

Prime Minister Vajpayee had presided over a fragile coalition government. Indeed, in 1999, this fragility culminated in a fall of his government. Elections were held again that year and he returned to office with a slightly stronger mandate, allowing him to pursue an

---

111 Bhagwati and Panagariya, 2004, first enunciated this hypothesis. Gupta and Panagariya, 2014, tested the hypothesis empirically.

112 At the centre, the UPA was voted out in 2014 while Modi was voted back in 2019. States in which competent governments have been repeatedly returned to power include Bihar, Odisha, Madhya Pradesh and Gujarat. States in which poorly performing governments got thrown out include Uttar Pradesh, Maharashtra and Chhattisgarh.

extensive reforms agenda. In 2004, when elections were held again, however, some of his coalition partners broke away, which tipped the balance in favour of the opposition. Growth acceleration to 8 per cent during the last year of his rule had come much too late to benefit him electorally.

In May 2004, the Congress-led UPA came to power. In 1998, Sonia Gandhi had wrested back the control of Congress party and was now at the helm. Though she opted to have Dr Manmohan Singh, a technocrat, as prime minister, she remained the real power behind the throne. Fully wedded to Prime Minister Indira Gandhi's socialism, she steered economic policies during the following ten years with the help of the National Advisory Council whose members were more or less committed to socialist ideology. Apart from continuation of trade liberalization and trimming the small-scale-industries list, reserving labour-intensive products for exclusive manufacture by very small enterprises, the reform process came to a standstill once again. Much of the progress was in expanding social spending, including the launch of the National Rural Employment Guarantee Scheme under which one member of every rural household was guaranteed 100 days of employment at a specified wage.

Robust growth on the back of the Rao–Vajpayee reforms greatly contributed to a rapid decline in abject poverty. This growth also yielded rising volume of tax revenues, allowing the government to expand social programmes aimed at combating poverty. These factors greatly helped UPA return to office in the 2009 parliamentary elections.

During its first term, while the UPA had not advanced the reforms agenda to any significant degree, it also did not reverse earlier reforms or introduce anti-growth policies. This allowed the Rao–Vajpayee reforms to perform their magic. But the policy stance took a turn for the worse in the second term of the government. Socialism, which had remained confined to expanding social spending in the first term, now began to penetrate policy. Four key legislations—the Land Acquisition

Act, the Right to Education Act, National Food Security Act and an amendment to the Income Tax Act of 1961 giving the government power to tax retrospectively—fell into this category. The last of these measures, which gave the government powers to collect taxes on transactions going back several years, even decades, seriously damaged investor sentiment. Large fiscal deficits to finance rapidly expanding social schemes, virtual standstill on environmental clearances for infrastructure and other projects, and paralysis in decision-making in the central government culminated in poor economic outcomes. During the last two years of the UPA government, inflation hit double-digit levels, the current account deficit ballooned and growth fell below 6 per cent. It was under these circumstances that Prime Minister Modi, who contested the 2014 elections on a development platform, came to power.

Growth and Development in the Modi Era

The arrival of a new prime minister who was determined to transform India economically and socially changed the course of policy yet again with prospects for reforms greatly improved. The Modi government moved quickly to restore macroeconomic stability. It adopted an inflation-targeting framework early in its term and successfully brought inflation as well as the current account deficit down. It committed to fiscal discipline, to which it adhered during its five years. It also successfully ended paralysis in the government and speeded up the decision-making process. During the full five-year term, GDP growth averaged 7.5 per cent.

Three features distinguish the approach to development by Modi from those of all of his predecessors. First, he completes his major projects and programmes in a time-bound manner. Second, he does projects on scale. And finally, his approach is holistic in terms of coverage of economic sectors as well as geographical regions.

On the first point, perhaps the best example is the Swachh Bharat Mission. Under the mission, Modi set the deadline of 2 October 2019 to end open defecation. At the time of the launch, this had seemed mission impossible. But he took up the project on a war footing and successfully completed it. Some gaps may remain and changed behaviour will have to be sustained over time but the basic fact that toilets are now available to all Indians in rural areas is generally accepted.

Modi has also shown the ability to do projects on scale. Four projects illustrating this side of his work style are: building of toilets under SBM, spread of Aadhaar identity cards to 1.2 billion Indians, opening of bank accounts for all and delivery of cooking-gas stoves to all poor households in a record time. Each of these projects covered hundreds of millions of households and individuals. In his second term, Modi has now set for himself the task of bringing piped water to all rural households, an even bigger challenge than SBM.

Finally, Modi has a holistic approach to development whereby he casts the net widely across sectors and regions. In infrastructure, while accelerating the building of roads and railways, he has connected numerous previously unconnected cities by air and has taken the initiative to develop transportation by waterways. Within railways, he has worked on not just the expansion of the railway network but also increasing the speed of trains, their electrification and modernization of railway stations.

For ordinary citizens, Modi has digitized numerous government services to improve the ease of living. For businesses, he has worked with states to improve the ease of doing business. He has taken the fight against corruption head on. He has made focused effort to develop the northeastern states with perceptible success. For the first time, he has also taken up the task of developing islands. He has reached out and built bridges to other nations on a scale not done by any other past leader. Finally, on the reforms front, he has enacted the Insolvency and Bankruptcy Code, National Medical Commission Act and the Goods and Services Tax while also cutting the corporate profit tax to

25 per cent with all exemptions ended. He has also steadily opened the Indian market wider to foreign investors in numerous areas, most notably e-commerce.

Those who see the glass half full under Modi would say that given the inheritance of an extremely fragile economy and low morale of not just businessmen but even bureaucrats, these are impressive achievements. Those who see the glass half empty would argue that Modi failed to implement deeper reforms that would have launched the Indian economy into a robust 8 per cent plus growth, which it had clocked during 2003/04 to 2011/12. They would also point to the slowdown in growth during the year ending on 30 June 2019 to 6.1 per cent. During the last two quarters of this year, growth rates had fallen successively to 5.8 and 5 per cent.

I place myself in the optimistic camp. Given where the Modi government started, restoring and maintaining macroeconomic stability along all major dimensions during the entire five-year term and accelerating growth to 7.5 per cent per year is no mean achievement. Pessimists have more of a case when they point to the slowdown in growth in the first year of his second term. But this must be seen in the light of two major factors impacting growth: ongoing clean-up of NPAs in public sector banks and the assault on corruption.

Among the many problems inherited by the Modi government was the vast stock of restructured loans at public sector banks that was on its way to turning into NPAs. Unfortunately, both the Department of Financial Services in the Ministry of Finance and the RBI were negligent of the problem until, in early 2017, data convincingly showed that growth of credit by public sector banks had collapsed. At that point, the government did move swiftly but the problem had become much larger by then. The process of clean-up is now well under way, but it will take a year or more for the financial sector to return to its normal operation.

The clean-up of NPAs and follow-up tightening of rules governing defaults have impacted economic activity in at least four ways. One, many leading entrepreneurs and corporations must absorb the lost value of their assets, which is testing their will to undertake new investments. Two, on the supply side, with the rules of the game having changed, banks are being a lot more cautious in lending. Three, balance sheets of the banks are still in the process of recovery so that the capacity of banks to expand credit is limited. Finally, entrepreneurs no longer have the option to restructure loans and continue business as usual that they used to have through regulatory forbearance by the RBI.

Turning to the second factor, in the early years, entrepreneurs underestimated the resolve of the prime minister to combat corruption. Many among them thought that demonetization, a key step in this fight, resulted from bad advice to the prime minister and that once the economy had been remonetized, they would return to business as usual.[113] But that is not how the reality unfolded.

The government continued to close loopholes in laws and tighten enforcement including through information and data it collected from bank accounts into which discontinued high-denomination rupee notes had been deposited after demonetization. The space for money laundering both internally and externally was also steadily reduced. Tax evasion has been made difficult. As a result, the manner in which transactions take place has been undergoing a fundamental change. For instance, in real estate, it is no longer the case that buyers can make half or more of the payment for house purchase in cash and escape the tax due on that part of the price.

Both of these factors—the NPA clean-up and fight against corruption—are forcing economic restructuring in the economy.

---

113 In November 2016, the government ended the legal tender status of the two highest denomination currency notes valued at ₹500 and ₹1,000. The idea was that those holding these notes in vast volumes would have to account for how they got them. If these sources of income had gone unreported in the past, those depositing the notes would then be subject to prosecution.

Developments in the banking sector are almost certain to help raise productivity in the medium to long run though they do set back growth in the short run. Under the new rules, banks can no longer lend or restructure loans irresponsibly. Symmetrically, entrepreneurs cannot borrow and invest recklessly in the hope of ever greening of loans with no consequences. More productive projects rather than well-connected entrepreneurs will have priority in banks' lending operations.

The impact of the fight against corruption on productivity is more uncertain, especially in the short and medium run. A key role of bribes is to speed up the decision-making process. They motivate bureaucrats who do not take decisions or take them slowly to move speedily. Therefore, as bribe-giving and bribe-taking become more difficult, the impact on productivity would be negative unless officials are held accountable for delays in decision making. Increased fear of being charged of wrongdoing when rules are not clearly spelt out would also make investors hesitant to undertake certain transactions.

Despite these adverse effects on growth, the case for Prime Minister Modi's anti-corruption drive remains strong for three reasons. First, ending corruption helps improve the moral fabric of the nation. An honest nation is a prouder nation. Second, corruption rewards the dishonest who willingly break the law knowing that they can bribe their way out of punishment even if caught. By most metrics of ethics, this is an unfair system. The law should reward the honest and punish the dishonest. Finally, in the long run, eradication of corruption is almost certain to improve productivity. Once the principle that those caught breaking the law will be punished is firmly and credibly established, decision makers in the government will come to accept the reality that there is no money to be made by delaying or blocking decisions. Indeed, they would themselves come under the scanner for delaying decisions. That would pave the way for a clean and swift decision-making system of administration.

Looking Ahead

Based on the experiences of countries that have sustained high growth rates for two or more decades, India has the potential to grow at near double-digit rates in the next two decades. India's own growth at 8 per cent-plus during 2003/04 to 2011/12 on the back of the Rao–Vajpayee reforms reinforces this proposition. The slowdown to 6.1 per cent rate during the full year ending on 30 June 2019 has shaken the confidence of many observers of the Indian economy but their judgement has been coloured by immediate weakness in the economy.

Fundamentally, the Indian economy remains sound and will return to a 7 per cent-plus growth in another year. One important indicator pointing in this direction is that Gross Fixed Capital Formation in 2018/19 at 29.3 per cent of GDP at current prices and 32.3 per cent at constant 2011/12 prices remains robust. With investment staying at this high level, financial markets improving and the government taking corrective actions, growth is unlikely to stay tepid for long.

This being said, India cannot take rapid growth and transformation as a given fact. Instead, it will require concerted reforms and steady progress in building infrastructure. Setting aside details, which I have already spelt out in the preceding pages, eight broad points are worth underlining as I conclude this volume.

First, it is necessary to recognize the importance of policy reform for faster growth. The projects and programmes on which the Modi government has laid heavy emphasis in its first term are necessary but not sufficient. The government represents only one of the two legs on which an economy walks. People, consisting of farmers, workers, professionals and businessmen, represent the other leg. Mobilization of their energies and talents requires a liberal policy framework.

Over the past seven decades, India has put far too many laws, rules and regulations in place that unduly constrain private actors. There has been a tendency to enact another law or write another regulation whenever faced with an issue without thinking through the effects that the law or regulation may have in other areas. Laws and regulations should be written to deal with situations that arise frequently. A one-time anomalous situation, which existing laws and regulations happen not to cover, need not trigger the addition of another law or regulation. Instead, it should be flexibly dealt with within the existing legal framework with the precedent recorded for future reference.

Second, policymakers must not lose sight of the fact that if they want to steadily expand government spending, they also need to continuously undertake policy reforms to accelerate and sustain high growth. When the economy is growing at a healthy pace, it is easy for the government to take it for granted and become complacent. But the economy is not like the mythological Kamadhenu that would keep giving the desired volume of revenues in perpetuity without due nurturing.[114]

The UPA government made precisely this mistake in its second term by returning to dirigiste policies while continuing to increase social spending to win elections. The strategy backfired with growth receiving a setback and inflation touching double-digit levels.[115] When an economy with a long history of command and control policies grows in response to reforms, new bottlenecks emerge, requiring further reforms. During the past several decades, India has built so many layers of regulation in nearly all areas that removal of a few of layers in a few areas is insufficient to give the energies of entrepreneurs full play.

Third, the government must recognize the importance of policy stability. When a government changes policy retroactively, subjecting investors to costs that did not exist at the time they made investment decisions, it has a chilling effect on future investments. For instance, the decision by the government in 2012 to amend the Income Tax

---

114 In Indian mythology, Kamadhenu is a goddess in the form of a cow who provides her owner whatever the latter desires.

115 Panagariya, 2019c.

Act of 1961 with retrospective effect sent shivers down the spines of investors. The decision by the Supreme Court in 2014 cancelling all allocations of coal blocks during 1993–2012 had a similar effect.

Though the Modi government put a lid on retrospective taxation under the amended law and brought a law under which coal blocks are now auctioned rather than administratively allocated, it too has had its share of actions contributing to policy uncertainty. An example is the policy on electric vehicles. The government announced, without due analysis, target dates for conversion of cars and motorbikes from internal combustion engine to electric ones. These dates were far more ambitious than even those the United States is predicted to achieve. Those announcements created much uncertainty regarding future investments in the minds of auto manufacturers. Though the targets have since been withdrawn, the announcements have not been without cost. Along the same line, frequent changes in GST rates and personal income tax rates, delayed implementation of the announcement of reduction in the corporate profit tax rate and frequent renegotiations of power purchase agreements have contributed to uncertainty in the minds of entrepreneurs.

Fourth, policymakers need to come to terms with the fact that without creating conditions for the migration of half or more agricultural workforce out of agriculture into industry and services, India cannot make them prosperous. The output per worker in agriculture remains low so that redistributing this output in favour of farmers and away from intermediaries in the supply chain through marketing reforms cannot go very far. Nor is the increase in productivity in agriculture a viable solution to the problem of low incomes of farmers. Any output increase will bring a decline in price that would wipe out the gains from increased output. Redistribution from non-agricultural workers to agricultural workers also has its limits since the overall income in India is low. Indeed, excessive reliance on this redistribution can undermine incentives to work and invest in industry and services and compromise growth.

Fifth, policymakers must further recognize that the bulk of the current employment in industry and services is concentrated in micro and small enterprises. These enterprises are characterized by low productivity, high underemployment and barely subsistence-level wages. The prospect of employment in them is not enough of an attraction for most agricultural workers to migrate out of their current employment. Therefore, the key to pulling the economy out of the current equilibrium is a set of reforms that would help firms grow larger, especially in sectors with high employment per unit of investment such as apparel, footwear, furniture and other light manufactures.

Sixth, export markets remain the key to bringing about the transformation India seeks and needs. Survival in the export market requires high productivity and steady increases in it. It also requires continuous product innovation to retain existing customers and win new ones. Enterprises that rely on export markets are typically large and therefore better able to exploit scale economies. The existence of these firms plays a critical role in creating a competitive ecosystem in which smaller firms also become more productive.

Seventh, contemporary developments in the Chinese economy offer a rare opportunity to bring many multinationals currently operating in that country to Indian shores. Real wages in China are now two to three times those in India on average. This has made many large enterprises in China, especially in employment-intensive activities, uncompetitive. They are seeking alternative production locations.

The trade war between the United States and China has given yet another reason to many enterprises currently in China to migrate elsewhere. India can greatly benefit from this situation by making India an attractive destination for these enterprises. The latter bring capital, technology, management techniques and valuable links to the world markets in a single package. By making India an attractive production centre for these enterprises, India can create vast volume of job opportunities for its workforce while also capturing the global export markets for many products.

The eighth and final point is something for Indian entrepreneurs to ponder. It is a paradox that in an economy in which capital is scarce and entrepreneurs continuously complain about high interest rates, they also overwhelmingly opt for highly capital-intensive sectors and technologies. For instance, as of 2018, India's largest corporation, Reliance Industries Limited (RIL), has $110 billion in assets but employs just 250,000 workers in total. This translates into just five jobs for each $2.2 million in assets. In comparison, India's largest exporter of apparel, Shahi Exports, employs 1,260 workers for each $2.2 million in assets. But most formal-sector entrepreneurs in India choose to invest in RIL-like capital-intensive industries. Those following the lead of Shahi Exports are few and far between.[116]

Indian entrepreneurs need to ponder why they do not invest more in employment-intensive sectors in which the country has a clear comparative advantage. If there are specific regulations that deter them from entering these sectors, they must seek their removal. For spreading India's scarce capital over a larger workforce is a win-win. It would not only go a long way towards accelerating growth on a sustained basis but also bring genuine prosperity to millions of its currently underemployed workers. After all, in today's world, true glory to a nation can come only when everyone gets to share in it.

116 Panagariya, 2018

REFERENCES

Agarwal, Pawan. 'Higher education in India: the need for change', Working Paper No. 180, New Delhi: Indian Council for Research on International Economic Relations, 2006

Ali, Mohammad. '23 lakh apply for 368 peon posts in Uttar Pradesh,' *The Hindu*, 17 September 2015: https://www.thehindu.com/news/national/other-states/23-lakh-apply-for-368-peon-posts-in-uttar-pradesh/article7660341.ece (accessed on 5 January 2019)

Amladi, Durgadas Ramkrishna. 'Mumbai's first bank, 1720: The beginning of banking on the Bombay island,' *Prajnan*, Vol. 43 (1), National Institute of Bank Management, Mumbai, 2014, pp. 9-49

Bertraud, A. 'Mumbai FAR/FSI conundrum: The perfect storm: the four factors restricting the construction of new floor space in Mumbai', 2011: http://alainbertaud.com/wp-content/uploads/2013/06/AB-Mumbai-FSI-Conundrun-Revised_June-2013_kk-ab1.pdf (accessed on 27 August 2019)

Bain, Marc. 2017. 'One very basic job in sneaker manufacturing is testing the limits of automation,' *Quartz*, 24 April 2017: https://qz.com/966882/robots-cant-lace-shoes-so-sneaker-production-cant-be-fully-automated-just-yet/ (accessed on 22 November 2018)

Bhagwati, Jagdish and Padma Desai. *India Planning for Industrialization, Industrialization and Trade Policies since 1951*, London: Oxford University Press, 1970

Bhagwati, Jagdish N. and Arvind Panagariya. 'Great expectations,' *Wall Street Journal*, 24 May 2004

Bhagwati, Jagdish N. and Arvind Panagariya. *Why Growth Matters*, New York: Public Affairs, 2013. Also published in India under the title *India's Tryst with Destiny* by HarperCollins

Chakraborty, Subhayan. 'Piyush Goyal takes 12 major decisions to boost exports, industrial growth,' *Business Standard*, 1 July 2019: https://www.business-standard.com/article/economy-policy/piyush-goyal-takes-12-major-decisions-to-boost-exports-industrial-growth-119060800034_1.html (accessed on 4 September 2019)

Chandramouli, C. 'Housing stock amenities & assets in slums—Census 2011', 2011: http://censusindia.gov.in/2011-Documents/On_Slums-2011Final.ppt

Cohen, Stephen. *India: Emerging Power*, Washington, D.C.: Brookings Institution, 2001.

Dehejia, Rajeev and Arvind Panagariya. 'The link between manufacturing growth and accelerated services growth in India,' *Economic Development and Cultural Change*, Vol. 64 (2), University of Chicago Press, 2016, pp. 221–264

Economic Advisory Council to the Prime Minister. *Report of the Logistics Development Committee on Key Challenges in Logistics and Development and the Associated Commerce-Policy reforms for Ease of Doing Business/Trade in India*, Government of India, October 2018

Fields, Gary. *Poverty, Inequality and Development*, Cambridge: Cambridge University Press, 1980

Foster, Andrew and Mark Rosenzweig. 'Are Indian farms too small?: mechanization, costs, and farm efficiency': http://www.bu.edu/

econ/files/2009/09/Rosenzweig_Seminar-Paper.pdf (accessed on 18 December 2018).

Gupta, Nandini. 'Selling the family silver to pay the grocer's bill? The case of privatization in India' in Jagdish Bhagwati and Arvind Panagariya, editors, *Reforms and Economic Transformation in India*, New York: Oxford University Press, 2013.

Gupta, Nandini and Arvind Panagariya. 'Selling PSEs improves efficiency, frees government to do the business it is meant to do,' *Economic Times*, 18 October 2019: https://economictimes.indiatimes.com/news/economy/policy/view-selling-pses-improves-efficiency-frees-government-to-do-the-business-its-meant-to-do/articleshow/71655897.cms

Gupta, Poonam and Arvind Panagariya. 'Growth and election outcomes in a developing country,' *Economics & Politics*, Vol. 26, Issue 2, 2014, pp. 332-354

Hull, Dana. 'Musk says excessive automation was "My mistake,"' *Bloomberg*, 13 April 2018: https://www.bloomberg.com/news/articles/2018-04-13/musk-tips-his-tesla-cap-to-humans-after-robots-undercut-model-3 (accessed on 22 November 2018)

Insolvency and Bankruptcy Board of India. *Quarterly Newsletter October-December 2018*, Volume 9: https://www.ibbi.gov.in/publication (accessed on 1 September 2019).

Ito, Takatoshi and David E. Weinstein. 'Japan and the Asian economies: A "miracle" in transition,' *Brookings Papers on Economic Activity*, Vol. 1996, No. 2, pp. 205– v 272.

Kapur, Devesh and Pratap Mehta. 'Mortgaging the future? Indian higher education', *India Policy Forum*, 2007, pp. 101–157.

Khatkhate, Deena. 'Indian economic reform: A philosopher's stone,' *Economic and Political Weekly* 41, no. 22: 2203–05, 2006.

Kingdon, Geeta Gandhi. 'Put the onus on teachers,' *Indian Express*, 14 January 2017: https://indianexpress.com/article/opinion/columns/education-schools-children-board-exams-mass-cheating-put-the-onus-on-teachers-4473156/

Kishore, Adarsh. 'India – The emerging giant or has it emerged?' *Business Standard*, 8 May 2008: https://www.business-standard.com/article/opinion/adarsh-kishore-india-the-emerging-giant-or-has-it-emerged-108050801066_1.html

Kletzer, Kenneth. 'Liberalizing capital flows in India: Financial repression, macroeconomic policy and gradual reforms', *India Policy Forum*, 1: 227–75, 2005

Kux, Dennis. *India and the United States: Estranged Democracies 1941–1991*, Washington DC: National Defense University Press, 1992.

Kwon, Huck-ju and Ilcheong Yi. 'Economic development and poverty reduction in Korea: Governing multifunctional institutions,' *Development and Change* 40, No. 4, July 2008, pp. 769–792.

Maddison, Angus. *The World Economy, 1-2001 A.D.*, Volume 2, Paris: OECD, 2006. Available at https://www.oecd-ilibrary.org/development/the-world-economy/the-world-economy-1-2001-ad_9789264022621-21-en

Mishra, Prachee. 'Overview of the power sector,' PRS working paper, September 2019: https://tinyurl.com/y3p869hy

Li, Haizheng. 'Higher Education in China: Complement or Competition to US Universities?' In Charles T. Clotfelter, ed., *American Universities in a Global Market*, Chicago: University of Chicago Press, 2010, pp. 269-304.

Li, Mei and Rui Yang. 'Governance reforms in higher education: A study of China,' IIEP research papers, International Institute for Educational Planning, UNESCO, Paris, 2014

Mahalanobis, P.C. 'The Asian drama: An Indian view,' *Economic and Political Weekly 4*, Special Number, 1119-32, 1969

Ministry of Finance. *Economic Survey 2017–18*, Government of India, New Delhi, 2018

Ministry of Finance. *Economic Survey 2018–19*, Government of India, New Delhi, 2019

Ministry of Housing and Urban Poverty Alleviation. *National Urban Rental Housing Policy (Draft)*, October, Government of India,

New Delhi, 2015: http://mohua.gov.in/upload/uploadfiles/files/National_Urban_Rental_Housing_Policy_Draft_2015.pdf (accessed on 9 June 2019).

Ministry of Human Resource Development. *Education Statistics at a Glance 2016*, Government of India, 2016: https://mhrd.gov.in/educational-statistics-glance-2016 (accessed on 2 September 2019)

Ministry of Human Resource Development. *All-India Survey on Higher Education 2016-17*, Government of India, 2017: http://aishe.nic.in/aishe/reports (accessed on 2 September 2019)

Muralidharan, Karthik and Venkatesh Sundararaman. 'The aggregate effect of school choice: evidence from a two-stage experiment in India,' *Quarterly Journal of Economics*, Volume 130, Issue 3, August 2015, Pages 1011–1066.

National Statistical Office. *Drinking Water, Sanitation, Hygiene and Housing Conditions in India: July 2012-December 2012*, Ministry of Statistics and Program Implementation, Government of India, New Delhi, 2014.

National Statistical Office. *Key Indicators of Unincorporated Non-agricultural Enterprises (Excluding Construction) of India: July 2015-June 2016*, Ministry of Statistics and Programme Implementation, Government of India, 2017.

National Statistical Office. 2019. *Periodic Labor Force Survey: July 2017-June 2018*, Ministry of Statistics and Programme Implementation, Government of India.

Panagariya, Arvind. 'Bringing competition to bureaucracy,' *Economic Times*, 27 September 2000.

Panagariya, Arvind. 'Bringing competition to the top civil service,' *Yojana*, New Delhi: Planning Commission, August 2005, pp. 9–13.

Panagariya, Arvind. *India: The Emerging Giant*. New York: Oxford University Press, 2008.

Panagariya, Arvind. 'Apparel industry holds the key for India's job creation requirements,' *Economic Times*, 18 January 2018:

https://economictimes.indiatimes.com/news/economy/policy/apparel-industry-model-holds-the-key-for-indias-job-creation-requirements/articleshow/62514682.cms

Panagariya, Arvind. *Free Trade and Prosperity: How Openness Helps Developing Countries Grow Richer and Combat Poverty*, New York: Oxford University Press, 2019a

Panagariya, Arvind. 'Reforms, please, not stimulus: Sagging sectors of the economy should not expect bailouts from the government,' *Times of India*, 21 August 2019b: https://timesofindia.indiatimes.com/blogs/toi-edit-page/reforms-please-not-stimulus-sagging-sectors-of-the-economy-should-not-expect-bailouts-from-the-government/

Panagariya, Arvind. 'India's choices in 2019: Modi has reforms to his credit, UPA free rode on Vajpayee's reforms,' *Times of India*, 6 February 2019c: https://timesofindia.indiatimes.com/blogs/toi-edit-page/indias-choices-in-2019-modi-has-reforms-to-his-credit-upa-free-rode-on-vajpayees-reforms/

Panagariya, Arvind, Pinaki Chakraborty, and M. Govinda Rao. *State Level Reforms, Growth, and Development in Indian States*, New York: Oxford University Press, 2014

Panagariya, Arvind and B. Venkatesh Kumar. 'Liberating India's best colleges: HRD minister Javadekar has just announced the most far-reaching reforms in higher education,' *Times of India*, 15 February 2018a: https://timesofindia.indiatimes.com/blogs/toi-edit-page/liberating-indias-best-colleges-hrd-minister-javadekar-has-just-announced-the-most-far-reaching-reforms-in-higher-education/ (accessed on 2 September 2019)

Panagariya, Arvind and B. Venkatesh Kumar. 'It's time to replace the UGC Act,' *Hindu*, 17 April 2018b: https://www.thehindu.com/opinion/op-ed/its-time-to-replace-the-ugc-act/article23565106.ece (accessed on 2 September 2019)

Panagariya, Arvind and B. Venkatesh Kumar. 'A path-breaking legislation: HECI Bill can uplift Indian higher education, but requires some correctives before enactment,' *Times of India*, 5 July 2018c: https://timesofindia.indiatimes.com/blogs/toi-edit-page/a-path-breaking-legislation-heci-bill-can-uplift-indian-higher-education-but-requires-some-correctives-before-enactment/

Panagariya, Arvind and B. Venkatesh Kumar. 'How autonomous colleges are breaking India's rigid degree system,' *Economic Times*, 17 May 2019: https://economictimes.indiatimes.com/industry/services/education/how-autonomous-colleges-are-breaking-indias-rigid-degree-system/articleshow/69380082.cms?from=mdr (accessed on 2 September 2019)

Panagariya, Arvind, and Vishal More.'Poverty by social, religious and economic groups in India and its largest states: 1993–94 to 2011–12.' *Indian Growth and Development Review* 7, no. 2: 202–30, 2014

Panagariya, Avind and Dani Rodrik. 'Political economy arguments for a uniform tariff,' *International Economic Review*, Volume 34, No. 3, 685-703, 1993

Planning Commission. 'Report on Indian Urban Infrastructure and Services,' New Delhi: Government of India, March 2011

Prasad, Ravi V. '30th year of assassination: memoirs of Indira Gandhi,' 2015: https://www.news18.com/news/india/30th-year-of-assassination-memories-of-indira-gandhi-723277.html
(Accessed on 17 August 2019).

Rangan, M.C. Govardhana. 'Thank RBI's February 12 order for Jet Airways' rescue,' *Economic Times*, 26 March 2019: https://economictimes.indiatimes.com/markets/stocks/news/thank-rbis-february-12-order-for-jet-airways-rescue/articleshow/68571804.cms?from=mdr (accessed on 1 September 2019).

Reserve Bank of India. *Report on Currency and Finance 2006-08*, Bombay, 2008: https://www.rbi.org.in/Scripts/AnnualPublications.aspx?head=Report+on+Currency+and+Finance (accessed on 30 August 2019).

Reserve Bank of India. *Report on Trends and Progress in Banking 2017-18*, 2018: https://www.rbi.org.in/scripts/AnnualPublications.aspx?head=Trend%20and%20Progress%20of%20Banking%20in%20India

Varshney, Ashutosh. *Democracy, Development, and the Countryside: Urban Rural Struggle in India*. New York: Cambridge University Press, 1995.

Yoo, Jungho. 'Neoclassical versus revisionist view of Korean economic Growth,' Development Discussion Paper No. 588, Harvard Institute for International Development, Harvard University, Cambridge, MA, 1997.

Zhang, Han, Donald Patton and Martin Kenney. 'Building global-class universities: Assessing the impact of the 985 Project,' *Research Policy* 42, 2013, pp. 765–775.

INDEX

ABOUT THE AUTHOR

ARVIND PANAGARIYA is a professor of economics and the Jagdish Bhagwati Professor of Indian Political Economy at Columbia University. He is also the Director of the Raj Center on Indian Economic Policies at Columbia University. He served as the first vice-chairman of the NITI Aayog from January 2015 to August 2017. He is the author of more than fifteen books, among them *India: The Emerging Giant* (2008), *Free Trade and Prosperity* (2019) and *India's Tryst with Destiny* (2012) with Jagdish Bhagwati (also published under the title *Why Growth Matters*) which has been called 'a manifesto for policymakers and analysts'.

The Government of India honoured him with the Padma Bhushan in 2012.